D0110491

MODERN AUSTRIA

Modern Austria
Empire and Republic, 1815–1986

Barbara Jelavich

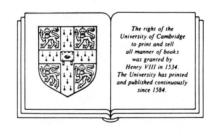

The right of the
University of Cambridge
to print and sell
all manner of books
was granted by
Henry VIII in 1534.
The University has printed
and published continuously
since 1584.

CAMBRIDGE UNIVERSITY PRESS

Cambridge
New York   Port Chester
Melbourne   Sydney

91-957

Published by the Press Syndicate of the University of Cambridge
The Pitt Building, Trumpington Street, Cambridge CB2 IRP
40 West 20th Street, New York, NY 10011, USA
10 Stamford Road, Oakleigh, Melbourne 3166, Australia

First published 1987
Reprinted 1988, 1989

Printed in the United States of America

Library of Congress Cataloging-in-Publication Data
Jelavich, Barbara, 1923-
Modern Austria: empire and republic, 1815 – 1986.
Bibliography: p.
Includes index.
1. Austria – History – 1815 – 1848   2. Austria – History –
1848 – 1867   3. Austria – History – 1867 – 1918.
4. Austria – History – 20th century.   1. Title.
DB80.J38   1987   943.6′04   86-33371

ISBN 0 521 30320 6 hard covers
ISBN 0 521 31625 1 paperback

British Library Cataloging-in-Publication applied for

CONTENTS

Contents

Contents

ILLUSTRATIONS

FIGURES

Illustrations

PREFACE

IN this history of modern Austria the emphasis has been placed on the years after 1918. It is, however, impossible to understand this period without a description of the Habsburg imperial past. In the first section of this book, dealing with the monarchy, the narrative concentrates on the affairs of the German-speaking population and on the imperial institutions that influenced the Austrian republic. Thus no attempt has been made to describe in detail other important aspects of Habsburg history, such as the intricacies of the monarchy's foreign relations and the complications of the nationality problem. Some of these questions have been discussed in two of the author's previous works: *The Habsburg Empire in European Affairs, 1814–1918* (Chicago: Rand McNally and Co., 1969), and the Habsburg sections of *History of the Balkans*, 2 vols. (Cambridge: Cambridge University Press, 1983).

The necessary limitations on length in this book have caused certain problems, in particular in the treatment of cultural history. It is difficult to conceive of an Austrian history that would omit the contributions in music and the arts. The subject has been covered here in a central section, whose content spans the years from the late eighteenth century to the interwar period, with the principal attention devoted to music, literature, art, and architecture in Vienna. It has, unfortunately, been impossible to do more than mention the major musicians, artists, and writers and indicate some of their works. A discussion of philosophy, medicine, and other fields in which Austrians excelled has, of necessity, been omitted.

The same considerations have precluded an inclusion of Austrian regional history. The author would have preferred to provide more information about events in the provinces, some of which, for instance, Tirol and Salzburg, have important histories of their own. Vienna and the actions of the central government thus receive the chief attention, an approach that in some aspects may distort the picture given of modern Austrian society.

Throughout this narrative Austria is treated as an independent state that is part of the wider German cultural nation. With full recognition that this question has caused controversy, the author believes that this definition is the best one for a study that endeavors to indicate the leading role that the Habsburg Empire has taken historically in Central Europe and to underline the argument that had events taken a different turn, German unification could have been achieved by Vienna and not by Berlin. It also reflects the strong Austrian desire for *Anschluss* in the interwar years and the present close relations between Austria and the Federal Republic of Germany.

The bibliography included here is designed to provide the reader with a list of books in English that can be consulted for further information on the various topics and periods covered. Books in languages other than English have not been included, although they – in particular works by German authors – have been used extensively in the preparation of the text. Footnotes are limited to the identification of the sources of the quotations.

In the spelling of place names, the form adopted is usually the one most familiar to present-day English-language readers. When the choice is not clear, the German spelling, with possible alternative national forms, is used for the sections on the imperial period to 1918. After the dissolution of the monarchy the appropriate national spelling is adopted for each succession state.

ACKNOWLEDGMENTS

The author would like to thank Professors Klemens von Klemperer, Smith College; Enno Kraehe, University of Virginia; R. John Rath, University of Minnesota; Karl A. Roider, Jr., Louisiana State University; and Alfred Diamant and Jane Fulcher, both of Indiana University, who read all or part of this manuscript. Their care and criticisms are greatly appreciated. Charles, Mark, and Peter Jelavich made major suggestions on the style and content.

Much of the basic reading and research for this book was completed in Vienna. The author would like to acknowledge the assistance of the staff of the Haus-, Hof- und Staatsarchiv, the Kriegsarchiv, and the Library of the Historical Institute of the University of Vienna. She is also particularly grateful to Dr. Karlheinz Mack of the Osterreichische Ost- und Südosteuropa-Institut for his aid and advice. In addition, Nancy Cridland, Indiana University Library, helped greatly with the acquisition of the necessary books; the Office of Research and Advanced Studies, Indiana University, gave welcome research grants.

In the publication of this book the author has been fortunate to have again the assistance of Frank Smith and the expert editorial reading of Janis Bolster. The manuscript was typed by Debbie Chase; the maps were drawn by J & R Art Services; the index was prepared by Lin Maria Riotto. She also thanks Dr. Wolfgang Petritsch, director, and Mrs. Dagmar Baldwin, press attaché, Austrian Press and Information Service, New York, for providing most of the illustrations.

The illustrations were included with the kind permission of the following:

Austrian Press and Information Service, New York: figures on pp. 15, 19, 24, 35, 53, 109–112, 114, 174, 193, 246, and 300

Bildarchiv der Osterreichischen Nationalbibliothek, Vienna: figure on p. 223

Fotostudio Schikola, Vienna: figure on p. 16

Galerie St. Etienne, New York: figures on pp. 115 and 119–121

Indiana University Art Museum, Bloomington, Indiana: figures on pp. 117–118

VOTAVA, Intern. Presse-Bild-Agentur, Vienna: figure on p. 243

ACRONYMS

CARE	Cooperative for American Remittances to Europe
COMECON	Council for Mutual Economic Assistance
DDSG	Donaudampfschiffahrtsgesellschaft: Danube Steamship Company
EEC	European Economic Community
EFTA	European Free Trade Association
FPO	Freiheitliche Partei Osterreichs: Freedom Party
KPO	Kommunistische Partei Osterreichs: Communist Party
NATO	North Atlantic Treaty Organization
OECD	Organization for Economic Cooperation and Development
OEEC	Organization for European Economic Co-operation
OGB	Osterreichischer Gewerkschaftsbund: Austrian Federation of Trade Unions
OIAG	Osterreichische Industrieverwaltung: Austrian Corporation for Industrial Administration
OPEC	Organization of Petroleum Exporting Countries

OVP	Osterreichische Volkspartei: Austrian People's Party
PLO	Palestine Liberation Organization
SA	Sturmabteilung: Storm Troops
SALT	Strategic Arms Limitation Talks
SMV	Sowjetische Mineralölverwaltung: Soviet Mineral Oil Administration
SPO	Sozialistische Partei Osterreichs: Austrian Socialist Party
SS	Schutzstaffel: Nazi elite guard
UN	United Nations
UNRRA	United Nations Relief and Rehabilitation Administration
USIA	Upravlenie Sovetskogo Imushchestva v Avstrii: Administration of Soviet Property in Austria
VdU	Verband der Unabhängigen: Union of Independents
VEW	Vereinigte Edelstahlwerke: United Specialty Steel Works
VOEST	Vereinigte Osterreichische Eisen- und Stahlwerke: United Austrian Iron and Steel Works

PART I

THE HABSBURG EMPIRE

Introduction

WORLD POWER AND
ENLIGHTENED DESPOTISM

THE lands of the present Austrian state have provided remnants of human habitation since the Early Stone Age. The Celts, invading around 400 B.C., established the first known political organization in that region, the Kingdom of Noricum. Around 15 B.C. the area south of the Danube fell under Roman rule. Among the important Roman centers were Carnuntum near Hainburg and Vindobona on the present site of Vienna. Pressure from German tribes and the Huns forced an abandonment of the area by the Romans in the fifth century A.D. Thereafter the territory was in contention among Slavs, Avars, and German tribes. Of the last, the Bavarians settled throughout the region, whereas the Alemanni concentrated in the present-day province of Vorarlberg. A major change occurred during the reign of the Frankish emperor Charlemagne (771–814). After defeating the Bavarians and the Avars, he established in 788 an administrative division, or March, as a defense against future invaders, in particular the Avars. The center included Upper and Lower Austria, the two regions being separated by the Enns River. Subsequently, the Austrian lands fell under the control of the Moravian kingdom and then of the Magyars.

The first important ruling family, the Babenbergs (976–1246), received the land as an imperial fief from the Holy Roman Emperor Otto II, whose father, Otto I, had freed the area from Magyar control. In the twelfth century Styria and other lands were added to the Babenberg possessions. At this time Vienna became the capital; the cathedral of St. Stephen's and the Hofburg (the court residence), henceforth central Viennese landmarks, date from this time. In 1246, as a result of a disputed inheritance, the Babenberg lands were taken by the Bohemian king, Přemysl Otakar II (1253–1278).

The Habsburg rule over the Austrian lands was established soon after Rudolph I (1273–1291) was elected Holy Roman Emperor in 1273. The Habsburg family, whose name was a contraction of the name of their Swiss residence, Habichtsburg or Hawks Castle, built about 1020, held territory principally in Alsace as well as in Breisgau and Aargau in present-day Switzerland. In 1276 Rudolph forced Otakar II to surrender his Austrian possessions, and in 1278 he defeated and killed the Bohemian king on the Marchfeld near Vienna. Thereafter the Austrian lands became the base of power for the House of Habsburg, which was also called the House of Austria. The Habsburg position, however, was circumscribed by the fact that the rulers were feudal lords and in no sense national monarchs; as such they met with constant opposition from the local aristocracy. Their position was further weakened by the family's failure to adopt the principle of primogeniture. Since at the death of the head of the family all sons had equal rights to the inheritance, the Habsburg lands suffered repeated partition. Although over the years the territories tended to merge again, this legacy of repeated redistribution weakened Habsburg power and influence.

The center of the family possessions nonetheless remained Upper and Lower Austria, with Vienna as the capital. Other regions were acquired in permanent possession in the fourteenth century and came henceforth to be considered as part of the Hereditary Lands: Carinthia (1335), Carniola (1335), Tirol (1363), and Vorarlberg (1375). Whether these regions were governed by the head of the house or by an archduke, the ruler had to take into consideration the views of the local diets. As elsewhere in Central Europe, these were composed of representatives from the nobility and landed aristocracy, the clergy, and the city dwellers.

GREAT-POWER ASCENDANCY

In the sixteenth century immense territories were to be added to this base. The Habsburg Monarchy became the major world power largely as a result of chance and of the marriage policies of Maximilian I (1493–1519). In 1477 Maximilian married Mary of Burgundy. When she died he claimed the Netherlands and part of Burgundy as Habsburg possessions. His children, Philip and Margaret, were married to John and Johanna, whose parents were Ferdinand and Isabella; their possessions included not only Spain and extensive lands in Italy, but also the great Spanish conquests in the newly discovered Americas. Of Maximilian's grandchildren, Charles married Isabella of Portugal, whereas Ferdinand and Mary were betrothed to the children of Louis II, the Jagiellon king of Hungary and Bohemia. The immense heritage of these marriages was brought under Habsburg control during the reign of Charles V (1519–1556). At his accession he acquired Spain with its Italian and American possessions, Burgundy, the Netherlands, the Austrian Hereditary Lands, and other scattered regions. In 1526 at the battle of Mohács the Ottoman army defeated Louis II, who died during the fighting. Bohemia and the part of Hungary not under Ottoman occupation thus came into Habsburg possession.

In addition to holding these vast domains Charles V continued the Habsburg tradition, which had been broken only twice since 1273, of being elected Holy Roman Emperor, an office signifying that the holder was in theory the chief temporal ruler in Western Christendom. Contemporaries regarded it not only as the highest secular position, but also as having been created by God. At this time the emperor was chosen by three ecclesiastical electors (the archbishops of Mainz, Cologne, and Trier) and four secular rulers (the duke of Saxony, the count of the Palatinate, the margrave of Brandenburg, and the king of Bohemia). Charles V was crowned by the pope, but his successors were not. The position gave Charles heavy additional obligations, which were not offset by similar advantages. As a result of his imperial responsibilities he was continually drawn into German affairs, but his influence here was curtailed by the opposition of local and regional authorities, jealous of their privileges. Moreover, the fact that the emperor held large non-German territories limited his ability to stand as a symbol of German unity or to bring the states closer together. This situation was to the interest of the German princes, but it contributed to a delay of German national consolidation and thus made it more difficult for the area to withstand intervention by outside powers.

The position of Holy Roman Emperor, with its combination of religious and secular obligations, made it inevitable that Charles V would be a major figure in the controversies of the Reformation. In 1517, two years before Charles came to the throne, Martin Luther posted the Ninety-Five Theses on the door of the church in Wittenberg, thereby challenging the Catholic authorities. Charles and his successors, although deeply aware of their responsibilities toward the church, were not always obedient servants of the papacy and were often in conflict with it. The religious disputes also had a profound political significance, since Protestant doctrines appealed strongly to those German rulers who favored feudal decentralization or who wanted to confiscate church lands.

The intertwining of religious questions with power politics was to damage further the ability of Habsburg rulers to control German events. In the Peace of Augsburg of 1555 the German princes won the right to decide their religion and that of their subjects, thus weakening the imperial tie.

When Charles V abdicated in 1556, the Habsburg family lands, which had already proved too extensive to govern from a single center (see Map 1), were finally divided. Philip II (1556–1598) received the more valuable share: Spain with its dependent lands in America, the Italian possessions, and the Netherlands. For the next years the Spanish court was the true center of Habsburg family power. Ferdinand I (1556–1564) was given the Austrian Hereditary Lands, the Bohemian and Hungarian heritage, and he became Holy Roman Emperor. As before, the Austrian provinces were ruled by archdukes. Despite the division of its territories the House of Habsburg retained a strong internal unity. Family relations were close between the Spanish and Austrian branches.

Although Charles V surrendered to some Protestant demands in Germany, Catholicism remained supreme within the family lands despite the early successes of the Reformation in certain areas. After around 1570 the Counter-Reformation took hold in most Habsburg territories, but it did not eradicate Protestantism everywhere. Indeed, the Thirty Years' War (1618–1648) commenced in Bohemia with a rebellion involving Catholic–Protestant antagonisms made complicated by political issues. The imperial victory at the Battle of White Mountain (1620) enabled Ferdinand II (1619–1637) to take over the Bohemian lands as a hereditary kingdom. Rebellious Protestant noble landowners were forced to emigrate and were replaced by Catholics, some of German but others of Spanish, Dutch, Italian, Scottish, or Irish descent. In the next years a large number of loyal state officials were to come from this group. Although the period of war-

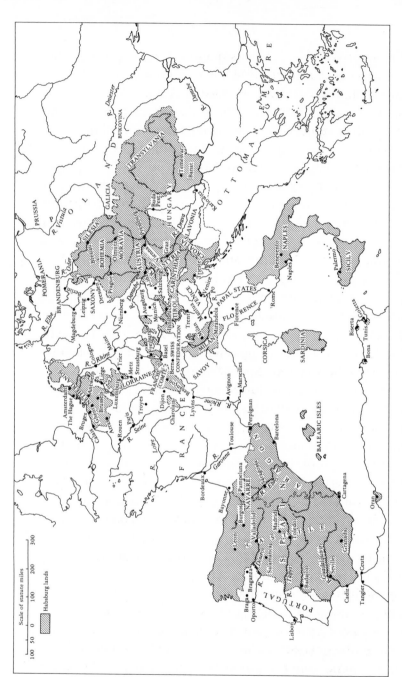

Map 1. The Habsburg Empire at the abdication of Charles V

fare resulted in the victory of the Catholic church in the Habsburg lands, the Peace of Westphalia (1648) was a further blow to the influence of the emperor and the unity of the German lands. Habsburg control over the family possessions was, however, strengthened.

In foreign affairs, Habsburg monarchs, either as kings of Spain or as Holy Roman Emperors, had to face severe challenges from France to the west and the Ottoman Empire to the east, powers that were sometimes in alliance. Despite the convinced Catholicism of the French rulers, they showed little hesitation in cooperating with Protestant Germans or the Muslim Ottoman Empire when it served state interests. The greatest threat to Habsburg lands came during the reign of Louis XIV (1643–1715), when that monarch attempted to achieve what he defined as France's "natural frontiers" on the Rhine, and at the Alps and the Pyrenees. The Ottoman threat remained almost constant throughout the fifteenth and sixteenth centuries. Under the leadership of Suleiman the Magnificent, Ottoman armies reached as far as Vienna at the end of September 1529, but the siege was broken in October. Although the Ottoman front remained relatively quiet during the Thirty Years' War, a revival of activity occurred after 1660. In July 1683 Ottoman armies under the command of Grand Vizir Kara Mustafa again besieged Vienna. With the aid of Polish forces and some German troops, the imperial army was able to lift the siege in September. Thereafter, the monarchy joined Venice and Russia in a counteroffensive, which by 1687 had taken most of the Hungarian lands. In 1699 the Habsburg and Ottoman governments signed the Treaty of Karlowitz (Sremski Karlovci), the most important agreement ever negotiated between the two states. This pact established a common boundary, which, with the exception of the Habsburg annexation of the Banat in 1718 and Bukovina in 1775, was to last until 1878.

Not only was the eastern border established at this time, but as a result of the War of Spanish Succession (1701–1714), other lasting changes were made in the composition of the territories under Habsburg rule. With the death of Charles II in 1700 the Habsburg line in Spain came to an end. The attempt of Louis XIV to place a Bourbon ruler on the throne involved the European powers in another long period of warfare, at the end of which the Spanish inheritance was divided in the Treaty of Utrecht (1713). Although a Bourbon king was indeed to rule in Madrid, the Habsburg Monarchy received as compensation the Spanish Netherlands (Belgium), Sardinia, and important territory in Italy, including Milan, Mantua, and Mirandola.

Despite the division of Habsburg lands during the reign of Charles V, a move taken in the interest of administrative efficiency, little else had been done toward facing the problem of organizing and defending scattered lands with differing national compositions and historic traditions. As we have seen, the Habsburg possessions had been acquired through marriage, war, or chance. Each area had retained its traditional system, or it had been assigned a Habsburg administrator. No great imperial institutions had been developed that could bring the Habsburg lands under a common system. At the time that the Treaty of Utrecht added the Italian and Flemish lands to the monarchy, the Habsburg Empire consisted of three major divisions: first, the Hereditary Lands, comprising primarily the provinces of Vorarlberg, Styria, Upper and Lower Austria, Carniola, and Carinthia, together with the scattered German possessions known as the *Vorlande;* second, the Kingdom of Bohemia (also known as the Lands of the Crown of St. Wenceslas), including Bohemia, Moravia, and Silesia; and third, the Kingdom of Hungary (or the Lands of the Crown of St. Stephen). Included in the Hungarian heritage, in addition to Hungarian lands, were two distinct areas, Transylvania and the Kingdom of Croatia, known before the Ottoman conquest as the Triune Kingdom of Croatia, Slavonia, and Dalmatia.

Since no attempt had been made to establish a uniform administrative system, and since most regions maintained their historic political organizations, the major link connecting the Habsburg possessions was the person of the ruler. However, despite his apparently exalted position and his great personal prestige, the emperor had, in fact, only limited powers. His most important duties were linked to foreign affairs and the military; he could declare war, make peace, and sign treaties and alliances. Here the emperor did indeed have autocratic powers. Nevertheless, even in these matters there were limits on his effectiveness. Although he was supreme commander of the armed forces, he had to rely for the most part on the provincial diets for recruits and the tax money needed to pay them. In fact, the limited financial resources available to the emperor weakened his power in almost all areas of government. Imperial administrative officers had the right to collect some taxes, such as customs dues. There was also the Habsburg family wealth and possessions, but these resources were usually so badly administered that they did not yield an adequate income.

With this situation it is easy to understand why major state functions rested in the hands of the nobility and why this estate was so powerful. It was in fact this group that was in close relationship with and had effective control over the mass of the population. As lords of their manors the nobles had direct authority over the peasants on their estates; they administered justice and provided what social services there were. As members of the provincial diets the nobles decided the political affairs of their regions, and, as previously mentioned, they voted the taxes and recruits needed by the monarch. They also held the high church and state posts, and they served as the diplomats and army officers. Their special privileges, which differed in various parts of the empire, included the right to pay taxes at a reduced rate or not at all. They could be tried only by their equals, and they had no set military obligations.

Like the other social divisions, the noble estate was extremely varied in character throughout the empire. Those of noble birth could control vast estates or small or medium farms, or they could be landless. They could be of noble lineage for many generations or newcomers who were advanced in status as a reward for service to the court. There were, of course, countless divisions in between. Important for Habsburg authority was the large group of service nobility, many of whom were of foreign background. The origin of the new nobility in Bohemia after the Battle of White Mountain has been noted. Over the years the Habsburg court retained the services of able men from all over Europe. This multinational group and the native service nobility constituted a strong support for the central authority, especially when confronting local interests with deep roots in their home provinces.

The great majority of the population consisted of enserfed peasants. In the Alpine regions, notably in Tirol, there were free peasant households, but most peasants were tied to the land and subject to heavy taxation in kind, money, and labor. This group provided financial support to the nobility and the central government and recruits for the army. Subject to the will of the local nobility, the peasantry had little contact with representatives of the central administration. Most estates were economically self-sufficient, with the individual peasant family producing enough to satisfy its own needs and to pay the required dues to the lord, the church, and the state.

The relatively small intermediate class of merchants, artisans, and professional men lived in towns and cities, some of which had considerable rights of self-government. Merchants and artisans were organized into guilds that supplied the local market. At this time the cities, like the state as a whole, suffered because the Habsburg central lands lay outside the main routes of trade; the one major European road in the Hereditary Lands ran through Tirol and linked the German and Italian lands. The repeated wars and the presence of rapacious armies on Habsburg soil had also drained the economy and disrupted normal trade relations in many regions.

THE BAROQUE AGE

Despite the past fluctuations of fortune, by the end of the seventeenth century the Habsburg leaders had much about which to congratulate themselves. Not only had the monarchy maintained itself as a great power against assaults from east and west, but the Catholic church, closely associated with the state, had emerged triumphant in the Habsburg lands. The court, the church, and the nobility celebrated their accomplishments with the adoption of lavish and outwardly extravagant ways of life, which were best expressed in the large-scale building of the period. The Baroque building style, imported from Rome, fitted well with the spirit of the time; its aim was to combine religious piety with worldly grandeur. Its art and architecture paid tribute to saints, military heroes, and Habsburg rulers alike. It dominated the reigns of Leopold I (1658–1705), Joseph I (1705–1711), and Charles VI (1711–1740).

The construction in Vienna was particularly impressive. The second siege of Vienna had caused massive damage; the city's suburbs were in ruins. After the signing of the Treaty of Karlowitz, when the threat of further Ottoman raids appeared ended, the way was clear for a rebuilding program. Moreover, there was now little hesitation about constructing large and expensive buildings outside the city walls. Although the Italian influence remained strong, three native artists created what have remained until today Viennese and Austrian landmarks. Johann Bernhard Fischer von Erlach (1656–1723) is perhaps best known for the design of the Karlskirche, built as the result of a vow taken by Charles VI during the plague year of 1713. Fischer also commenced work on the palace of Schönbrunn, which was supposed to outshine Versailles; it was finished by his son. Johann Lukas von Hildebrandt (1668–1745), among other buildings, designed the splendid Belvedere Palace for Prince Eugene of Savoy, the most famous Habsburg military hero of this time. The third important architect, Jakob Prandtauer (1660–1727), directed the rebuilding of the Benedictine Abbey at Melk, situated on the Danube River about fifty miles west of Vienna, and the completion of the work on the Abbey of St. Florian.

Although the greatest achievements of Austrian Baroque were in architecture, interior decoration was also a major concern of the time. Artists and sculptors provided rich ornamentation to the new churches and buildings, using themes from history, religion, and classical civilization. The court, the church, and the aristocracy were patrons of all aspects of Baroque art. Not only did they support the elaborate building program, but emperors, clergy, and nobility alike collected paintings, statuary, and tapestries; their residences were conspicuous for their rich and elegant furnishings.

In this atmosphere theater and music naturally flourished. Opera was in great favor, since it combined music, dance, drama, and spectacle. Music held a special position at court; Ferdinand III (1637–1657), Leopold I, and Joseph I were all composers. In general, Italian and French imports predomi-

14

Karlskirche

The Abbey of St. Florian

nated, but an Austrian composer, Johann Josef Fux (1660–1741), wrote masses, operas, and oratorios for the court and the church. He was also the author of one of the most famous treatises on counterpoint, *Gradus ad Parnassum* (1725).

Baroque as a style fitted only an aristocratic culture. It was also expensive to maintain. As long as the patrons could afford the cost, building programs could be continued. Soon, however, the immense burden of continual warfare, joined to domestic crises, caused a halting or a modification of plans. Moreover, tastes changed with time; Schönbrunn was completed, for instance, in the lighter Rococo style. The Baroque period was the great age of Habsburg architecture. At the beginning of the twentieth century another important school was to emerge, but without similar imperial and historical associations.

ENLIGHTENED DESPOTISM: MARIA THERESA AND JOSEPH II

The eighteenth century, a period of almost continual warfare, was to witness the adoption of a series of reforms, whose nature was to shape the character of the monarchy until its downfall. Dangerous developments in foreign affairs at this time made it clear that changes would have to be made so that the state would be strong enough to meet challenges from abroad. After the conclusion of the Treaty of Utrecht in 1713 the next major threat came not so much from the traditional opponent, France, as from a German power, Prussia. Moreover, despite the decisive Treaty of Karlowitz, the monarchy was at war with the Ottoman Empire in the years 1716–1718, 1737–1739, and 1788–1791. At the end of the century, with the commencement of the wars of the French Revolution and Napoleon, France once again became the main enemy.

That major changes in the organization of the monarchy were essential was made clear during the reign of Charles VI (1711–1740) when it became apparent that the male line of the family was threatened with extinction. Fearing a partition of the Austrian lands and a fate similar to that suffered by Spain with the demise of the dynasty there, Charles in 1713 proclaimed the Pragmatic Sanction, a document which declared that the Habsburg lands were indivisible and hereditary in both the male and the female line. This arrangement was in fact the first legally binding document that was applied equally in all the lands of the monarchy. At first it was issued as a family compact, but after his only son died at a young age, Charles sought its acceptance by the provincial diets and foreign governments. Although his estates agreed to it, the Hungarian diet did so only after forcing him to recognize the special position of that kingdom in the Habsburg domain.

In 1740 Charles was thus succeeded by his daughter, Maria Theresa (1740–1780), who was twenty-four years old when she came to the throne. In 1736 she married Francis Stephen of Lorraine; the name of the dynasty became thereafter the House of Habsburg-Lorraine. In 1745 Stephen was elected Holy Roman Emperor. In nineteen years the couple had sixteen children. The empress had not been trained for her position, since as long as her father was alive there was a chance that he would have a son. She, nevertheless, had excellent advisers, and she was to prove herself an able ruler. When her husband died in 1765, her son, Joseph II (1780–1790), became co-regent and Holy Roman Emperor.

Immediately upon her accession the weak position of the Habsburg lands was clearly demonstrated. Despite the agreements that they had made with Charles VI recognizing the Pragmatic Sanction, the monarchy's avaricious neighbors at once took advantage of the situation. Prussia, under the leadership of Frederick the Great, immediately seized Silesia and thus started the War of Austrian Succession (1740–1748); France, Spain, Saxony, and Bavaria subsequently joined the Prussian side. In this crisis the monarchy found

Maria Theresa

itself virtually isolated, although some support came from other German states, and Britain provided subsidies. In a desperate situation, Maria Theresa had to appeal to the estates for soldiers and money; once again assistance was not obtained without further concessions to Hungarian particularism. The war ended with the Treaty of Aix-la-Chapelle, which confirmed the Prussian possession of Silesia. In the next year, identifying Prussia as the prime enemy, the empress and her foreign minister, Wenzel von Kaunitz, prepared to avenge this defeat. In a diplomatic revolution that ended the previous Austrian–French antagonism, the two states in May 1756 signed the Treaty of Versailles; in the same year Prussia allied with Britain. Thus in the Seven Years' War (1756–1763) Austria and France, joined by Russia, fought against Prussia and Britain. Despite his often dangerous situation, Frederick was able in the final peace to retain almost all of Silesia, a rich province that was to add immeasurably to Prussian strength.

The two wars over Silesia were to have important consequences for the monarchy. First, Prussia was henceforth to emerge ever more strongly as a challenger to the previous Habsburg primacy in the German lands. Second, the loss of the predominantly German-populated Silesia was to shift the balance of the population in the Bohemian kingdom in favor of the Czech inhabitants, a change whose repercussions were not to be clearly felt for almost a century.

Although the monarchy surrendered Silesia to Prussia, gains were made in other areas. From the Ottoman Empire Austria acquired the Banat in 1718 and Bukovina in 1775. After the War of Bavarian Succession (1778–1779) the Inn Quarter was annexed. Even more important, Austria participated with Prussia and Russia in 1772 and 1795 in two of the three partitions of Poland. The newly acquired territory, with a Polish and Ruthenian population, was organized as a province under the name of the Kingdom of Galicia and Lodomeria, with a governor and a diet in Lvov. The wars of the eighteenth century thus altered the ethnic composition of the monarchy, in that a large German population was lost whereas the numbers of Poles, Ruthenians, and Romanians were increased.

As significant as the acquisitions of land were the great reforms inaugurated in the reign of Maria Theresa and completed by Joseph II. An Austrian historian has aptly summed up their importance for the future: "A study of any aspect of modern Austrian history – public administration, finance or economic policy, public education, military organization, jurisprudence, or public health – leads to the inevitable conclusion that the most energetic reforms and the most beneficent institutions date back to the reign of the great Empress."[1]

Like their contemporaries Frederick the Great and Catherine the Great, Maria Theresa and, in particular, her son were influenced by the ideas of the Enlightenment. As other Enlightened Despots did, they believed that it was their duty as monarchs to devote their lives to the service and betterment of the condition of their subjects. The state and state power were to be used as instruments to achieve social progress through direct intervention in the lives of the people. It was not a democratic age: the principle of everything for the people but nothing by the people predominated. The aim was to change the system, previously described, whereby the monarch ruled in conjunction with a nobility that had control over the peasants under its jurisdiction. The reforms were designed to overthrow this feudal structure and to insert the state and its agents between the noble and peasant and above both; the majority of the population would therefore be under direct central supervision. The position of the noble would indeed be curtailed, but he could serve in the bureaucracy and in other state institutions. Although the age of reform was inaugurated to enable the state to meet the Prussian

---

[1] Adam Wandruszka, *The House of Habsburg* (Garden City, N.Y.: Doubleday and Co., Anchor Books, 1965), p. 119.

challenge, the measures themselves were similar to those adopted in Prussia.

The first reforms, undertaken during the reign of Maria Theresa and then continued during her joint rule with her son, resulted in changes in the administrative and legal systems and in the relationship of church and state, as well as measures to aid the peasantry. The administrative acts, which were not applied in Hungary, Belgium, or the Italian lands, were aimed at placing the Hereditary and Bohemian lands under the control of a centralized bureaucracy and thus limiting the activities of the diets. The legal reforms were in the same direction, with the first changes enacted in 1769. In 1787 a general penal code was issued that eliminated the application of the death penalty. The laws reflected the ideas of the age in accepting the principle that equal punishments would be applied for equal crimes no matter what the social status of the convicted was.

In the church reforms Maria Theresa followed what had become a Habsburg tradition of favoring state control over those aspects of religious life that did not strictly involve doctrine. A devout Catholic, she, like previous Habsburg monarchs, was convinced that the dynasty had a special mission and that she was directly responsible to God for its fulfillment. A major problem at this time was the church's domination of education. With the reforms it was clear that the schools would have to undertake new tasks, such as, for instance, the training of bureaucrats. The opportunity to establish a state system was offered in 1773 when the pope abolished the Jesuit order, which had been very influential in Austrian education. Following this example Maria Theresa seized the property of the order and used the income to provide secular schooling. Henceforth, elementary education was in theory at least to be available for all Austrian citizens.

Both Maria Theresa and Joseph II were concerned about the condition of the enserfed peasantry, which provided both taxes and soldiers. Under Maria Theresa's rule an attempt was made to establish a uniform system governing the relationship of the peasant and the noble and to obtain a clear statement of peasant obligations. The principle of state intervention between the peasant and his overlord was thus established.

After his mother's death Joseph II continued the reforms, but in a more radical direction. Both he and his brother Leopold II were convinced adherents of the ideals of the Enlightenment. Both considered themselves primarily servants of the state, justifying their high position not by the principle of divine right, the basis of absolute monarchy, but by their assigned task of bettering the condition of their people. Well aware of the wretched condition of many of the enserfed peasants, Joseph felt an obligation to work especially for the interest of this class. In his administrative reforms he showed his dislike of feudal privilege and the accompanying provincial autonomous rights. During his reign he did not convoke the diets, and he refused to be crowned separately, as was customary, in Hungary and Bohemia. Instead he organized a centralized administrative system in the Hungarian kingdom; its lands, including Transylvania and Croatia, were divided into ten regions. His actions trod on local aristocratic sensibilities not only because he revoked traditional privileges, but also because his centralized bureaucracy used German as the official language. This issue was to become a major point of dispute in the next century in the nationality conflicts.

In his religious reforms Joseph went even further than his mother in asserting state control over religious institutions. In a major move he dissolved over seven hundred convents and monasteries that did not provide social services, such as

Joseph II

medicine or education. He used the money acquired from this action for charitable purposes or to build new churches in areas where a sufficient number did not exist. His great measure, however, was the Toleration Patent of October 1781.

According to its terms, Lutherans, Calvinists, and certain other Protestant sects, as well as Orthodox citizens, were to be free to exercise their religion and to build churches. They could also hold state offices. At the same time some measures that restricted the Jews were removed.

Joseph's greatest achievement was the abolition of serfdom. The Serfdom Patent of 1781 freed the peasants except in the Hungarian lands; soon similar measures were enacted there too. The Austrian peasants thus no longer suffered from assignment to a hereditary servile status; they could marry, change their professions, or leave the land, if they had replacements, without the lord's permission. They still, however, had to pay dues for the use of the land. Joseph would have liked to introduce reforms here too. However, his radical plans to replace the many taxes and payments still collected from the peasant with a single sum could not be implemented before his death in 1790.

As well as in these specific reforms, the firm directing hand of the central government was also felt in general economic planning. The mercantilist policies adopted under both Maria Theresa and Joseph II resembled those followed by the other great powers and did not cause controversies similar to those aroused by the previously described changes. Like the reforms, the economic measures were designed to promote the general welfare, but most significantly to prepare the state for war. At this time it was believed that these goals could be best achieved through economic self-sufficiency and the adoption of commercial policies that would result in a surplus of exports over imports. A favorable balance of trade was expected to bring an inflow of gold, which could in turn be used for armaments or other expenditures that would increase state power. This program obviously called for state direction and measures to improve the domestic economy. Of first importance was the abolition of barriers to domestic trade. Almost all internal tariffs were eliminated in most of the Hereditary Lands and Bohemia by 1775 and in the Hungarian kingdom by 1784. The division between Hungary and the rest of the monarchy lasted, however, until 1851. Whereas measures were taken to foster trade within the monarchy, great efforts were made to protect domestic interests from foreign competition through high tariffs, quotas, and some prohibitions on the import of certain goods.

Another series of measures was adopted that was to have a lasting influence on internal development. With a clear program for the future of their country, the Habsburg officials expected that the eastern regions would be the chief source for food and raw materials to supply the manufacturing centers, which would be concentrated in certain areas in the west. This attitude meant that early industrial development occurred chiefly in the Alpine lands, in the region around Vienna, and in Bohemia and Moravia. The government gave loans and tax exemptions to those nobles who wished to establish workshops on their estates and to middle-class businessmen; it also supported efforts to lure skilled workers from abroad with the promise of high wages and good housing. The textile industry, producing wool, cotton, and linen cloth, became of first importance in Bohemia, Moravia, and Vienna. The Alpine regions, particularly Styria and Carinthia, produced iron and steel products, such as cutlery and basic farm implements. Although this period marked only the weak beginnings of industrialization, the Austrian economy was advanced for its time. In 1767, for example, Styria produced as much pig iron as England.

Despite the advancements made in the reform era and the popularity of many of the changes, particularly those accomplished during the reign of Maria Theresa, the radical nature of many of Joseph's measures caused such a strong reaction that he not only had to stop further action, but also had to withdraw some of his controversial enactments. At the end of his reign his Belgian lands were in revolt, Hungary was on the edge of rebellion, and there was widespread dissatisfaction with his rule. Nevertheless, his two great acts, the Toleration and Serfdom patents, remained as lasting monuments to his rule. His successor, his brother Leopold II (1790–1792), shared Joseph's enlightened goals, but a greater sense of political realism induced him to accept further retreats. He thus, for instance, reinstated the previous administrative organization of Hungary, so that the diet resumed its former authority. When Leopold died suddenly at the age of forty-five, the reform era came to an end.

Leopold was succeeded by his son Francis (1792–1835). The first period of his reign was dominated by the repeated disasters occasioned by the wars of the French Revolution and Napoleon. Soon after his accession he had to face the shock of the execution of his brother-in-law, Louis XVI, in January 1793, followed by that of his sister, Marie Antoinette, in October. Over the next years Austrian armies were repeatedly defeated by the French Army, and Habsburg territory was partitioned to French advantage. Moreover, the revolutionary ideas associated with France at this time went far beyond anything ever advocated by Joseph II and did indeed endanger the social order in the monarchy. The threats to Austrian possessions, to the social and political order, and to the Habsburg family scared most of the Austrian citizenry.

No attempt will be made here to describe the complicated events of over a quarter century of revolution and war. For future Habsburg history, however, two major changes occurred. First, in reordering the map of Europe Napoleon made significant alterations in the political organization of the German states. In July 1806, with the formation of the Confederation of the Rhine, about three hundred political jurisdictions in Germany were abolished. At the end of the fighting, thirty-nine states remained, of which four were free cities. Second, in May 1804 Napoleon made himself emperor in France. Foreseeing the inevitable loss of his position as Holy Roman Emperor, Francis in the same year assumed the title of emperor of Austria. After the formation of the Confederation of the Rhine, the medieval association was indeed brought to an end.

Despite its bad military record previously, the monarchy joined in the great coalition with other European powers in the final campaign against Napoleon. In March 1814 the victorious allies entered Paris, thus ending the long series of wars that had dominated European international relations during the previous century. The new era began with peace negotiations, held in Vienna, that were to create a territorial and political situation in Europe to the Habsburg advantage.

Although much of Habsburg history had in the previous century been dominated by warfare, it was the reform period that was to be most significant for the future of the state. Serfdom had been abolished, although some problems connected with it remained. A modern administrative system with an efficient, educated bureaucracy had been introduced in the Hereditary Lands and Bohemia. The legal system, placing all citizens on the same level, was one of the best in Europe. The assertion of state control over the church and the establishment of a secular school system were also steps forward. Most important was the recognition of the principle that the state could and should intervene to protect certain classes of the population from exploitation from others and to offer basic social services. This attitude was to become an attribute of Austrian government even after the dissolution of the empire.

1

THE AUSTRIAN EMPIRE, 1815–1867

T HE Congress of Vienna, which met from September 1814 to June 1815, resulted in a European settlement that was to lay the groundwork for a long period of peace. Another period of massive conflict, involving all of the great powers, was not to come until 1914. In the treaty some adjustments were made in the territory under Habsburg control (see Map 2). No attempt was made to retain the Austrian Netherlands and scattered German territory that had been lost during the war. However, Dalmatia, Venetia, Istria, and Salzburg, which had been held intermittently in the previous years, were now annexed. Some Polish territory was given up and Cracow was made a free city, but the major portion of the Galician acquisitions remained under Habsburg jurisdiction. The settlement reached in regard to the German and Italian lands was particularly advantageous to the monarchy. No attempt was made to revive the Holy Roman Empire or the multitude of prewar political jurisdictions. Instead a new organization, the German Confederation, joined the German states together. The Habsburg Empire and Prussia were given controlling positions, with Austria assigned the permanent presidency. The confederation also had a diet, which met in Frankfurt, composed of envoys instructed by the German princes. This weak union was empowered to send and receive ambassadors and to make war and sign treaties. This

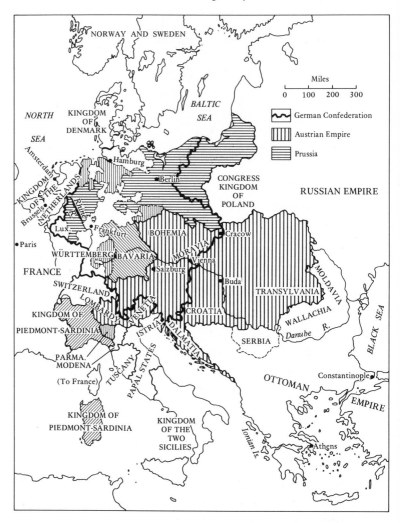

Map 2. Europe in 1815

arrangement placed the former territories of the Holy Roman Empire under the dual control of the two great powers, but also gave the smaller states of Germany some protection.

The Italian peninsula was similarly organized in a manner

30

favorable to Habsburg interests. Venetia was joined with the new acquisition of Lombardy to form the Kingdom of Lombardy-Venetia. The Italian states, with the exception of Piedmont-Sardinia, all had rulers who were either Habsburg relatives, as in Tuscany and Modena, or friendly allies, such as the Bourbon ruler of the Kingdom of the Two Sicilies and the pope for the Papal States. Parma was given to Francis's daughter, Maria Louisa, who had been married to Napoleon for a brief period.

At the conclusion of the conference the monarchy signed two general treaties. The first, the Quadruple Alliance, joined Austria with Britain, Russia, and Prussia in an agreement designed to protect the peace settlement and to guard against renewed French aggression. The second, the Holy Alliance, a pet scheme of Tsar Alexander I, was simply a declaration that the European rulers would conduct their policy according to Christian principles. Although this document had many signatories, only Alexander took it seriously. In later years the term *Holy Alliance* was used to designate the close alignment of Austria, Russia, and Prussia in international affairs.

CONSERVATIVE RULE: THE AGE OF METTERNICH

With the defeat of Napoleon and the negotiation of a stable peace settlement, the long period of stress and turmoil that had threatened not only the Habsburg government, but also the social and political system, came to an end. Throughout the Habsburg lands, as in Europe in general, there came a relaxation of tension, accompanied by a feeling of fatigue and a desire for stability: the Napoleonic age was over. In such circumstances Francis I was not ill fitted for his position. A plain man with an unassuming manner, but a strong sense of duty, he certainly had no dreams of imperial expansion or glory; military affairs did not interest him. Moreover,

Francis "the Good" had habits that were appealing in an age of quiet and comfort. Court life was kept simple. The emperor gave audiences freely and walked unescorted in the city parks of Vienna. His convictions and manner of life won him the approval of those who, like himself, wanted to keep everything in Austria as it was.

The rest of Francis's reign was certainly not a period of revolutionary striving or heroic activity. The Biedermeier period, whose name came from that of a fictional school-teacher, reflected the recognition among much of the population of the joys of peace and the moderate prosperity of the time. It was an age that placed an emphasis on simple pleasures, on family life, and on comfort and happiness. Influenced by the Romantic movement, Austrians became deeply interested in the natural world and came to appreciate the beauty of their spectacular Alpine regions. Reflecting the preferences of what was a middle-class as well as an aristocratic clientele, artists produced, in particular, landscape paintings, such as those by Georg Waldmüller, and miniatures and lithographs, often endowed with a picturesque or sentimental quality. Biedermeier furniture, a modified version of Napoleonic imperial styles, reflected the values of simplicity, comfort, and quiet beauty.

The reign of Francis I marked the end of Enlightened Despotism and radical reform, but it was not a period of intense repression. There was, however, certainly a reaction against the ideas of the French Revolution, which had been spread as a result of Napoleon's conquests. The major reforms remained, but the spirit in which they were administered changed. This modification was caused in part by the shift in the attitude of the aristocracy toward the court. Joseph II, it will be remembered, had attacked the special position of the nobility and had attempted to break down the historic privileges not only of this class, but of regions such as the

Hungarian kingdom. During his reign the nobility thus tended to be in opposition to the central government. The French Revolution affected the attitudes of both parties. The external and internal dangers showed the court and the nobility, closely attached to the provincial diets, that they needed each other. The centralists and those who wished to defend local historic rights thus learned to cooperate; the central government institutions came to act more often in the interest of the aristocracy. The feudal estates society was not restored, but the conservative direction of government policy appeared to guarantee the maintainance of the aristocratic privileges that remained.

The determination of the government to keep conditions as they were and to prevent the influx of revolutionary ideas was backed by positive actions. The school system was used to indoctrinate proper attitudes; the church aided in this task. Censorship and police interference, which had also been a part of life under Joseph II, remained. Although the offices of repression were in place, they were in fact seldom used in a drastic manner. Although prior censorship of publications was extremely annoying to writers and newspaper publishers, and the existence of controls undoubtedly repressed and discouraged literary activity, these measures were not accompanied by obvious outward violence. There were also no political trials during the last twenty years of Francis's reign.

Although the Habsburg Empire was served by a large bureaucracy, there were no adequate central offices. The emperor alone was in a position to survey the work of all the departments and to make the basic decisions. To meet the demands of his office, Francis worked very hard. Leopold II had seventeen children, so there were also always archdukes available for state service. In addition to the members of his family, Francis relied chiefly on two able ministers – Count

Franz Anton Kolowrat and Clemens von Metternich, two men who usually disagreed on fundamental questions. Kolowrat was especially effective in internal administration; in fact, until 1848 he exerted the major influence over domestic affairs. A great Bohemian landowner, with some liberal ideas, he objected to many points in Metternich's foreign policy. He opposed, for instance, an active involvement in affairs that would require large expenditures on the army. During his period in office the Habsburg armed forces declined in strength and effectiveness. A centralist in administration, he disagreed with Metternich's conception of the proper organization of the monarchy.

The dominant figure in Austrian history at this time and one of the greatest European statesmen of any period, Metternich gave his name to the era. Born in Coblenz in the Rhineland in May 1773, Metternich, like his father, entered Austrian state service. Rising fast in the diplomatic corps, he became ambassador to France in 1806 and came to know Napoleon well. In 1809, when the monarchy was in a condition of demoralization and defeat, he became foreign minister. Attempting at first to appease the French conqueror, he negotiated the marriage of Maria Louisa and then tried to exploit the relationship. In August 1813 he brought Austria into the final coalition against France. The Austrian Army thus fought in the decisive Battle of the Nations at Leipzig in October 1813. After the victory Metternich presided over and was a major influence at the Congress of Vienna; the settlement reached there reflected many of his views. As a representative of the generation of the aristocracy that had been most deeply injured by the French wars, he too believed that the revolutionary doctrines of liberty and equality would inevitably lead to internal and foreign disasters.

At the Vienna conference Metternich strongly supported the restoration of the balance of power and the maintenance

Clemens von Metternich

in many cases of changes accomplished during the Napoleonic period as the best way to preserve order. His attitude
was clearly shown in his program for the German area. He
made no attempt to restore the Holy Roman Empire, and he
accepted the secularization and mediatization that had been

accomplished under French direction. He, however, wanted national consolidation to go no further, although a certain measure of federal unity among monarchical states under Habsburg leadership was acceptable to him, a condition that he achieved with the formation of the German Confederation. In Germany, as in the Habsburg Monarchy, he could thus be called a federalist. He was also quite willing to allow Prussia an important role in German affairs, especially in programs to prevent revolutionary activity in Central Europe. In this endeavor, and to preserve the Vienna settlement, he favored the cooperation of the five great powers.

Despite the major role that Metternich played in foreign affairs, his influence within the government was limited. Although the final years of Francis's reign were in general a peaceful period, a problem did arise over the question of succession. The eldest son, Ferdinand, was epileptic and retarded. Since the heir was under his influence, Metternich nevertheless stood strongly by the hereditary principle. When Francis died in February 1835, Ferdinand (1835–1848) did indeed become emperor, but the power in the government was placed in the hands of a State Conference, appointed in December 1836. Although Ferdinand was supposed to preside over this body, his duties were taken over by his uncle, Archduke Ludwig. Ferdinand's brother, Archduke Franz Karl, Metternich, and Kolowrat were all members of the State Conference. Ferdinand's inability to fulfill the obligations of his office was damaging to Austrian imperial interests; the absolute monarchy was now without a functioning monarch.

Meanwhile, despite the political stalemate, life was changing, and most important, the influences of the new industrial age were becoming apparent. The late 1820s to 1840s were marked by continuing and even accelerating progress in exactly those areas whose beginnings in the eighteenth century have been previously noted. However, unlike the situation in the mercantile age, the government did not act to further industrial progress. Francis and his advisers could not be expected to support developments that might upset the internal order. Nevertheless, the textile industry continued to expand, with the centers still in Bohemia, Moravia, and the Vienna region. Machinery, often imported from England, was used for cotton and wool spinning. Iron and steel production increased, particularly in the Alpine regions, but the lack of convenient coal supplies hampered its development.

The period also witnessed rapid improvements in transportation, most notably the building of railroads. Here the government did take a leading role, since it quickly understood the military and economic significance of an adequate rail system. Both state and private capital were involved in financing the railroads, but a decree of 1841 established that the government would have the deciding voice in planning. Austria, in fact, had the first continental European railroad. In 1832 a horsedrawn train was in operation between Budweis (České Budějovice) and Linz, a distance of about seventy-eight miles. Vienna was and remained the center of the railroad network. In a parallel development, the government concerned itself with the improvement of roads and canals. In this period steam navigation began on the Austrian rivers; in 1829 the Danube Steamship Company (Donaudampfschiffahrtsgesellschaft or DDSG) was founded, which was to play a major role in the commercial life of the river.

With the growth in industry, the working class naturally increased in size and significance. In Austria, as elsewhere, early industrialization was accompanied by bad working conditions. Long hours, crowded housing, and low pay were the rule. The urban population also rose: Vienna grew from a city of over two hundred thousand in 1780 to one of more than four hundred thousand around the middle of the century. Nevertheless, the monarchy remained a basically agricultural country; in 1846 about 74 percent of the population was engaged in farming or related occupations, with just under 17 percent in industry and mining.

The heavy emphasis on agriculture made it important that conditions in the countryside be satisfactory. However, neither the noble landowners nor the peasants were happy with the situation. The reforms of the eighteenth century had given the peasant personal freedom, but not land. He objected in particular to the continuation of the heavy labor service, the *robot,* which he owed in return for the use of his plot of land. Many progressive landlords also desired a new system; they wished to follow in the path of their counterparts in Britain and Prussia and organize their estates as producing units, employing farm laborers and introducing scientific improvements. In general, the nobles too wanted the robot replaced; they, however, wished to be indemnified in cash. The peasant, without monetary resources, and the landlord both looked to the government to arrange a new relationship.

By the 1840s the peasantry was faced with additional problems. The rural population was growing, but the industrial development was not adequate to absorb the excess. Payments and taxes rose during the century, but agricultural prices did not show a similar increase. By this time also the individual peasant had lost his faith in the system; he did not believe that God had placed him in a subservient position and that he should accept his lot. He was now more willing to adopt aggressive and violent measures to achieve his major goal: the full possession of the land he worked.

Whereas the grievances of the peasants were closely tied to their economic and social disabilities, other sections of the population wanted political reform. Two great revolutionary ideologies, liberalism and nationalism, both with their origins in the time of the French Revolution, continued to attract passionate adherents. The Austrian middle class – composed of merchants, manufacturers, artisans, bureaucrats, and those in professions, including lawyers, doctors, and teachers – was particularly attracted to liberal doctrines. Since members of this class were primarily German-speaking, they felt few national pressures. They did, however, suffer from the consequences of inefficient government and state regulation. Moreover, they had access to books, papers, and pamphlets propagating revolutionary ideologies. Austrian censorship was never particularly effective; it was difficult to deny access to foreign books to an educated middle class. The more politically involved of this group became extremely attracted to the standard liberal program of the era. The emphasis was on political reform with the goal of establishing constitutional government, including representative institutions that would give the taxpayer some control over public expenditures and a voice in the formulation of national policy. Liberals were not democrats; they usually favored a franchise with strict property or tax qualifications. In addition, they also supported the adoption of a standard program of civil liberties, including the guarantee of the right to free speech, assembly, and an uncensored press. They also supported agricultural reform and the end of robot services, not only for ideological reasons, but because they knew that an efficient farming system would ensure the availability of cheap food. The city working class had similar interests. The adoption of the liberal program would cause major modifications in Habsburg political institutions, but it did not call for a basic social or economic revolution.

If liberalism appealed to some elements of the middle class, nationalism was bound to attract adherents among the politically active, non-German people, particularly among the Hungarians. As we have seen, in the past the Hungarian nobles had consistently fought for an autonomous relationship with Vienna and what they defined as their historical rights. Hungarian nationalism at this time showed some new features, which reflected current nationalist ideology. In the nineteenth century language became one of the major criteria to determine national identity. In 1843 the Hungarian diet replaced Latin with Hungarian as the official language to be used in administration and education in the lands of the kingdom. This measure affected adversely the non-Hungarian nationalities, who made up half the population. In addition, radical Hungarian liberal leaders called for a reorganization of the monarchy, with the Hungarian crownlands, including Transylvania and Croatia, organized as a centralized, autonomous state, which would then be joined only by weak links to the rest of the monarchy. Hungarian liberals thus called for major changes in the state structure, and they supported many of the same political ideals as did their German and Italian counterparts.

Although no revolutionary movements disturbed Austrian domestic tranquility before the middle of the century, Metternich in foreign relations was forced to deal with a series of revolts in the German and Italian lands, where direct Habsburg interests were involved and where liberalism and nationalism were indeed revolutionary ideals. He was able to control the situation and to manipulate events primarily because he could work closely with Tsars Alexander I (1801–1825) and Nicholas I (1825–1855) and with the Prussian king, Frederick William III (1797–1840). Joined together in the Holy Alliance, the conservative rulers accepted the principle that they, representing the majority of the great powers, had the right and duty to intervene to prevent the overthrow of legitimate governments by force and violence. The French and British governments often cooperated with them in these endeavors.

Of first concern to Metternich were the revolutionary manifestations in the German states connected with the national and liberal revival that commenced in the Napoleonic period and continued into the conservative era. The most obvious signs of subversive activities occurred in the universities and in student organizations. Deeply affected by the spirit of the Romantic age, some groups adopted signs and symbols from the past, including the use of the colors red, black, and gold, associated with the Holy Roman Empire and medieval German greatness. Moreover, certain rulers in the middle states, in particular in Bavaria, Baden, and Saxe-Weimar, were willing to grant liberal institutions. At the same time, some public celebrations, for example, the Wartburg Festival of October 1817, held to commemorate the Reformation and the Battle of Leipzig, seemed to present dangerous revolutionary challenges. Metternich was able to use such events to persuade Frederick William III to join him in instituting repressive measures. In August 1819 representatives of the German states met at Karlsbad, where they passed a series of decrees designed to curb revolutionary activity and to control the universities and student activities. The diet of the German Confederation accepted these measures. The Habsburg government was thus able to assert its leadership in the area, but at the same time it alienated German national and liberal sentiments.

Similar events occurred in Italy. Here the first revolts were not so much national as directed against native repressive regimes, in particular those in the Papal States and in the Kingdom of the Two Sicilies. When a revolt broke out in Naples and King Ferdinand appealed for aid, a Habsburg army marched down the peninsula to restore his autocratic powers. Metternich also approved of French intervention in Spain in 1823 to suppress a revolutionary movement there. He was, however, to be disappointed by the reaction of the powers to the Greek revolution of the 1820s; here France, Russia, and Britain cooperated to establish an independent Greece in 1830.

The revolutionary wave of the 1830s brought similarly mixed results. Once again Habsburg troops entered Italy, this time to put down revolts in Parma, Modena, and the Papal States; the German Confederation again moved to suppress revolutionary activities within the member states; and the Russian Army crushed a revolt that broke out in the Russian-controlled parts of partitioned Poland. However, an insurrection in Paris succeeded in bringing a new monarch, Louis Philippe, to the throne, and an anti-Dutch uprising led to the establishment of an independent Belgium in 1831.

Nevertheless, until the late 1840s Metternich was able to contain the revolutionary elements in the two areas of major concern – the Germanies and the Italian peninsula. In addition, no rebellions had occurred in the Habsburg domains despite the growing discontent with conservative rule. Metternich's ability to control Prussian policy had certainly been a major element in his success; Frederick William III had not challenged the Austrian leadership. Nevertheless, in one field the Prussian position in Central Europe was strengthened. Starting in 1819 Prussia began to sign a series of commercial agreements with other German states, thus establishing a customs union (*Zollverein*) that by 1848 included most of the German states, but not Hanover and the Habsburg Empire. Prussian–Habsburg relations were also affected when Frederick William IV (1840–1861) became king. A difficult and erratic ruler with contradictory ideas, he was affected by the spirit of the Romantic age. He respected the Habsburg Empire as the first of the German powers, and he was attracted to the concept of the Holy Roman Empire, but he was not as pliable and open to Austrian suggestions as his predecessor. Similarly, in Italy new leaders assumed office. In 1846 Pope

Gregory XVI, who had been close to Vienna, died; he was followed by Pius IX, who was expected to introduce reforms. Even more significant, Charles Albert (1831–1849) was now king of Piedmont. A new era was about to open in German and Italian affairs.

These changes abroad were paralleled by a growing discontent at home. Not only had nationalist ideologies affected, in particular, many Hungarians and Italians, but the peasantry was becoming increasingly restive. In 1845, 1846, and 1847 a series of natural disasters caused a dramatic fall in farm production. Hunger joined social discontent to turn the peasant into a potential revolutionary. Moreover, Vienna, the seat of the government, had also become a possible powderkeg. The city had a middle-class intellectual leadership, well versed in revolutionary doctrine and tactics; it could count on the support of a discontented and exploited working class, which had also been made aware of radical action programs. The stage was thus set for the revolutionary year of 1848.

THE REVOLUTIONS OF 1848

Similar conditions existed throughout Europe; everywhere popular discontent and radical organization created a propitious atmosphere for revolution. The first revolts occurred in Sicily in January; in Paris in February Louis Philippe was overthrown. The revolutionary wave next engulfed the German states and the Habsburg lands, with revolts breaking out simultaneously in Vienna, Prague, and Budapest, as well as in Lombardy-Venetia. In the cities the leadership was in the hands of the liberal middle class, supported by students and workers; in the countryside the peasants joined the rebellion and demanded the end of the robot.

For the Habsburg government the events in Vienna were

most disturbing. On March 13 the streets filled with crowds demanding reforms, in particular the enactment of a constitution that would meet liberal demands. A national guard was formed; students were organized into the Academic Legion. Since the Habsburg Army was concentrated in the Italian and Hungarian lands, the court did not have troops to use against the armed revolutionaries, and concessions had to be made. Metternich, the symbol for the crowd of reactionary rule, was forced to flee; a reorganized ministry, under pressure, then agreed to the convocation of a representative assembly that was to formulate a constitution. Most important, on March 28 a rescript was issued accepting the abolition of the robot in principle, with compensation to be given the landlords. Censorship was also ended. On April 25 the government issued a preliminary constitution for the Habsburg lands with the exception of Hungary, which by now had its own revolutionary regime. According to this document Austria was to become a constitutional monarchy with a bicameral legislature chosen on a restricted franchise. When these provisions met with popular disapproval, and when more rioting in the streets occurred, the constitution was changed to provide for a single-chamber assembly elected without a property qualification for voting.

Despite the concessions, the court felt that the situation in Vienna was too dangerous, so it moved to Innsbruck on May 17, leaving the revolutionary leaders in control of the city. Elections were held in June and July everywhere but in the Italian and Hungarian lands, where fighting had broken out. On July 22 the first parliament in Habsburg history opened under the presidency of Archduke Johann. The deputies were not radicals. Of the 303 elected, the majority came from the educated professional middle class, but 94 were peasants; there were 160 Germans, with the rest Slavs, Italians, or Romanians. At Custozza three days later, on July 24, the Habsburg army defeated Charles Albert and the Piedmontese Army, which had come to the aid of the rebels in Lombardy-Venetia. This military victory, combined with the capture of Prague in June, greatly improved the position of the conservative forces; in August the court judged it safe to return to Vienna.

The great achievement of the assembly was the full emancipation of the peasants, except in Hungary. The robot and other obligations were abolished; as far as compensation was concerned, in return for a recognized full ownership of their land, the peasants paid a third of the cost, with the state and the lords contributing the rest equally. The measures took years to work out in detail, but the relative smoothness by which the task was accomplished had a negative effect on the revolutionary movement. The peasants, having what they wanted, tended to become nonpolitical and to withdraw from participation in further revolutionary activities. Moreover, many felt that the benefits had been a gift from the court rather than an accomplishment of the revolution.

With this major question settled, the assembly began a long period of debate on other issues. Meanwhile, revolutionary activity revived in Vienna. The renewed violence and the street demonstrations began to alarm some middle-class property owners, natural champions of law and order. They as well as the peasants began to move to the right. Feeling threatened by the renewed agitation, the court in October moved to Olmütz (Olomouc); at the same time the assembly was prorogued to meet again in November in Kremsier (Kroměříž) in Moravia. The court was now in an even stronger position. Not only had the loyal Habsburg army been victorious in Italy, but the troops had taken control in Prague.

The revolutionary movement in Bohemia produced an event that was to influence subsequent Habsburg history. In Prague a Slavic conference opened on June 2 that was intended to be the counterpart to the German national assembly that had been called to convene in Frankfurt. This meeting, under the leadership of František Palacký, demanded the organization of the empire on a multinational basis. It enunciated the concept of Austroslavism — that is, that the Habsburg Slavs should seek an autonomous organization within the monarchy rather than independence. The delegates expressed their opposition to German or Magyar domination, but they feared that should the state break up, the small nationalities would fall under Russian or German rule. Although Austroslavism thereafter remained an important alternative in the various discussions on the reorganization of the Habsburg Empire, the assembly was unable to achieve any practical goals before it was disbanded by the army. Riots and demonstrations, similar to those in Vienna, broke out in Prague. When students and workers clashed with the soldiers, Gen. Alfred Windischgrätz took control on June 17, established a military government, and put an end to all revolutionary manifestations. Having accomplished this task, Windischgrätz led the army to Vienna, where it acted in a similar manner. Once the revolutionary regime in that city was suppressed, the court could again return.

Despite the military victories, it was clear that the central government would have to be strengthened. The monarchy could not continue to function with a mentally incompetent emperor. Members of the Habsburg family thus cooperated with strong ministers, among whom were Felix Schwarzenberg, Franz Stadion, Alexander Bach, and Karl Bruck. In December Ferdinand was persuaded to abdicate in favor of his eighteen-year-old nephew Franz, who took the name Joseph after that of the reforming emperor. In the first years of the new reign the emperor was strongly under the influence of Schwarzenberg, who proved to be an able minister in the mold of Kaunitz and Metternich.

The elected assembly, meeting in Kremsier, began debates on a constitution in January 1849 and by March had produced a draft. The arguments over the provisions showed a major division of opinion on the future organization of the state: the chief question at issue was whether the historic provinces should be retained or be replaced by new divisions drawn along ethnic lines. A compromise was reached by which the historical divisions were to remain, but they were to be subdivided according to nationality. A similar middle path was followed on the issue of a centralized or decentralized government. As far as the monarch's power was concerned, the constitution allowed him only a suspensive veto over legislation, but a large measure of control over foreign policy and the military. Ministers were to be responsible to the two-house legislature, elected on a generous franchise. The Kremsier constitution, as can be seen, expressed the liberal program.

Meanwhile, the court under its rejuvenated leadership was drawing up its own constitution. In contrast to the Kremsier delegates, the ministers favored a centralized regime, and they wanted the monarch to have an absolute veto. With the army under their control, they were able to dissolve the assembly in March; the delegates were told that they should go home and that the emperor would issue a constitution of his own. This document, drawn up under the direction of Stadion, called for a strongly centralist regime; there was to be one citizenship, one legal system, and one assembly. The monarch was to be crowned only as emperor of Austria; he was to have an absolute veto, and he could issue emergency decrees. This document, never put into effect, was formally rescinded in December 1851.

Although in full control in the rest of the monarchy by the end of 1848, the government was to find Hungary a more difficult matter. In March 1848, under extreme pressure on all fronts, the court had been forced to concede autonomous rights to the revolutionary Hungarian regime. That government, under the leadership of Lajos Kossuth, proceded to create the type of state preferred by the strong Hungarian nationalists. With the adoption of the March Laws a liberal constitutional system was indeed introduced, but the historical divisions of Croatia and Transylvania were abolished. With their nationalist convictions overriding their liberal sympathies, the leaders attempted to govern as if indeed the lands of the Crown of St. Stephen were inhabited only by Magyars. As a result, the Romanian and Slavic populations turned against the revolution and sought aid from Vienna. Even in this situation the Habsburg government could not put down the rebellion. In May 1849 Franz Joseph asked Nicholas I to aid him. Russian forces then joined with the Habsburg Army in an invasion of the Hungarian lands; the revolt was crushed in August. Although Nicholas I thus did indeed come to the aid of a fellow monarch facing a rebellion, this action was to cause problems for the future.

With the revolutionary activities within the monarchy ended, the government could turn to completing the task of reestablishing control in the Italian peninsula and the Germanies. The Italian revolt, which had commenced in the Kingdom of the Two Sicilies in January 1848 spread rapidly to other states. In March Charles Albert gave in to the demands of the revolutionaries and granted a constitution. His action gave Italian nationalists a leader. When Lombardy-Venetia revolted, he agreed to come to the aid of the province. At first the Habsburg government had attempted to negotiate, but it could not accept the Piedmontese demands for the independence of Lombardy-Venetia and the cession of southern Tirol. The victory of Field Marshal Joseph Radetzky at Custozza in July and the subsequent Habsburg occupation of Milan resulted in the negotiation of an armistice.

Fighting flared up again in March 1849, but Charles Albert was once again defeated. Peace was subsequently made on the basis of the status quo ante and the payment by Piedmont of an indemnity. Charles Albert then abdicated; he was followed by Victor Emmanuel II (1849–1878), who kept the constitution and thereby won the approval of Italian liberals and nationalists.

For Habsburg history the events in the Germanies had even greater significance. As has been seen, after 1815 the monarchy did indeed hold supremacy in the Germanies; Prussia did not directly challenge Habsburg primacy. Although Metternich favored cooperation among the German princes, he strongly opposed national movements, particularly those with a popular base. German national revolutionary forces thus could not look to Vienna for support or inspiration, but they had more to expect from Berlin. For some this second German state seemed more German-national in character, despite its Polish minority, than did the multinational Habsburg Empire. Once the revolution broke out, Prussia appeared also to be liberal. In March Frederick William IV accepted the demands of the revolutionary leadership for a constitution and the eventual merging of Prussia into a united Germany.

The central event in the German revolution was, however, the convocation of delegates from the various states in an assembly in Frankfurt whose task was to be to prepare a constitution for a united Germany. Archduke Johann, whose views did not conform with those of most of the Habsburg family, became head of the executive branch of a provisional regime established in July. The diet of the German Confederation was suspended. The first moves toward national unity had thus been taken, but there were certain grave weaknesses in the revolutionary camp, in particular its lack of a military force. Moreover, not only did many of the delegates not have the full backing of their own states, but, coming from only a narrow social and economic segment of German society – mostly university-educated teachers, lawyers, doctors, writers, and civil servants – they had few links with the majority of the people. The assembly also could not agree on a single program. The major debate came over the question whether Germany should be united on a *grossdeutsch* basis, that is, with the inclusion of Habsburg German and Bohemian territory, or on the *kleindeutsch* alternative, which, by excluding the monarchy, would give Prussia the predominating position. The victory in October of the kleindeutsch camp showed the relative weakness of Habsburg influence in nationalist circles.

In March 1849 the assembly finally agreed upon a constitution creating a united Germany without the Austrian lands. The crown was then offered to Frederick William IV, who refused. With no viable alternative as chief executive, the revolutionary movement collapsed. Although the Prussian king would not accept a German crown from a revolutionary assembly, he was willing and eager to receive a similar invitation from the German princes. The Prussian action, however, came too late. Having defeated its major internal enemies, the Habsburg government could turn to the task of reestablishing its position of leadership in the Germanies; Franz Joseph and his advisers saw the German question chiefly as a struggle between the two princely houses of Habsburg and Hohenzollern. Not only did they wish to restore the German Confederation, but Schwarzenberg, presenting a vision of a great empire of seventy million stretching through the center of Europe, wanted to include in it all of the Habsburg lands. In this quarrel between Prussia and the Habsburg Empire, the Russian government, to protect its own interests, used its influence to persuade both powers to accept the re-formation of the German Confederation on the basis of 1815. The Habsburg government also failed to gain another objective. Aware of the significance of the Prussian-led Zollverein, Bruck, the minister of commerce, attempted unsuccessfully to bring Austria into this economic union. Austria and Prussia did, however, sign a commercial treaty in 1853.

The revolutionary era in Central Europe thus was brought to a close with the restoration of the old order. No problems had been solved. Neither liberalism nor nationalism had lost its appeal as an attractive political program. Italian, Hungarian, and German nationalists could not be expected to abandon their struggles for unified national states. Nor had the Habsburg government solved the problem of developing political institutions that would bind more closely together its various nationalities, with their differing political, economic, and social interests.

NEOABSOLUTISM: THE UNIFICATION OF ITALY

With the reestablishment of its control over the domestic situation and with the regaining of predominance in the German and Italian areas, the Habsburg government still had to face the problem of how best to deal with both the internal and the foreign situations in the future. The revolutionary years had, as we have seen, brought a new emperor to the throne. Given the nature of the Austrian state, with the central position of the ruler in the political system, the character and attitude of Franz Joseph were of immense importance. Born in August 1830 in Schönbrunn, he had received the rigorous and careful training given a possible heir to the throne. He had served in the army, fighting in Lombardy-Venetia in 1848. He had also, of course, experienced the extreme danger that the revolutionary years had posed for the dynasty and the country. Thereafter he was deeply involved in all decisions affecting matters of state. Although he proved to be a competent administrator, he was to face a period in which Habsburg power declined rapidly, both in international relations and in its ability to assure internal cohesion and tranquility. The emperor also did not have a particularly fortunate personal life. In 1854 he married his sixteen-year-old first cousin Elisabeth, of the Bavarian Wittelsbach family. An exceptionally beautiful woman, with whom Franz Joseph was deeply in love, Elisabeth was neither willing nor able to accept the responsibilities of her imperial position. She spent much of her time traveling and was finally assassinated in Geneva in 1898. The emperor's children also caused him grief. A daughter died in infancy, and his only son, Rudolf, who resembled his mother, had difficulty adjusting to the life required of an heir to the throne. Married to a Belgian princess he did not like, he ended his life in January 1889 by shooting himself and his mistress, Marie Vetsera, in a hunting lodge at Mayerling. The new heir, Franz Ferdinand, displeased the emperor by insisting upon contracting a morganatic marriage; he and his wife were assassinated in 1914, an act leading to the outbreak of World War I. It should also be remembered that Franz Joseph's brother, Maximilian, was executed by a firing squad in Mexico in 1867.

The emperor faced his personal problems by burying himself in his work. Having received the upbringing of a prince of the old school, he had deeply ingrained in him a strong sense of duty toward the dynasty and the state, concepts that were identical in his mind. He considered the Habsburg Empire a natural unit. Although he felt himself to be a German prince and preferred that language, he had no deep feelings on the matter and felt instead that his obligations extended to all of his subjects. He personally lived a simple life, but he insisted upon a strict observance of court etiquette and ceremonial. He was tactful, self-disciplined, and practical, with

Franz Joseph

a strong sense of honor. He was not doctrinaire; ideas as such did not much interest him. Many felt that he was cold, and he had few close associates. His main endeavor was to hold the empire together. With this goal he hesitated to accept any major changes that might disrupt the internal order, and he did not support an active or expansionistic foreign policy. Like Queen Victoria in Britain, he gave his name to an era in his country's history. During these years he won the respect and affection of a great part of the Austrian population.

With the victory of the court and a young ruler on the throne, the Habsburg leadership attempted to establish a system that would ensure domestic order and be strong enough to maintain its primacy in Central Europe and the Italian peninsula. Until his death in 1852 Schwarzenberg exerted the chief influence in the government. He worked closely with Franz Joseph, who in turn trusted and respected him. Thereafter, the emperor in practice became his own chief minister. The solution to the empire's myriad problems was again seen in the establishment of a centralized administration that would be strong enough to demonstrate to the internal and external enemies that the state was unified and indissoluble. In June 1849 Alexander Bach became minister of interior; his name is usually given to the new period of neoabsolutism. The Stadion constitution, despite its conservative and centralist nature, was abandoned, and instead the Sylvester Patent was issued on December 31, 1851. Under its terms the emperor held supreme power; there were no representative institutions.

The new regulations were directed in particular against Hungarian separatism. Like most of the rest of the state, the Hungarian kingdom was divided into districts; Croatia-Slavonia, Transylvania, and Vojvodina were now separate units. The local administrations were abolished and the country was placed under the direct control of the bureaucracy in Vienna. Since it was difficult to find Hungarians with the necessary knowledge of German, men of other nationalities, often Czechs, were brought in. It should be noted that the system was applied not only to the Hungarians who had rebelled, but also to Romanians, Serbs, and Croats who had supported the court against the Hungarian revolution. They therefore could complain that they won in return for their aid and assistance exactly what the Hungarians received for their rebellion. Indeed, this centralized administration was introduced throughout the empire, with two notable exceptions: Lombardy-Venetia, which retained its organization as a separate kingdom; and Galicia, where, under the governorship of Agenor Goluchowski, the Polish aristocracy was able to maintain almost full control of its own affairs.

The Bach period also witnessed a strengthening of the position of the Catholic church, which wished to use the opportunity to regain its influence over matters such as family law and educational policy. It also wished to rid itself of state interference and to be able to remain in close touch with the Vatican. After 1850 many of its desires were fulfilled. With the signing of the Concordat of 1855 the church regained some of the privileges that it had lost during the reform period in the eighteenth century. In education it again had the right to oversee the content of instruction to assure that the subjects taught and the materials used were not in conflict with its teachings.

Despite the return to a system of stricter political controls and centralized administration, this period was characterized by strong efforts to modernize the economy, with many measures corresponding to current liberal economic theory, including a drastic reduction in the tariffs. The railroad network continued to expand. Here the most spectacular Austrian achievement was the completion in 1854 of the first mountain railroad, which ran from over the Semmering Pass and connected Vienna with Trieste. This city was the single Habsburg commercial seaport of significance. At this time also the measures fully emancipating the peasants, passed previously, were carried through.

The Bach system was designed to assure a period of stability and calm. Unfortunately for official policy, the years from 1853 to 1859 were marked by continual crises in foreign policy. Although nationalism within the empire had been contained, it continued to be the great doctrine of liberation movements not only in German and Italian lands, but also among the Christian people of the monarchy's Ottoman neighbor. Throughout the nineteenth century the Habsburg Empire was involved in the Eastern Question, that is, with the problems that arose in connection with the weakening of the Ottoman Empire and the revolt of some sections of its population. For Vienna prior to 1853 the most important events were the Serbian uprisings of 1804 and 1815, which resulted in the establishment of a semiautonomous principality and, even more significant, the formation of an independent Greek state in 1830. In regard to the Greek revolution of 1821, a major event in European diplomatic history, Metternich, who opposed all revolutions and feared increasing Russian influence in the Balkans, first had tried to restrain tsarist intervention and then had left the major responsibilities in the hands of France, Britain, and Russia. The monarchy played a larger part in the Egyptian crises of the 1830s, but its role in the Eastern Question remained subordinate to that of the other three great powers, who at this time were in strong competition over who should dominate and direct Ottoman affairs.

The Crimean War of 1853–1856 was to place the Habsburg Empire directly in the center of this rivalry. In 1853 Russia and the Ottoman Empire went to war; in 1854 France and Britain and in 1855 Piedmont joined on the Ottoman side. Although the basic issue in the conflict, the relation of Russia to the Balkan Orthodox Christians, was of deep concern to Vienna, the Habsburg statesmen were placed in an extremely difficult situation. The basic Habsburg alignment in foreign policy was still the Holy Alliance, involving a close relationship with Prussia and Russia. In addition, the Russian government, expecting a repayment for the assistance that it had given in crushing the Hungarian revolt, wished the Habsburg government to adopt a policy of benevolent neutrality, not active intervention. Prussia, in fact, did assume what the Russian government regarded as a satisfactory attitude.

Pressure, however, also came from the opposing side. The Western allies were faced with the difficult problem of finding a suitable battlefield on which to fight their adversary.

Should the monarchy enter the war, a direct route into Russia would be opened. Habsburg forces would then, of course, face the unpleasant prospect of fighting on the front lines. Britain and France had effective weapons with which to put pressure on Vienna: for instance, the French government threatened to support Italian national forces fighting Habsburg rule. Piedmont was, after all, a Western ally, and its government was eager to use the occasion to forward nationalist interests.

Faced with equally impossible choices the Habsburg government wavered and finally, by issuing an ultimatum to Russia, forced it to make peace. In 1855 Nicholas I died; his successor, Alexander II, was extremely bitter about what he regarded as an Austrian betrayal. The breaking of the Holy Alliance and the subsequent Russian support for French policy in Italy and for Prussia in the German question were to have disastrous consequences for Habsburg interests in these areas. With Russian acceptance, national unification movements were henceforth to proceed in the Danubian Principalities, the Italian peninsula, and the Germanies. In each case, the results were detrimental to the monarchy's internal and external situation.

The first event in this new era of national consolidation occurred in the Danubian Principalities of Moldavia and Wallachia, where in the winter of 1858–1859 the same man, Alexandru Cuza, was elected as prince in both provinces; in 1861 the administrations were amalgamated. The leaders of the Romanian movement had participated in the 1848 revolutionary activity. Liberal and national in conviction, they and their successors were bound to consider Transylvania, where the majority of the population was Romanian, as one of their future objectives. Although the Habsburg government opposed the double election, it could not act because of the situation in Italy.

Since 1815 the Habsburg Empire had been faced with the danger of revolt in the Italian peninsula. After its victory in 1848–1849, the monarchy continued to collaborate closely with the conservative regimes in the Kingdom of the Two Sicilies, the Papal States, Tuscany, Parma, and Modena. The intense national feeling of the previous years had, of course, in no sense been stifled. Moreover, the revolutionary leaders knew who their principal opponent was: the Habsburg Empire. In direct control of Lombardy-Venetia and the chief support of the reactionary regimes in Italy, the monarchy was the obvious target for attack. In contrast, Piedmont served as a point of attraction. Victor Emmanuel II had kept the constitution of 1848, and he was served by a brilliant premier, Camillo di Cavour. Understanding the workings of the international system, Cavour first brought Piedmont into the Crimean War to gain attention to the Italian cause. He then assiduously courted his ally, France, whose ruler, Napoleon III, not only had come to power because of the events of 1848, but also was sympathetic to national movements. In July 1858 Napoleon met Cavour at Plombières and promised French support to Piedmont if war should break out with Austria, but only if that state appeared to be the aggressor. After the war was won, Napoleon wished the peninsula to be organized as a confederation of states, much like that in the Germanies. France also negotiated to assure the neutrality of Russia.

The Habsburg Empire was not prepared at this time for a military confrontation with a major power. Expenditures on the army had not been sufficient to ensure a first-class fighting force. Nevertheless, the monarchy allowed itself to be provoked into declaring war, and it invaded Piedmont at the end of April 1859. Honoring his agreement, Napoleon came to the support of the Italian national cause. The Habsburg effort was also hampered by doubts about the reliability of the empire's Italian and Hungarian troops. Napoleon had been in touch with Kossuth and other Hungarian leaders who were in exile. Although France won battles at Magenta and Solferino, the victories were not decisive. Unsure of the attitude of the German states should war continue and unenthusiastic about the course events were taking, Napoleon III met with Franz Joseph at Villafranca, where the two monarchs drew up a compromise arrangement without Piedmontese participation. Their agreement, which called for little more than the Habsburg cession of Lombardy to Piedmont, was overturned by the actions of revolutionaries in the other Italian states, in particular by those of Giuseppe Garibaldi in the Kingdom of the Two Sicilies. By 1861 the Italian states were unified under the leadership of Piedmont with two exceptions – Venetia, still under Habsburg control, and Rome, which was occupied by French troops.

CONSTITUTIONAL EXPERIMENTATION:
GERMAN UNIFICATION

The loss of Italy, a Habsburg humiliation, reflected on state administration às well as on the military. Since the Bach system had proved a failure, a better alternative had to be found. The government had faced three centers of opposition to its centralizing policies. First, the landed aristocracy, conservative in conviction, wanted the provincial diets, which they dominated, to regain their lost authority. Second, the Liberals, a party composed primarily of middle-class Germans and bureaucrats, liked the centralized monarchy, but, as believers in the principles of 1848, wanted its power limited by a constitutional system and a guarantee of civil liberties. Neither of these groups was nationally minded, although Germans were predominant in both. In contrast, the third, composed of Hungarians, small landowners in the

59

majority, wanted a restoration of the March Laws of 1848 and autonomy for the lands of the Hungarian crown. They preferred that the link with the rest of the empire be primarily through the person of the monarch.

To face this opposition the court did not have and never acquired its own organized party. It did not, for instance, attempt to call for support from the peasants or the smaller nationalities, such as the Croats, Serbs, Romanians, and Czechs, the majority of whom had certainly proved their loyalty to the crown in 1848–1849. The government preferred to work with and to try to balance those political forces which already had considerable influence and power, namely, those representing the German aristocracy and middle-class and the Hungarian and Polish nobility. From 1860 to 1867 various alternative proposals were examined to replace the existing system. Franz Joseph, after wide consultation with his advisers, made the final decisions. New measures were introduced by decree and often suddenly. Two basic questions were at issue with each change: the first involved the degree to which the empire should be centralized or federalized, the second the extent to which liberal measures should be introduced.

The first reorganization proposal, the October Diploma of 1860, declared "permanent and irrevocable" but never put into actual practice, reflected the interests of the old aristocracy, including the Hungarian, and marked a shift from centralized absolutism to conservative federalism. Bach was replaced by the Polish aristocrat Goluchowski. In a move toward representative government, Franz Joseph accepted some restrictions on his power in some areas, but he maintained his full authority in foreign policy and military affairs. Previously, in 1851, an advisory council of officials had been established, to which later representatives from the diets had been added. Under the October Diploma the membership of the Reichsrat (Imperial Council) was set at a hundred, and it was empowered to deal with the problems of the entire empire in an advisory capacity. The diets at the same time acquired more control over local affairs. The intent was to appease the Hungarians, whose administration now resembled that in effect before 1848, except that the nobility could be taxed and the peasant emancipation measures were retained.

The October Diploma, which favored the large landowners, displeased other groups. The German Liberals were unhappy with measures that reduced the authority of the bureaucracy and favored the nobility in the provinces. Even the Hungarian leadership was divided; many desired no common institutions such as the Reichsrat. Since the court could not afford to estrange its German Liberal supporters, Goluchowski was replaced in December by Anton von Schmerling, the choice of the German centralists, and another reorganization was undertaken.

The February Patent of 1861 was presented as the enactment of the October diploma, but in fact it reversed the aristocratic and conservative direction of that document and turned back to a liberal centralist orientation. The Reichsrat became a regular parliamentary body with the power to pass laws and approve the annual budget; its two houses consisted of a senate (Herrenhaus), composed of archdukes, high church officials, and nominees of the monarch, and an assembly (Abgeordnetenhaus) whose delegates were chosen by the provincial diets under an electoral system that assured the domination of the landed aristocracy and the German middle class. Franz Joseph retained his autocratic powers in foreign affairs and the military; he could also convoke, prorogue, or dissolve the Reichsrat.

Although Schmerling remained in office from 1860 until 1865, the government did not function smoothly. The Hungarian leaders, refusing to cooperate, did not send delegates to the Reichsrat, and finally their diet was dissolved. Czechs and Croats attacked the centralizing features and felt some sympathy for the Hungarian objections. Even the German Liberals contributed to the ultimate failure of the system. Their hostile attitude toward the church split them from one of the main props of the monarchy. Their failure to fight for a wider franchise and a more democratic system alienated others. Their most destructive position, however, was that taken toward the Habsburg armed forces, whom they held responsible for their defeat in 1848. Liberals consistently opposed expenditures on the army, which thus still lacked essential equipment. It was not, for instance, supplied with the breechloading needle guns so important in future Prussian victories.

The situation obviously could not continue. After the unification of Italy it was clear that the next crisis would involve a struggle with Prussia over supremacy in Germany. Franz Joseph and many of his ministers felt that the Hungarian demands would have to be met at least in part; Austria could not resist Prussian pressure in Germany with a Hungary in revolt at its back. Such a possibility had caused apprehension previously in the war in Italy. Negotiations between Habsburg and Hungarian leaders thus started in 1862; Ferenc Deák became the most important representative for the Hungarian side. By the spring of 1865 it was clear that the Hungarian demands would be met. In July the Reichsrat was dissolved and Schmerling was replaced by a Moravian noble, Richard Belcredi, whose principal task was to reach a settlement in view of the impending war with Prussia; as a first step the February Patent was suspended. When a newly elected Hungarian diet met in December 1865, most of the representatives supported Deák's program, which called for a reorganization of the empire on a dualist basis with the lands of the Hungarian crown joined to the monarchy only through the person of the emperor and a common policy on foreign affairs and defense. Discussions were still in progress when Austria and Prussia went to war in 1866.

By this time the rivalry with Prussia over German affairs dominated Habsburg foreign policy. Until the middle 1850s, as we have seen, the Habsburg monarchy, despite an often unfavorable military position, had been able to control events in Central Europe. This position was maintained largely through the skill of a series of ministers, in particular Metternich and Schwarzenberg, who knew how to play the international balance and thus compensate for Habsburg weaknesses. However, for the next years the talent was to reside in Berlin in the person of Otto von Bismarck, who became Prussian minister-president in 1862. The dominating figure in European relations until 1890, Bismarck was to have as his first major accomplishment the establishment of Prussian hegemony in Germany and the removal of Habsburg influence from the region. He was successful to a large extent because he was able to obtain the support of Russia, whose statesmen deeply resented the Habsburg "betrayal" at the time of the Crimean War. As a former Prussian ambassador in St. Petersburg, Bismarck was in a good position to use the long-standing Russian–Prussian relationship. The friendship was strengthened in 1863 when a revolt broke out in the Russian Polish territories. Whereas Austria joined with France and Britain in expressions of sympathy for the rebels, Prussia firmly backed the Russian measures of suppression.

The Habsburg government was well aware of both the growing influence of Prussia and the strong desire throughout the German states for a closer union. The unification of Italy had shown the true strength of the national idea. The monarchy, however, could neither directly challenge Prussia on the battlefield nor lead a movement for German unification. With its multinational population, the Habsburg Monarchy could not stand as the principal sponsor of a purely German movement. Moreover, most German nationalist leaders, the heirs of 1848, were also liberals. The Bach regime and Austrian absolutism did not attract them. Hampered in this manner, the monarchy could only respond to nationalist demands for action with suggestions of reform for the German Confederation. In August 1863 the Habsburg government sponsored a conference of German princes to discuss a strengthening of the organization. Among the Habsburg proposals was the establishment of a central parliament composed of representatives from the assemblies of the member states. Disliking this assumption by Austria of leadership, Bismarck, although with difficulty, persuaded the Prussian king, William I (1861–1888), not to attend the gathering. With the absence of the largest German state, the other princes could not well proceed with reform plans.

The series of events that led to the exclusion of Habsburg influence in Germany commenced with the war fought by Prussia and Austria against Denmark over the duchies of Schleswig and Holstein. Thereafter both powers, foreseeing a possible future clash, made diplomatic preparations for it. The Habsburg government concluded an agreement with France assuring its neutrality; Prussia signed a treaty with Italy promising it Venetia in return for military aid.

When the Seven Weeks' War broke out in June 1866, the Habsburg Monarchy had the support of the major German states, including Baden, Hanover, Hesse-Cassel, Saxony, Bavaria, and Württemberg, but of these allies only Saxony gave significant military support. The war with Prussia was a disaster for the allies and another humiliation for Habsburg arms. Victories were, however, won against Italy both at Custozza in June and in the naval battle of Lissa (Vis) in

July. The decisive engagement was the Prussian victory at Königgrätz (Hradec Králové) in Bohemia. Thereafter Bismarck persuaded his reluctant Hohenzollern king, who wanted to press on to inflict a crushing defeat on the rival Habsburg dynasty, to make a moderate peace that would encourage a renewal of good relations. The Treaty of Prague, signed in August, required Austria to surrender Venetia to Italy and to pay a small indemnity. Prussia took some territory from the Habsburg allies, but its major objective was the exclusion of Austria from Germany. The German Confederation was dissolved and replaced by the North German Confederation. This organization, under Prussian leadership, included all of the German states except Bavaria, Baden, Württemberg and Hesse-Darmstadt. These four states were joined to Berlin by defensive–offensive alliances.

Thus the Habsburg Empire surrendered the position of primacy that it had held in the German lands for six hundred years. As Holy Roman Emperors the Habsburg rulers had been the first among the German princes; the office of president in the German Confederation had maintained at least a symbolic leadership. The loss of this source of prestige and power affected not only foreign relations, but also the ability of the central government to control its own lands. Nationalism had triumphed in Germany and Italy; it was to win a further victory in Hungary with the completion of the negotiations on the reorganization of the empire.

THE AUSGLEICH

The *Ausgleich* or Compromise of 1867 was the last of the major constitutional reorganizations; the state structure established at this time was to last until the collapse of the monarchy. The provisions were a victory for the Hungarian moderates, such as Deák and Gyula Andrássy, who desired full internal autonomy, but not a complete break with the rest of the Habsburg lands. The Ausgleich divided the monarchy into two parts, with the Hungarian kingdom established as a separate unit. To head the state three administrative authorities were set up, of which the first consisted of the monarch and the common offices. Franz Joseph held the title of emperor for the Austrian lands and king for the Hungarian. He appointed the ministers for the three ministries with jurisdiction over the entire state: foreign affairs, defense, and finance. The minister of finance's duties, however, concerned only the funding of the diplomatic and military establishments. Other matters of common concern were to be discussed at the meetings of the delegations, separate committees whose members were appointed from the two parliaments, with forty chosen from the lower chambers and twenty from the upper. The delegations, meeting alternately in Vienna and Budapest, were instructed to sit separately and communicate only in writing. Should a deadlock occur, they could meet together. If they still disagreed, the monarch would make the final decision. The three common ministers were responsible to the delegations.

The other ties were weak. The two parts were to have the same currency and postal system, but there was no common citizenship. Although a customs union was established, its terms were to be renegotiated every ten years, as were other commercial and financial questions. This division also brought up a difficult problem of terminology. The Kingdom of Hungary was an obvious choice, but an alternative name for the rest of the state was not so clear. The official title was the awkward "the Kingdoms and Lands represented in the Reichsrat." Other designations could also be used. Since the river Leitha separated the two sections, they were also called Cisleithania and Transleithania. More convenient, however, was the use of the name Austria for the non-Hungarian lands.

Austria-Hungary was the accepted designation for the state (see Map 3).

In addition to the common offices, two separate governments were established in Budapest and Vienna. Most of the lands of the Hungarian kingdom were placed under a centralized administration; a separate agreement, the *Nagodba* (Arrangement) of 1868, gave certain limited autonomous rights to Croatia-Slavonia. The establishment of the Austrian administration caused more difficulties. The Ausgleich had been negotiated by bargaining between the Hungarian leaders and the emperor, who consulted certain close advisers. The Austrian parliamentary institutions had not taken part in the discussions, but their approval was necessary. To obtain the agreement of the Reichsrat the court had to grant large concessions to the German Liberals, whose support was essential. The new political system, introduced in December 1867, was based on the February Patent. It made Austria a constitutional monarchy and met the Liberal demands for strong guarantees of civil liberties. Franz Joseph nevertheless retained many of his former powers, particularly in regard to foreign affairs and the military. He could still select and dismiss ministers, who were, however, to be responsible to the lower house; he also summoned and dissolved parliament.

The dual structure of the state was to have decisive significance for the future viability of the monarchy. The major problems in the future were, as shall be seen, to involve the demands of other nationalities for a similar political arrangement that would give them a position equal to that of the Germans and the Hungarians. Although the government in Austria was at times willing to make wide concessions, the Hungarian leaders, who represented only a minority of their population, were determined to maintain their privileges. Because of the terms of the Ausgleich, they were able to

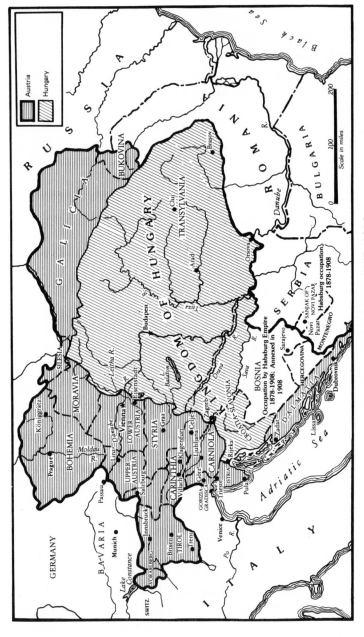

Map 3. Austria-Hungary, 1867–1918

block reform in Austria as well as in Hungary and thus to prevent a reorganization that would have allowed other nationalities, for example, the Czechs or South Slavs, to enjoy similar rights. The Ausgleich also made impossible any attempt to reverse the decision of 1866. In October 1866 Franz Joseph appointed Ferdinand von Beust, who had been in the service of the king of Saxony, as foreign minister. It was widely surmised at the time that this strong opponent of Bismarck would make it an objective of his policy to regain the former Habsburg supremacy in Germany. Such a goal was, however, difficult to contemplate, since it would have involved an alliance with France, popularly regarded as a German national enemy. Even more important, Hungary, in touch with Prussia, opposed the policy. Although some Austrian leaders favored a strong anti-Prussian stand, the minister-president of Hungary did not.

Austria-Hungary thus played a relatively minor role in the final stages of German unification. The declaration of war by France in 1870 was sufficient to rally German national feeling behind Prussia. The Russian support of Berlin, expressed in a clear warning to Vienna and a concentration of troops on the border, helped to paralyze the Habsburg government. The Prussian victory on the battlefield made any further attempts to hinder German unification impossible. An obvious sign of the shift in German leadership from Vienna to Berlin was the crowning of William I as German emperor in Versailles in 1871. The imperial German title, abandoned by the Habsburgs in 1806, was thus revived by the rival Hohenzollern dynasty. Moreover, the Prussian kleindeutsch, not the Habsburg-sponsored grossdeutsch, basis of German unification had prevailed.

As chancellor of the unified German state Bismarck was well aware of the importance of maintaining good relations with Vienna. In 1871 he met with Beust at Gastein; Franz

Joseph and William I held a similar conference at Salzburg. Although fences were to some extent mended, a basic rapprochement was achieved only after Andrássy was appointed foreign minister in November 1871. A Hungarian nationalist and a revolutionary of 1848, he regarded Russia as the principal opponent and would have liked to see the formation of an alignment joining Austria, Germany, Britain, and Italy. He nevertheless accepted Bismarck's proposals to reconstitute the former Holy Alliance. The Three Emperors' Alliance of the 1870s was based not on a written agreement, but rather on the common policies adopted in Vienna, Berlin, and St. Petersburg, reinforced by exchanges of visits among the monarchs and foreign ministers. No major crises troubled the European scene or the relations among these allies until 1875, when a revolt in Bosnia and Hercegovina reopened the Eastern Question.

The conclusion of the Ausgleich ended an era in Habsburg history. In considering the years after 1815, it can be seen that the conservative period before 1848 was marked by stability and calm in internal and foreign affairs, a condition that, however, reflected the failure to make progress in significant areas. In 1848 the repressed desires for liberal reform and national rights broke forth in a great revolutionary movement that put the monarchy in grave danger. Although the revolutions organized from below on a popular or middle-class basis failed, many of the objectives were achieved in the next two decades by other means and with another leadership. The Italian and German national unification movements, accomplished at Habsburg expense, were carried through not by the people but by the Piedmontese and Prussian governments, led by the ingenious statesmen Cavour and Bismarck. Within the monarchy, after the initial absolutist period, Habsburg ministers attempted to work out some constitutional arrangement that would satisfy the demand for representative institutions. Here Hungarian national convictions prevented a solution that could be applicable to the entire state. The Ausgleich, as we have seen, was negotiated by the court with the Hungarian political leaders. Representatives of the other nationalities, including the Germans, were either conciliated afterward or not consulted at all. The Ausgleich, which gave the controlling position in Austria to the Germans and in Hungary to the Hungarians, was bound to arouse the animosity of the other nationalities. Until the fall of the empire the national question was to dominate Habsburg history.

2

THE DUAL MONARCHY,
1867–1918

THE last half century of the monarchy was to witness
bitter internal struggles; the new arrangement in fact
created more problems than it solved. The Ausgleich did not
even guarantee good relations between Austria and Hungary; instead, almost immediately intense conflicts took place
over the interpretation and implementation of the terms of
the agreement. For the Austrian government, in particular
for Franz Joseph, the Ausgleich represented the maximum
concession to Hungarian opinion. In contrast, some Hungarian leaders wished not only a further separation, but even
full independence.

The great problem in both parts of the empire, however,
was the position of the non-German and non-Hungarian
nationalities, representing together well over half the population. The controversies over this issue were eventually to
paralyze the Austrian government and to arouse sharp controversy in Hungary. The Hungarian nationality policy, particularly, was to cause difficulties for both parts of the monarchy. Although Hungarians constituted less than half of the
population of the kingdom, Hungarian leaders embarked upon
a policy of intense magyarization, which was to cause bitter
animosity and to raise the national consciousness of the other
peoples. Not only did this situation create problems for Budapest, but the Hungarian leadership used the dual arrange-

ment to block national reforms in Austria. Legalistic in attitude, it could always argue that if the Austrian state structure
were altered – for instance, if a special agreement were made
with the Czechs – then the terms of the Ausgleich would be
violated, since the nature of one of the parties had changed.

In this chapter the major emphasis is on the developments
in Austria, particularly those affecting the Austrian Germans, since events here form the background for the postwar Austrian republic. The national conflicts and the political crises in Austria, but not in Hungary, will thus be treated
in detail. However, before we consider these questions, a
brief review of foreign policy is in order. Although no major
dangers threatened the state from abroad, many issues in
foreign affairs played a part in domestic policy.

FOREIGN RELATIONS TO 1908

After the loss of influence in Germany and Italy, Habsburg
interest in Eastern and Southeastern Europe, particularly in
the territory under Ottoman control, became greater. Thus
when in 1875 a rebellion broke out in Bosnia and Hercegovina, Andrássy was eager to cooperate with Germany and
Russia to attempt to find a solution acceptable to both the
rebels and the Ottoman government. The situation became
more serious when in the summer of 1876 Serbia and Montenegro, autonomous states under Ottoman suzerainty, declared war on the Ottoman Empire. The subsequent Serbian
defeats, combined with the public reaction to reports of
widespread massacres of Bulgarian civilians by Ottoman ir-
regular troops, placed great pressure on the Russian government to act to defend these Slavic Orthodox people. After
making an agreement with Austria-Hungary over a future
peace settlement, Russia declared war on the Ottoman Empire in April 1877. The Russian military victory enabled that

state to conclude in March 1878 the advantageous Treaty of San Stefano, whose terms, however, violated previous understandings with Austria-Hungary and upset the balance of power in the Near East. Under extreme pressure from Britain and Austria-Hungary, Russia consented to attend the Congress of Berlin and agreed to a modification of the peace terms.

The Treaty of Berlin of July 1878 created a new Balkan map: Romania, Serbia, and Montenegro became independent; an autonomous Bulgarian state was established north of the Balkan Mountains, with a semiautonomous province, Eastern Rumelia, to the south; Greece, Serbia, Montenegro, and Romania all received additional territory. For Austria-Hungary the most important section of the treaty was that which gave the state the right to occupy and administer Bosnia and Hercegovina and to occupy the strategic strip of land separating Serbia and Montenegro, the Sanjak of Novi Pazar. The control of the two former Ottoman provinces was assumed only after much domestic disagreement. Franz Joseph, among others, would have liked to annex the territory; the great powers would probably have agreed. However, both the German Liberals and the Hungarian government, which did not want more South Slav lands added to the empire, opposed their acquisition. After an occupation had been agreed upon, another serious problem arose. The provinces could not be added to either Austria or Hungary without upsetting the balance between them. Finally, it was decided that they would be put under the jurisdiction of the joint minister of finance, who had very little to do anyway.

The Berlin settlement caused great resentment among the Russian leaders, who felt that Germany had not given sufficient support at the congress to their position. For a short time thereafter the close relationship between Berlin and

74

St. Petersburg broke down. At this time and in the next three years the Habsburg Monarchy negotiated and signed the alliance agreements that were in effect at the outbreak of the First World War. The first, the Dual Alliance, was concluded with Germany in October 1879. A secret defensive agreement directed against Russia, it was to be renewed regularly at five-year intervals. In June 1881 the Three Emperors' Alliance of Russia, Germany, and the Habsburg Empire was revived, but this time a formal treaty was signed. A neutrality and consultative pact, it was to be renewed only once. The second major agreement with a lasting significance, the Triple Alliance among Germany, Austria-Hungary, and Italy, was concluded in May 1882. A defensive alliance directed against France, the treaty was renewed regularly and was in effect in 1914.

These three alliances gave Austria-Hungary a favorable diplomatic position. In addition, agreements signed in 1881 with Serbia and in 1883 with Romania tied these two states closely to Vienna. Although the clear direction of European diplomacy lay in Berlin, not Vienna, the monarchy was a member of the strongest European alliance system. This favorable situation, however, was soon to be endangered by another Balkan crisis, brought about when Eastern Rumelia revolted and declared its union with the autonomous Bulgaria. After its establishment by the powers at Berlin, that state had been under Russian influence. However, its prince, Alexander of Battenberg, and the leading political parties soon broke with the protecting power. When the revolt in Eastern Rumelia occurred, Russia thus opposed the union, since it would strengthen the position and prestige of the prince. In this first stage of the three-year Bulgarian crisis Austria-Hungary supported Russia. The union was, nevertheless, saved by the actions of Serbia, which launched an attack on Bulgaria. The subsequent Serbian defeat demonstrated to the great powers that it would be difficult to enforce the separation of the Bulgarian provinces. The Russian government, although accepting the union, was determined to oust the prince. In August 1886, with Russian prior approval, a group of army officers kidnapped Alexander and transported him outside the country. Although a counterrevolution brought him back, his subsequent injudicious actions forced him to abdicate. In July 1887 a Bulgarian assembly elected Ferdinand of Coburg as his successor despite strong Russian disapproval. In this second phase of the crisis, Austria-Hungary joined with Britain in support of Bulgarian defiance of Russian demands. As a result of this break, the Three Emperors' League lapsed in 1887. In that year the monarchy signed with Britain and Italy two Mediterranean agreements, which were designed to protect the status quo in the Black and the Mediterranean seas and were directed against both Russia and France.

Further changes in the European alliance system occurred in the next decade. In 1890, when Bismarck was forced out of office, William II dropped the German treaty connections with Russia, whose government in 1891 and 1894 negotiated a strong military and political treaty with France. In 1895 the Mediterranean agreements lapsed. Although the Triple Alliance at this time stood in apparent opposition to the Franco-Russian alliance, Russia and Austria-Hungary in 1897 agreed to cooperate to maintain the status quo in the Balkans. By this date Russian attention had turned to the Far East, whereas the Habsburg government was preoccupied with its internal problems. Their joint endeavors to solve the Macedonian problem in the first years of the twentieth century showed that the two countries could work together effectively when it was to their mutual interest. With this period of relative calm in its foreign relations, lasting from

1887 to 1908, the Habsburg Empire could concentrate on the solution of its growing domestic controversies.

INTERNAL DEVELOPMENTS TO 1914

Although Austria-Hungary was to remain primarily an agricultural country until 1914, progress toward industrialization was slow but steady before the middle of the century. The empire suffered from certain economic disabilities not shared by those countries whose industrialization advanced more rapidly in the nineteenth century. Most important was the fact that the empire was not a geographic unit; natural barriers divided certain provinces. Dalmatia and Lombardy-Venetia, for example, lay behind an Alpine wall; Vorarlberg belonged to the Lake Constance-Switzerland region; Galicia and Bukovina were separated from Vienna by both geographic and political obstacles. The rivers did not serve to unify the country; the Danube did not connect major industrial centers or lead directly to the world's great sea-lanes. The Bohemian-Moravian industrial regions were oriented northward, along the Moldau and Elbe to Hamburg, and hence to Germany and not Vienna. The empire also lacked a significant seaport. Although a railroad linked Vienna with Trieste after 1854, shipping by this means was expensive. Hamburg handled as much overseas Habsburg shipping as did the Adriatic city.

As we have seen, from the eighteenth century industrialization had advanced chiefly in Austria, while the lands of the Hungarian crown remained primarily agricultural. This division was to some extent maintained until early in the twentieth century, when Hungary made an effort to industrialize. Again the emphasis here will be on Austrian developments, particularly on those which influenced conditions in the postwar republic. In Austria the years between 1850 and 1873, the so-called *Gründerzeit* (Founders' Period), were marked by a steady expansion in industry and in railroad construction. However, henceforth the progress was greatest not in the Alpine and Vienna regions, but in the lands of the Bohemian crown. Here textiles remained of chief importance, but there were also metallurgical and chemical industries, food-processing plants, machine and glass manufacturing, and iron foundries. In Styria and Carinthia iron foundries and metallurgical industries continued to prosper. This region, however, suffered from the lack of coal; most iron was smelted with charcoal. The year 1881 saw the founding of what was to remain one of the major Austrian corporations, the Alpine Montangesellschaft, (Alpine Mining Company), which had works in Bohemia and Moravia, where adequate coal supplies were available. The Vienna basin was still the third industrial region. In addition, Vienna had by the late sixties become the center for finance and banking for the monarchy.

The advances after the middle of the century were also helped by the state's attitude. The era of absolutism in government, from 1848 to 1860, had been a period of liberalism in economic policy. During the ministries of Bach and Bruck tariffs were reduced and trade encouraged, a policy that was at first continued. Under the Ausgleich the tariffs became matters of constant contention between Austria and Hungary and were debated at the time of the renewal of commercial arrangements. Foreign trade, which did not play a large role in the Austrian economy, was dominated by Germany; from 1880 to 1914, 35 percent to 40 percent of the imports came from that country, which received 40 percent to 50 percent of the Austrian exports.

The period of economic prosperity coincided with the time when the German Liberals, representing the group that benefited most from the situation, dominated the government. However, the favorable economic situation was not to continue. In the monarchy, as elsewhere in Europe, the economic advances had made it possible for some to earn handsome profits, but many enterprises had not been organized on a sound footing; fraudulent practices and the corruption of public officials also characterized the operation of some businesses. The great crash of 1873 brought down the weaker of the enterprises, leading to a period of economic depression, widespread unemployment, and a fall in wages. The shock caused by this event damaged the Liberals and their laissez-faire economic program. The widespread demand for protection was reflected in the tariffs put into effect after 1878. Another period of marked prosperity occurred at the beginning of the twentieth century. By 1914 Austria thus had an industrial base and had experienced the problems of an industrial society. The center was in Bohemia and Moravia; the Vienna basin and the Alpine regions showed much progress, but enterprises here had to depend on the rest of the country for supplies, notably coal and basic foodstuffs. These economic advances were not paralleled in the rest of the country. Although the empire was an economic unit, the regions did not develop equally.

Austria, a country two-thirds of which was composed of mountains and hills, did not have a prosperous agricultural economy. The large estates throughout the empire functioned well, but the small units, particularly in the Alpine regions, in general did not. The end of the robot obligations in 1848 had indeed inaugurated a period of beneficial change in the countryside, but some groups were nevertheless harmed. The loss of labor services was damaging to the small landowner, who often sold out. In the same manner peasants with small holdings tended to lose their lands to their richer neighbors. As years passed and the population rose, family lands were divided or, where other inheritance laws prevailed, some children had to find different occupations. The condition of the peasant in the mountains was particularly hard; with the unfavorable climate and poor soil, he could not compete with the cereal or animal products of the large estates, in particular those of Hungary. The problem of peasant overpopulation involved both parts of the monarchy; industry could not absorb the excess. From 1871 to 1914, 1.3 million citizens emigrated from Austria, and about the same number from Hungary.

The changing economic conditions naturally affected the social balance in Austria. Economic prosperity and industrialization created a wealthy class of businessmen, industrialists, and bankers, but also a large working class concentrated in the cities. Attracted by the hope of employment, peasants increasingly came from the countryside to the industrial centers, sometimes altering their ethnic balance. In Bohemia, for instance, Czech peasants moving into Prague changed it from a German to a Czech city. Obviously some, for instance, wealthy entrepreneurs and large landowners in need of cheap labor, liked the situation; others did not. Landless or threatened peasants, unemployed workers and artisans, small shopkeepers and merchants who could not compete, and others in similar situations were all becoming increasingly restless.

Such social and economic dissatisfactions were alive in every national group, and they contributed to creating friction among the nationalities. However, what was to be notable in this situation was that there were few attempts to organize political associations along class lines on a supranational basis. Usually when any nationality felt its national position threatened, all members, no matter what their social position, tended to join together. Thus no great coalitions bridging the national divisions and linking, for instance, peasants of all nationalities, or all great landowners throughout the monarchy, were successfully organized. Only one major party, the Social Democrats, made a serious attempt in this direction, and it failed to achieve its basic objective.

After the Ausgleich the chief problem for the government was to maintain a balance between the major nationalities and try to conciliate the others. In Hungary, as has been mentioned and as we shall see in greater detail, the dominant nationality adopted a program of rigorous magyarization of its minorities in an attempt to assimilate them fully into Hungarian culture and society, and it attempted to alter the provisions of the Augleich in its favor. The situation in Austria was more complex because here the Germans, unsure of their own position, did not show the same determination to maintain superiority. The victory of the kleindeutsch idea for German unification affected not only the Habsburg state, but also its German citizens, who lost the psychological support that they had gained from Austrian leadership in the wider German community. Moreover, faced by the rising demands from other nationalities, they had to define their own objectives. Previously, Austrian Germans had been in the main not German-nationalistic, but loyal to their emperor and attached to the Catholic church. They had accepted their strong position as the natural result of what they considered a superior culture and as something that would last forever. They felt themselves the "state" people.

Under these circumstances, it was difficult to organize a German-national party as such. Moreover, of all the nationalities the Germans were the most socially differentiated. The major German parties, as will be shown, were based more on class lines than on a specific national program. The development of an acute German self-consciousness was also affected by the fact that the united Germany did not want to contribute to the breakup of the Habsburg Empire. It opposed any program that argued that the lands of the former Holy Roman Empire should be reassembled even under the leadership of Berlin. The Dual Alliance thus put a cap on extreme German nationalism. As we shall see, specifically German-national manifestations usually occurred in areas where the German population was on the defensive, such as in Bohemia, with its Czech majority, and Carinthia and Carniola, with their growing Slovene populations.

The position of the Austrian Germans was indeed difficult. Defined in the terms of the Romantic nationalism of the day, which put the emphasis on language, they should perhaps have felt primary loyalty to the German state, whose ruler had taken the title of German emperor. However, the great majority undoubtedly felt that their first allegiance was to the Habsburg monarch and to the state over which he ruled. Nevertheless, the problem of where the German homeland lay was to be a major question from this time forward. An attempt to formulate a specifically national program was made in the city of Linz in September 1882 by a group of intellectuals, including Georg von Schönerer, Viktor Adler, and the historian Heinrich Friedjung, three men who were to have widely divergent future careers. The Linz Program was designed to protect the German position, and it expressed the fears of those who felt that the Germans were drowning in a Slavic sea. It was proposed that the non-German areas of Galicia, Bukovina, and Dalmatia be detached from Austria and either given to Hungary or made autonomous. The remaining territory was to be organized as a German state, attached to Germany by a customs union and with German as the official language. The connection with Hungary should be maintained only through the person of the emperor. The Linz Program did not gain wide support, but its authors were to play a major role in the organization of various German parties in the future.

The national disputes were fought out in the Reichsrat with such animosity and bitterness that this body finally ceased to function as a governing institution. Before moving on to the specific issues that the Reichsrat faced, it is necessary to consider the nature of the major German and Czech political parties since they dominated parliamentary life. Until 1873 the representatives to the lower house of the Reichsrat were chosen by the provincial diets. In 1873 this system was changed, but the electoral law placed such severe restrictions on the franchise that only 6 percent of the adult male population participated in what were indirect elections. There were few large stable parties; instead the situation was chaotic. Until 1914 around fifty parties, organized into competitive parliamentary clubs, took an active part in politics. The membership in the parties and the coalitions among them shifted constantly. Only two, the Social Democrats and the Christian Socials, had established organizational bases. The term *party* is therefore used in this narrative to designate loose coalitions or factions as well as more formally organized groups with set programs.

For the Austrian Germans the principal political parties were the Liberals, the Social Democrats, and the Christian Socials. From 1867 to 1879 the German Liberals, owing to the restrictive franchise, were the predominant influence in the parliament. The party represented primarily the interests of industry, commerce, high finance, the professions, and the bureaucracy. As heirs of 1848 its members supported the classical liberal doctrines, including a laissez-faire economic system and a guarantee of civil liberties. As individuals they probably considered themselves above the national conflicts and believed that their policies were for the good of all. Not democratic, they aimed to replace the former aristocratic political predominance with the rule of men of education and property. They thus wished the suffrage to include the middle class, but to go no further. The narrow class basis of this party accounts for its decline with the widening of the franchise.

The Social Democratic Party was founded to give representation to the increasing working population. At first workers were prevented from organizing, but in 1867 laws were passed that allowed them to form associations. After April 1870 trade unions could be organized and workers could strike for better conditions. Following the example of Bismarck's Germany, Austria accepted the principle that the state should intervene to protect the worker. In the 1880s a series of measures, patterned on the German, were passed: conditions in mines and factories were regulated; insurance against accident and sickness was offered; old-age pensions were guaranteed; and the working day was set at eleven hours in factories and ten in mines.

The formal organization of the first workers' party took place at a congress of Socialist leaders held at Hainfeld in December 1888 and January 1889. The meeting was preceded by long negotiations among various factions over the many issues dividing Marxist socialists at this time. Although all accepted the basic Marxist program and agreed upon the ultimate goals, there was a strong division over the tactics to be adopted. The question was whether the party should concentrate on the overthrow of the existing governmental structure by revolutionary means or instead cooperate with the authorities, enter candidates in the elections, attempt to win benefits for the workers, and simply wait until the time was ripe for the assumption of full power in the state.

At Hainfeld the major influence was exerted by Viktor Adler. His aim was to bring the Socialists together and to avoid defining issues so closely that party unity would be impossible. He personally believed that capitalism was inevitably doomed to collapse, so he favored a moderate waiting policy. The party program agreed upon at Hainfeld put the emphasis on unity, but it did not directly meet the major issues. The Socialist aim was declared to be the ownership of the means of production by society, but at this conference and later the party leaders avoided openly choosing either a revolutionary or an evolutionary course of action to obtain their goals. The organization of a cohesive mass party was, of course, necessary whether the party intended to work within the existing system or to overthrow it. In the future Austro-Marxism was to represent a system of gradual reform, not violent change, although the party's program and policies were always the subject of lively debate among its members.

The Social Democrats, of course, had to deal with the nationality question. In theory the party was both supranational and international, but in practice it broke up into its national components. Officially it supported the reorganization of the empire and the replacement of the historic provinces with units set up on the basis of nationality, each with full autonomy. Austria would then become a federation organized on a national basis; the Ausgleich and the special connection with Hungary were to be ended. Some party leaders, notably Karl Renner and Otto Bauer, produced plans of reorganization that emphasized the nationality of the individual voter rather than his place of residence.

From its origin the party attempted to be more than just a political organization. Through the formation of special clubs and associations it offered both education and entertainment to its members; it organized activities such as choral groups, hiking expeditions, book clubs, theatrical events, concerts, and classes on various subjects, and it published books and newspapers, of which the *Arbeiter-Zeitung* (Worker's Newspaper) was the most important. The aim was to make the working-class member feel that the party was his second home.

The Liberal Party, as we have seen, provided representation for the successful middle class; the Social Democrats defended the interests of the workers. A third party, the Christian Socials, was to represent the "little man" in between. Certainly the Liberals and Social Democrats left out of their programs the interests of a large number of people – for instance, peasants, artisans, small manufacturers, and shopkeepers – who were often strongly attached to the dynasty and the Catholic church and who were neither rich nor revolutionary. In 1882 the franchise was extended to include this group, which was to be the main support of a new political party, the Christian Socials. Despite their later stand, at first this party was strongly critical of Austrian conditions. Convinced Catholics, its members opposed both the anticlericalism of the Liberals and the established Catholic church hierarchy, which had closely identified itself with the court and the government. Some agreed with Pope Leo XIII, whose encyclical *Rerum novarum* (1891) stated that employers had a moral duty to their employees and that church and state should join to improve the life of the working class. They were also influenced by the writings of Karl von Vogelsang, a German convert to Catholicism, who edited in Vienna a Catholic conservative newspaper, *Das Vaterland* (The Fatherland). Supporting social reform on Christian principles, he too argued that the state should act to protect the little man. The party, in line with these ideas, was strongly critical of the Liberal laissez-faire economic program and "capitalism," particularly as represented by the Jewish businessman and financier. It also favored close ties with Germany, and it had a sympathetic attitude toward the non-Hungarian minorities, but not toward the Ausgleich or Hungary. Christian Social candidates attacked Jews, Liberals, and Socialists, but gave strong support to Catholicism, the monarchy, and the extension of the franchise.

The party had a strong leader and spokesman in Karl Lueger, who appealed in particular to the Viennese voter. Although the movement was loyalist and clerical, the Christian Socials caused concern in the court and the church hierarchy. Lueger was chosen mayor of Vienna five times before Franz Joseph would confirm his election, in April 1897. An extremely popular figure, he made major improvements in Vienna. Under his direction the city took over the major utilities – gas, electric power, and water. A building program led to the construction of schools, hospitals, parks, roads, and bridges. Lueger was reelected in 1903 and 1909. After his death in 1910, no similarly appealing party candidate could be found, and control of the city administration was eventually surrendered to the Social Democrats.

The Christian Socials, it will be noted, like the Social Democrats, were for municipal socialism and the concept of the welfare state. They were similarly interested in and worked to improve the condition of the working class. In the 1890s a Catholic trade union was organized under the leadership of Leopold Kunschak.

Of the three parties, the Liberals and Social Democrats had programs that they believed bridged the national controversies; the Christian Socials supported a reorganization of the empire and the abandonment of the Ausgleich. Only one German-based party, the Pan-Germans led by Schönerer, had a strictly nationalist program, which called for the breakup of the empire, with the German-inhabited lands, including Bohemia, joining Germany. An erratic man, Schönerer founded a party that received much attention then and later, but that in its time had little political significance. In the 1880s it probably had no more than three followers in the Reichsrat; in 1888 its leader was publicly disgraced. Schönerer also had a program that was bound to alienate just about everyone. He stood not only against the dynasty and the state, but also against the Catholic church. Maintaining that Lutheranism was the true German religion, he tried to organize a *Los von Rom* (Away from Rome) movement, but he succeeded in winning only about fifty thousand conversions by 1910. His position was also fundamentally weakened by the fact that Germany did not want to annex the Austrian German lands in question. The eventual influence of these doctrines on Adolf Hitler and the party's strong anti-Semitism have earned for it perhaps more attention than it deserves. Its program represented the extreme German-Austrian position.

The German parties, as can be seen, were based primarily on social and economic factors. Nevertheless, as time passed national issues increasingly dominated political life. As the controversies intensified and as individual Austrian Germans felt themselves threatened by the demands of the other nationalities, they too became more aware of their German cultural background and less tolerant of others. Two conflicts in particular aroused strong feelings and bitter resentments, and they had consequences that have lasted to the present: first, the rise of feeling against the Jews and, second, the Czech–German struggle for the control of the Bohemian crownlands. The two issues were quite different in nature. The Jews were assimilated into German, as well as into Hungarian, society; the Czech question was a part of the larger nationality conflict, which involved the struggle of most of the small nations for parity with the Germans and Hungarians.

During the nineteenth century increasingly unfavorable conditions in Russia led to a large Jewish migration into the Habsburg Empire. Most of these Jews, while retaining their religious community, were assimilated into German society in Austria and became German-speaking. The bitter conflicts over the use of German as a state language that were at the center of other national controversies thus did not occur. Largely an urban people, the Jews were attracted in particular to Vienna: in 1870 there were 40,000 Jews forming 6.6 percent of the population; by 1880 this number had increased to 72,000, or 10.1 percent; and by 1890 it had grown to 118,500, or 11 percent. Although Jews could be found at all social levels, some were extremely successful. By the end of the century they held a dominant position in the central banking system, the wholesale and retail trade, and the press. They also had a leading position in the professions; in Vienna in the 1880s 61 percent of the doctors, 57 percent of the lawyers, and 86 percent of the law clerks were Jewish. As will be shown in the next section, assimilated Jews played a major role in the cultural achievements of this period.

As a group, Jews met no obstacles in certain circles; Jewish names predominate among the leaders of the Social Democrats and appear prominently among the Liberals. Where anti-Semitism became strong was in the parties with a populist base, such as the Christian Socials and the Pan-Germans. Some national groups also were anti-Semitic in that they resented the assimilation of so many Jews into the German and Hungarian societies. It must be remembered that although some German parties had programs that were anti-Semitic, in general Germans and assimilated Jews joined together in the conflicts with other nationalities, who, in turn, tended to see Germans and Jews as identical. The Jews themselves did not found organizations for political action of their own, but worked within the established parties. The Zionist movement of Theodor Herzl, which aimed at the establishment of a Jewish state in Palestine, originated in Vienna, but it was of little significance at this time.

Of the nationality conflicts in Austria the most bitter was

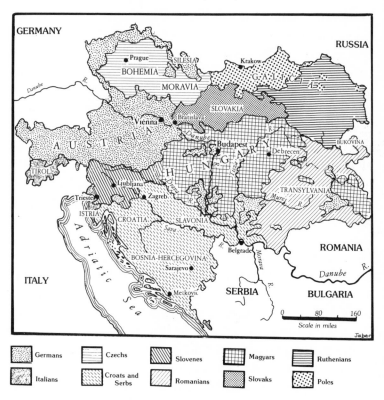

Map 4. Nationality map of Austria-Hungary

to be between the Czechs and Germans, although there were also controversies involving the Poles, Ruthenians, and South Slavs, which will be discussed later (see Map 4). As the second largest group in Austria, with a majority in the lands of the Bohemian kingdom, it could be expected that the Czechs would demand equal political rights and the use of their language in education and government. Previously, Bohemia had often been in opposition to the centralizing policies of Vienna. The multinational great landowners, in control of provincial affairs after the Battle of White Mountain, had consistently emphasized historical and local rights, a position also to be adopted by Czech nationalists.

In the lands of the Bohemian crown – Bohemia, Moravia, and Silesia – the Czechs were a clear majority, a position that would be strengthened if they could win the support of the kindred Slovaks. However, in these same lands the Germans composed a third of the population, and they could expect encouragement from the other Austrian Germans. In this situation Czech national leaders had three options: first, they could seek simple equality with the Germans in the Bohemian kingdom; second, they could favor a trialistic solution, that is, the joining of all the Slavic lands of the monarchy into a third unit; or third, they could seek to gain from Vienna a recognition of Bohemian provincial autonomy. Holding the majority, the Czechs could hope to dominate a separate government. Most Czech political groups favored the third solution.

The Old Czechs, the first national party of significance, was led by and represented the interests of the large landowners and prosperous members of the middle class, including businessmen, officials, and those in the professions. Austroslav in orientation, the Old Czechs were conservative, cautious, and loyal to the dynasty. They were soon challenged by the Young Czechs, led by Eduard and Julius Grégr. The members of this party were primarily artisans, peasants, tradesmen, and the less successful of the professional classes. Their political program was strongly nationalistic, and it supported moderate social reform. The party was strengthened by the change in the franchise in 1882, which allowed more of its supporters to vote.

The Czech national revival was also aided by the fact that the Bohemian lands were the center of Austrian industrialization. In the late 1860s the Škoda works of Pilsen (Plzeň) became the major arms manufacturer in the monarchy. As has been shown, the region was also predominant in the monarchy in heavy industry, textiles, and food processing. The lure of better-paying employment drew an increasing number of Czech peasants off the land into the cities, where they were more likely to become involved in political controversies. These Czechs did not assimilate; they kept their own language and became increasingly hostile toward what they regarded as an oppressive, German-controlled system.

The national question, in particular the Czech–German controversy, dominated Austrian parliamentary life after the Ausgleich. At that time a Liberal ministry under Karl Auersperg was in power, backed by a majority in the Reichsrat. This government first turned to the implementation of one part of its program that had not yet been accomplished: the weakening of church–state relations. The Concordat of 1855 was broken; schools were returned to state control. The education bill of 1869 made compulsory, free, secular education available for all children.

The government also gave consideration to the nationality problems, in particular to the status of the Poles and Czechs. The Polish problem proved relatively easy to settle: the province of Galicia was simply surrendered to the control of the Polish aristocracy. Although centralist in theory, the Liberal ministers gave the province an autonomous status; Polish was recognized as the language of administration, the legal system, and secondary education. Through this settlement the Ruthenian population was placed under Polish control. In the 1910 census there were in Galicia 4,672,500 Poles and 3,208,092 Ruthenians.

With full political control in Galicia the Polish aristocracy thereafter supported whatever government party was in power. This attitude made impossible any united front of Slavic nationalities. However, the Polish leadership had as its clear objective the reestablishment of partitioned Poland. Since this goal could not be obtained without a radical change in European conditions that would bring about not only Austria's but also Russia's and Germany's surrender of their Polish territories, the Polish leadership was content with establishing Galicia as a national center.

Matters did not proceed so smoothly in Bohemia. Between January 1870 and November 1871 the Liberals were out of power for a short time. In February 1871 Karl Hohenwart headed a government that was conservative and federalist. Faced with the rise of Czech national feeling, it recognized that some agreement should be made. After negotiations between government representatives and conservative Czech leaders, a program was formulated and presented to the Bohemian diet. Its terms included the establishment of a central assembly for Bohemia, Moravia, and Silesia; these lands, joined together, would have administrative autonomy and a role in determining foreign relations. As could be expected, the proposals touched off a violent reaction, particularly from the Germans and Hungarians; even the diets of Moravia and Silesia did not approve. Andrássy, now minister-president of Hungary, charged that the plan broke the Ausgleich since it changed the nature of one of the parties to the agreement; that is, it involved a basic alteration in the structure of the Austrian state. Faced with this uproar Franz Joseph abandoned the attempt to make an agreement with the Czechs at this time. Unsurprisingly, the failure of the negotiations weakened the position of the moderate groups on both sides.

The Liberals, this time under the leadership of Adolf Auersperg, in November 1871 returned to office, where they were to remain until 1879; Andrássy became the foreign minister. The main achievement of this period was the enactment of the franchise law of April 1873, whose terms resulted in an increased representation for the German middle class, the basis of the Liberal Party. The Liberal position was, however, weakened by the economic disaster of the great crash of 1873, which brought into question both the party's theories and its leadership. The immediate cause for its downfall was, however, its position on the occupation of Bosnia and Hercegovina in 1878. Violently opposed to the addition of more Slavs to the empire, the Liberals refused to vote the money needed by the government to take over the administration of the provinces. Franz Joseph had never liked the Liberals, though he had tolerated them as long as they voted the military budget and did not interfere in foreign affairs. The fall of the Auersperg government in 1879 marked the last time that a purely German ministry ran Austrian affairs; thereafter the governments were of mixed national composition or they were composed of court appointees.

As a replacement Franz Joseph called in his childhood friend, Eduard Taaffe, who in August 1879 formed a non-party ministry. After new elections were held, Taaffe was able to organize a coalition of clericals, German conservatives, and Polish and Czech representatives, a government known as the Iron Ring. This bloc controlled 168 seats as against the Liberals' 145. After the signing of the Dual Alliance between Austria-Hungary and Germany, there was little fear of outside German assistance to the Austrian German parties. Moreover, some German groups, particularly those from areas such as the Tirol and Styria, disliked the anticlerical attitude of the Liberals and thus voted with the coalition.

A main goal of this government was to win over the Czechs and to settle some of the other national controversies. It was in this era that the Czech national movement gained its greatest momentum. The heart of the conflict remained the language question. The Czechs insisted that their language be used in the external service of the administration, that is, where officials dealt with the public, even in areas where only a few Czechs lived. The problem facing the German officials was that whereas almost all educated Czechs knew German, relatively few Germans could speak Czech, since it was not taught in their schools. Not only jobs were at stake, but also German prestige. Moreover, during the Iron Ring administration, it was clear that the Czechs were gaining at the German expense. In May 1883 in the elections to the Bohemian diet, the Czech representatives won 167 seats as against 75 for the Germans. Aware that they could not hold control of all of the Bohemian lands, the German parties at this time came to favor a partition of the region along national lines, a solution that the predominant Young Czech party refused to consider. From this time on, both sides were to become increasingly militant.

The Taaffe government, weakened by the failure to bring the Czechs and Germans together, fell in October 1893 over the question of franchise reform. Franz Joseph and his advisers had come to the conclusion that the middle class was the main support of violent nationalism throughout the monarchy and that the situation would be improved if more people could vote. The proposal was made to extend the franchise to every literate male citizen over twenty-five, an idea that was opposed by a wide range of political opinion for different reasons. The departure of Taaffe, who had been in office for fourteen years, ended the last stable regime before the war.

The next ministry, headed by Alfred Windischgrätz, depended mainly on conservative support, such as that of the clericals and the Poles, but the Liberal Party worked with it. The national rivalries and franchise reform were the main questions facing it. This ministry was forced out over the relatively minor issue of the building of a Slovenian-language secondary school in Cilli (Celje), a German town set in a

Slovene countryside. When in 1895 the government accepted the Slovene position, the German Liberals withdrew their support.

Under the ministry of Kasimierz Badeni, formed in June 1895 and composed primarily of officials, a new franchise law was passed that was based on almost complete manhood suffrage. In the elections in March 1897 under this law, twenty-five parties chose representatives. The German parties won 202 of the 425 seats in parliament, but they were divided into nine factions. The wider franchise aided in particular the Young Czechs, who won 60 of the 62 seats held by Czechs. This situation was to cause a major political crisis. At this time the negotiations called for in the Ausgleich, which were held every ten years, were coming up. Since Badeni needed the support of the Czech representatives to obtain firm parliamentary backing, he gave them important concessions. In April 1897 two decrees were issued whose implementation would have required that all civil servants in Bohemia and Moravia, from the lowest worker to the highest official, be able to speak and write Czech as well as German by July 1901. All of the German parties joined to oppose this measure; their violence and their obstructionist tactics made parliamentary discussions impossible. Badeni was forced to resign, and the language decrees were not put into practice.

After the fall of the Iron Ring, Franz Joseph preferred to appoint officials rather than political leaders as ministers; there was no attempt to base the ministry on a majority in parliament. Moreover, when the government could not get bills through the legislature, it made increasing use of Article 14 of the 1867 constitution, in theory an emergency measure that allowed the emperor to enact laws when the Reichsrat was not in session. This system was at its height during the ministry of Ernst von Koerber from 1900 to 1904. In January 1907 another electoral law extended the suffrage to all males and abolished the indirect system of voting. The numbers of parties competing for representation was now increasing: in 1907 over thirty parties returned candidates; in 1911, the last prewar election, over fifty parties fought for 516 seats.

The Austrian government had to deal not only with its own national problems, but with the consequences of the magyarization policies in Hungary and with the constant attempts of its leaders to improve their position in the Ausgleich relationship. In Austria at least the attempt was made to meet the nationality problem, and universal suffrage was introduced; in Hungary, in contrast, the leadership endeavored to tighten its control over the non-Magyar people and to limit the franchise. The treatment of the minorities was also to have severe repercussions in foreign policy. The alliance of the Dual Monarchy with Romania, for instance, was severely strained by the way the Romanians in Transylvania were administered. The Hungarian policy toward Croatia-Slavonia, which had certain autonomous rights, hindered the resolution of the entire South Slav question, which will be discussed subsequently, and endangered the stability of the empire.

Although the Hungarian government made every effort to maintain the status quo in its own lands, some leaders attempted to move toward increasing independence from Vienna. After the conclusion of the Ausgleich its authors, Deák and Andrássy, held the chief positions in the state. After Deák retired and Andrássy became foreign minister, Kálmán Tisza became premier, a position that he held from 1875 to 1890. His supporters, the Liberal Party, were in control to 1918, with the exception of the years from 1905 to 1910. The government negotiated the renewals of the economic arrangements of the Ausgleich with Austria in 1877, 1887, 1897,

1907, and finally 1917. Although supporting the dual arrangement in principle, it attempted to win additional advantages whenever possible. Opposition to the Ausgleich came chiefly from the Party of Independence, headed by Lajos Kossuth, who was in exile. When he died, his son Ferenc took the leadership of the party.

Those who wished a weakening of or an end to the connection with Austria had their opportunity to act when in 1903 a bill was placed before the Hungarian parliament that called for an increase in the number of recruits. Opposition representatives at this time demanded basic changes in the army, which was, of course, under the joint ministry. They wanted the soldiers from the Hungarian lands to form separate units, to be led by Hungarian officers, to fly the Hungarian flag, and to use Hungarian as the language of command. These measures would be a step toward the dissolution of the union and would aid in the magyarization efforts.

Franz Joseph, always sensitive about interference in questions of foreign policy or the military, took a very strong stand on this issue, and the proposed changes were blocked. However, in 1905 the Liberal Party, now led by István Tisza, the son of Kálmán, lost its majority in parliament. Franz Joseph then appointed a nonpolitical ministry of officials; he was able to secure the passage of the military bill in the form he desired by threatening to use his power to introduce the secret ballot and manhood suffrage into the Hungarian kingdom. Since the Hungarians formed less than half of the population, these measures would have destroyed both the domination of this nationality and the hold of the aristocracy over the state. In 1910 the Liberal Party, reorganized as the National Labor Party, returned to power; in 1913 István Tisza was again premier. Parliamentary government in Hungary, however, remained an illusion; a small minority of the population ran the kingdom.

When considering the domestic affairs of the monarchy, particularly under the dual system, it is easy to paint a bleak picture of black hatreds and increasing division. Such a presentation would, however, be misleading. It is in fact just as possible to describe the era in the opposite terms – as a warm, idyllic, happy time whose innocent charms can never be recaptured, an era of the sort often portrayed in Viennese operettas. Certainly the average Austrian German had the opportunity to lead a very pleasant life. He lived in a strikingly beautiful region amid what were for the time comfortable material conditions. He could also enjoy the benefits of a good education and, if he chose, the products of the cultural flowering of his nation. In the nineteenth century Austria, in particular Vienna, held European preeminence in music and medicine and made important contributions in other fields. No Habsburg history would be complete without at least a brief discussion of some of these Austrian achievements.

VIENNA AS A CULTURAL CENTER

This section concentrates on Vienna in the nineteenth and early twentieth centuries for examples of Habsburg accomplishments. Although other cities (for example, Prague, Budapest, Salzburg, and Graz) and other centuries were also important, Vienna at this time had a particular significance for both European cultural history and postwar Austria. As the intellectual capital of a great power, the city not only drew upon the talent of the Habsburg lands, but also attracted gifted individuals from all the German-speaking regions. The following pages cover the careers of creative individuals who worked primarily in Vienna, although they may have been born and educated elsewhere; non-German-language contributions and the work of Austrian Germans who lived in other cities (like Rainer Maria Rilke or Franz Kafka) are omitted. No attempt is made to analyze the work of the musicians, artists, writers, and architects discussed; instead they are placed in their historical setting and a few of their major contributions are indicated. It is hoped that the reader will come to an understanding of their significance by reading the books listed, by listening to the music, and by looking at the paintings, graphics, and buildings.

In addition to the enormous contributions made by Vienna to the arts, it must not be forgotten that similarly significant work was accomplished in the humanities, in particular in philosophy; in the social sciences, especially in economics; and in the natural sciences in medicine and physics. Of these categories, only the work of Sigmund Freud is considered here, but the reader should remember that music, art, and literature were just part of a cultural flowering that included other branches of knowledge. Here too Austrian creativity and analytical ability had international impact.

Why Vienna became so well known for its music can be at least partially explained. Situated in a central position, between the Italian and German areas, and with a rich heritage of its own in the folk music of the empire's many nationalities, the city could offer its residents a richly varied and cosmopolitan atmosphere. Even more important, by the nineteenth century music had become an important part in the lives of the entire population. Rich and poor alike played instruments, sang, or became avid listeners. Music could be heard not only in the salons of the wealthy, but in parks, restaurants, inns, beer halls, and wine gardens. Popular demand assured that professional musicians, whether they sang, played, or composed, would have at least a hope of employment. The stormy controversies that often raged in connection with individual performers, conductors, and composers gave witness to the deep involvement of the city in musical achievement.

In the eighteenth century the main support for the serious musician continued, as before, to come from the court and the great aristocracy. The children in the large family of Maria Theresa received musical training and put on performances for visitors. Although subsequent rulers, from Joseph II to Franz Joseph, were not deeply involved personally, the court continued to provide money for theater, symphony, and opera performances. The great noble families, as a matter of prestige, maintained musicians and orchestras in their Vienna homes and on their estates. They also commissioned works and collected libraries of musical scores. Although a musician or composer in noble employ was often regarded as little more than an upper-level servant, even wearing the house livery of his aristocratic patrons, court and noble interest nevertheless did provide him with a means of support and an often appreciative audience for his work.

Most of the performances supported by the court and nobility were open to a favored few. Starting in the late eighteenth century the prosperous middle class began to follow the aristocratic example and duplicate the interest in and patronage of musical events. With the widening of the audience and the inauguration of public performances, musicians gained other means of support. They could now earn livings by giving concerts, which the great performers and composers did, not only in Vienna, but throughout Europe and America. They were also paid for their works. In this century music was part of social as well as family life; circles of friends were formed to play or to hear favorite compositions. The great literature of vocal and instrumental music available gave pleasure to the listener and amateur performer and an income to the composer. Music thus provided livelihoods for performers, composers, publishers, and those who organized musical events.

The Catholic church was also a source of support, since music was a necessary part of the masses and the special celebrations. On Sundays the churches became veritable concert halls. The greatest composers wrote masses and oratorios. Moreover, the church was not tradition-bound; its music reflected the changing cultural climate. This music, like the public concerts, was, of course, open to all sections of Viennese society.

The Viennese populace, noble and city dweller alike, generally preferred music when it was combined with theater and spectacle; opera was thus of central importance. In the Baroque age Italian influence predominated in opera as well as in instrumental music. A new age of German music drama began with the work of Christoph Willibald Gluck (1714–1787), who was employed at the court of Maria Theresa. His operas – for example, *Orfeo ed Euridice* (Orpheus and Euridice, 1762) and *Alceste* (1767) – had librettos in Italian or French, but they differed from previous works in that Gluck attempted to achieve a better balance between words and music. His aim, as he explained, was: "Always as simple and natural as possible, my music merely strives to achieve the fullest expression and to reinforce the poetic declamation."[2]

The greatest period of Austrian music lasted from the second half of the eighteenth century to the death of Schubert in 1828. Here four names dominate: Joseph Haydn (1732–1809), Wolfgang Amadeus Mozart (1756–1791), Ludwig van Beethoven (1770–1827), and Franz Schubert (1797–1828).

---

[2] Gluck to the *Mercure de France,* February 1773, private letter, Helga and E. H. Mueller von Asow, eds., *The Collected Correspondence and Papers of Christoph Willibald Gluck* (New York: St. Martin's Press, 1962), pp. 30–31.

Haydn, who came from a peasant family in Lower Austria, was supported through patronage from the Eszterházy family. Required to live on its estate in Eisenstadt, he regretted his isolation from the musical center of Vienna, where he moved only when he was sixty. He nevertheless was able to compose hundreds of works, both in the country and in Vienna, where he completed his two great oratorios, *Die Schöpfung* (*The Creation*, 1797) and *Die Jahreszeiten* (The Seasons, 1801). Composed in the age of the Enlightenment, his work showed the rational and optimistic spirit of the time. He enjoyed a successful and creative life, respected by his contemporaries and supported by noble patronage.

Mozart's career was quite different. Although he was one of Europe's greatest composers, his life was short and difficult. He was born in Salzburg, a musical center, and his father was an accomplished violinist and composer. A child prodigy, Mozart was taken by his father to perform in France, Britain, and the German states. Although he had excellent training and the opportunity to hear the best performers of his day, his genius and his experience did not win him a settled position. Financial problems haunted him until the end of his life. He had for a while the support of the archbishop of Salzburg, but the two quarreled and eventually parted company. Moving to Vienna, Mozart received money from private lessons, from concerts, and even from the court. However, the time had not yet come when a musician could enjoy an easy independent life. When he died at the early age of thirty-five, he left large debts and was buried in an unmarked pauper's grave.

Despite the difficulties of his personal life, this prolific composer produced a wealth of compositions, including forty-one symphonies as well as other instrumental works; masses, including the *Requiem Mass,* which was uncompleted at his death; and operas, which were his personal preference. After his arrival in Vienna in 1781 he received a commission to compose a German opera from the Deutsches Nationaltheater (German National Theater), which Joseph II had founded in 1776. This work, a *Singspiel,* or drama with music, *Die Entführung aus dem Serail* (The Abduction from the Seraglio, 1782), was favorably received. Mozart next collaborated with Lorenzo da Ponte, who wrote the librettos, for his three great Italian-language operas: *Le Nozze di Figaro* (The Marriage of Figaro, 1786), *Don Giovanni* (1787), and *Così Fan Tutte* (Thus Do All, 1790), which was also commissioned by Joseph II. His last opera, *Die Zauberflöte* (The Magic Flute, 1791), with its message of brotherhood and understanding, of the victory of light over dark, reflected the spirit of the Enlightenment as well as the influence of the composer's membership in the Freemasons.

Beethoven, in contrast, fully appreciated by his contemporaries, had no major financial problems. Born in Bonn, he moved to Vienna in 1792; here he lived a simple life and did not marry. Although he received generous aristocratic patronage, he could support himself through the sale of his compositions and, at first, by his concert performances. His relationship with his patrons showed that changes were taking place in the Viennese musical circles; they courted his favor and provided him with an orchestra and finally with a guaranteed income.

Beethoven was deeply influenced by his loss of hearing, which began when he was in his late twenties. Despite this handicap he wrote his greatest works in the last ten years of his life when he was totally deaf, though his affliction, which disturbed him deeply, caused him to withdraw from the outside world.

Beethoven's music dominated his period. His many compositions included, among other works, nine symphonies, piano sonatas, the opera *Fidelio,* and masses, in particular the great *Missa Solemnis* (1823). Previously, the emphasis had been on vocal music, with a preference shown for opera, oratorio, and cantata. Beethoven brought instrumental music to its highest point of development; his compositions could convey ideas and emotions without accompanying words. Although, like other composers discussed here, he did not participate in the political events of the day, his work often expressed contemporary concerns and attitudes. For instance, his third symphony, the *Eroica* (1804), was initially dedicated to Napoleon, although he soon became disillusioned with that "hero." His single opera, *Fidelio* (1805), placed emphasis on the idea of freedom and the necessity of rebelling against tyranny.

Whereas Beethoven was famous in his lifetime, Franz Schubert's short life prevented him from receiving similar recognition from his contemporaries. Born in Vienna in a musical family, he did, however, win the admiration of a circle of friends who lent him money. Even though he did not have noble patronage, he was able to earn a small amount by teaching and selling his compositions. Shortly before his death, his friends organized a highly successful concert which seemed to assure that he would not have further major financial problems. In November 1828 he died of typhoid fever at the age of thirty-one. Although he wrote choral, chamber, and piano music, operas, and eight symphonies, Schubert is best remembered for his development of the *Lied*, or art song. He set to music over six hundred poems, maintaining in his Lieder a balance between text and music. Two song cycles illustrate his preeminence in this form: *Die schöne Müllerin* (The Beautiful Mill Girl, 1823) and *Winterreise* (Winter Journey, 1827).

During this period, despite the superiority in music, Vienna did not have literary figures who compared, for instance, to Goethe or Schiller. As we have seen, the Metternich era was the time of extreme political conservatism. Literary production was no doubt hindered by the system of preventive censorship that, by requiring the submission of works for approval before they were published or presented in public, made it very difficult for writers to deal with political themes.

Franz Grillparzer (1791–1872), Austria's greatest dramatist, was born in Vienna and in 1813 entered government service, where he had a successful career. He also received recognition for his work: in 1859 he was awarded honorary doctorates from the universities in Vienna and Leipzig, and in 1864 he was made an honorary citizen of Vienna. Although he was an efficient and loyal state servant, he was critical of the political conditions of the day, including the Metternich system, but he expected little improvement to come through revolutionary action.

Grillparzer wrote thirteen plays – twelve tragedies and one comedy – some of which were not produced in his lifetime. In 1838, after his comedy failed, he decided to stop writing plays. He also had continual problems with the censors. Some of his dramas had mythological and psychological themes, including the trilogy *Das goldene Vliess* (The Golden Fleece, 1821) and *Des Meeres und der Liebe Wellen* (The Waves of the Ocean and Love, 1831); others had historical settings, such as *König Ottokars Glück und Ende* (King Ottokar's Happiness and End, 1825), which portrayed Rudolph I as a heroic figure, and *Ein Bruderzwist in Habsburg* (Strife in the Habsburg Family, 1848), which dealt with the Thirty Years' War.

Two other dramatists, Johann Nestroy (1801–1862) and Ferdinand Raimund (1790–1836), were performers as well as writers. Nestroy, extremely popular with his audiences, wrote in the Viennese dialect about the local people. His comedies not only were satires on social and political conditions but also made fun of historical and mythological figures. His targets for attack were widespread. Although he was a supporter of the revolution of 1848, he subsequently lost faith in much that it represented. In his eighty-three plays he introduced some new theatrical devices: for instance, his actors would step out of their roles and comment to the audience; he would try to avoid the censors by having the actors express their ideas through gestures, emphasis, or expression. Raimund gained fame as the era's greatest comic actor. His eight plays all dealt with the supernatural and were peopled with fairies and spirits; they also contained songs that became popular in their own right.

A new period in Austrian cultural history commenced in the last decades of the century. By this time Vienna had a prosperous middle class, deeply involved in the arts and willing to spend money on its houses, on interior decoration, and on theater and music. Viennese artists participated in the great European movement of impressionism and, later, that of expressionism. In literature writers expressed the doubts and uncertainties of the age; composers and performing artists introduced the second great period of Austrian music. Architecture became particularly important. Vienna was to acquire a new face for the modern age: the center of the city was completely rebuilt in a style that caused a strong reaction and the formation of a new, modern school, whose basic aims and assumptions were to predominate in the postwar years.

With the income of the state tied up in the wars of the eighteenth century and the French Revolution, the massive building of the Baroque era had come to an end. During the reign of Joseph II the emphasis had been on the practical and functional. The spirit of the Biedermeier period directed attention to the home and not to the construction of impressive public buildings. A change, however, came after the middle of the century, one that affected in particular Vienna.

There a massive construction program was inaugurated during the period of Liberal Party control established after 1860, when the city gained the right of municipal self-government. At this time, to meet the demands of a rapidly expanding population, certain vital improvements were made: a clean water supply was provided; the Danube, which before had often overflowed and flooded large areas, was channeled; a public health system was established; and the great parks were improved.

Most important, however, were the basic changes made in the city plan. In the middle of the century Vienna was still surrounded by the old city wall. An open area, the glacis, maintained primarily for military purposes, separated the center from the suburbs. In December 1857 Franz Joseph issued a decree that turned the glacis over for civilian use. A commission was established to decide what should be done with the land. The existence of this large tract made possible the laying out of the great boulevard of the Ringstrasse, which enclosed the central city on three sides, with the Danube Canal forming the fourth side. Some of the land was sold to private investors, and the income was used to construct the massive public buildings that were to give modern Vienna its present-day appearance.

The aim of the city planners was to have an architectural style suitable for an imperial capital. The principle of historicism was adopted, with no attempt to enforce uniformity or to introduce new and original conceptions. The style adopted for each building was that which was considered to best reflect its historical associations. Thus the town hall and the Votivkirche (a church built to commemorate an unsuccessful attempt to assassinate the emperor in 1853) were constructed in Gothic style; the university, the opera, and the art and natural science museums in Renaissance; the parliament building in classical; the Burgtheater (court the-

The Vienna Opera

ater) in Baroque. Land not occupied by the public buildings was devoted to private use. Apartment houses of four to six stories were built, which also could contain business offices and retail stores.

The buildings had elaborate facades; the interiors too were characterized by rich ornamentation in the spirit of the architectural style chosen. The aim of the architects was to create an impression of grandeur and magnificence. Cosmopolitan in nature, historicism looked to the past. Whether one admired the effect or not depended, of course, on personal preferences, but some artists and architects heartily disliked the result. They argued that architecture should express the needs of modern society and that the style of a building should reveal its function, which should not be concealed by decorative facades. Two architects of this group, Otto Wagner (1841–1918) and Adolf Loos (1870–1933), were to influence the architecture not only of Austria, but also of the world.

109

The Parliament Building

Between 1894 and 1901 a modern transit system was built in Vienna. Otto Wagner was appointed the artistic adviser of this project, and in the course of his duties he designed over thirty stations as well as bridges and viaducts. In his designs he placed emphasis on function rather than art, and he made use of the materials of the industrial age: steel, iron, glass, zinc, copper. Although he dispensed with much ornamentation, his work was deeply influenced by the *Jugendstil* (art nouveau) movement of the Secession, to be discussed shortly. Representative buildings are his railroad stations, the Postal Savings Bank, the building at Neustiftgasse 40, and his private houses, for example, the Majolica house. Adolf Loos, emphasizing simplicity and line, adopted similar principles, as is shown by his building on the Michaelerplatz. His work in interior decoration was also important; he is known for his use of rich materials and an insistence on craftsmanship.

110

The Imperial Station at Schönbrunn, designed by Otto Wagner

This new architecture, not the Ringstrasse style, was to become the standard for the future. It led to economical building, and cost and practicality were to become overriding concerns in the future. It should be noted that government contracts were given not only to those attached to traditional patterns, but also to architects of the new school.

Art underwent a similar period of evolution. In the Ringstrasse era public tastes were influenced by the critic and artist Hans Makart (1840–1884), who admired in particular Rubens, Titian, and Veronese. His painting, with its classical and historical themes, fitted the Ringstrasse style well. He was also the president of the Künstlerhausgenossenschaft (Artists' House Society), an association of artists, sculptors, and architects founded in 1861, which controlled the major exhibition building in Vienna. The influence of this organization was challenged at the end of the century by a gener-

Building on the Michaelerplatz, designed by Adolf Loos

ation of artists deeply affected by new European movements. In 1897 a group of these men withdrew from the Künstlerhaus and formed the Vienna Secession. Their aim was to open Austria to modern European art; their motto was "To the age its art, to art its freedom." Their first exhibition, held in rented rooms in 1898, was very successful. They recognized, however, that they needed their own building, as well as a journal in which to express their views. The Secession building, opened in 1898, reflected modernist concepts in art and architecture; the journal *Ver Sacrum* (Sacred Spring), published for five years after 1898, contained writings and drawings in the Secession style.

The major artist of this time, Gustav Klimt (1867–1918), reflected in his life and work the changing art climate. At the beginning of his career he was a Ringstrasse artist, and he was strongly influenced by Makart, as is shown in his ceiling paintings in the Burgtheater and the Kunsthistorisches Museum (Art History Museum). He then became the leading figure in the Secession movement. In 1894 he was commissioned to execute three murals for the university. His completed works, depicting Philosophy, Medicine, and Jurisprudence, caused such an uproar that the university refused to display them. Changing again, Klimt in his gold period turned to a more ornamental and decorative style. In the last fifteen years of his life he painted principally portraits and landscapes.

Two other Austrian artists of this time, Egon Schiele (1890–1918) and Oscar Kokoschka (1886–1980), were to become even more controversial. Schiele, influenced by the Secession and in particular by Klimt, produced works reflecting fear, desolation, and violence. Kokoschka spent his early life in Vienna. Here he wrote and illustrated his poem *Die träumenden Knaben* (The Dreaming Boys, 1908) and his play *Mörder Hoffnung der Frauen* (Murderer, Hope of Women,

Gustav Klimt

1907), which depicted an eternal struggle of the sexes in a style that prefigured expressionism.

Many artists under the influence of the Jugendstil movement turned to the decorative arts. In fact, a major Viennese

Egon Schiele, Secession Exhibition poster, 1918

contribution of this period is in the applied arts and interior design. Artists devoted their attention to the fashioning of furniture and household items like dishes, vases, glassware, and other tableware. Following the British example, they

The Secession Building

combined their call for the return to craftsmanship with an attack on the methods of mass industrial production. In 1903 the organization Wiener Werkstätte (Vienna Workshops) was founded, which provided studios for artists engaged in the crafts. Employing rich materials, including gold and silver, these modern artisans produced elegant furniture, jewelry, and household utensils. Deeply influenced by the Jugendstil movement, they too thought that they were designing for the modern world. Instead of imitating the styles of previous ages, as the Ringstrasse architects had done, they devised a new visual vocabulary based on vegetative, biological, and geometric forms. Because of their emphasis on craftsmanship and creative quality, with little reference to cost, their work could be purchased only by the very rich. Many of their designs, however, were to be used by the manufacturers of mass-produced goods.

Egon Schiele, portrait of Rupert Koller

Oskar Kokoschka, portrait of Walter Hasenclever

In music the critic Eduard Hanslick (1825–1904) held a position very similar to that of Makart in art. His support of certain musicians to the detriment of others aroused enormous interest in a society where music, composers, conduc-

Oskar Kokoschka, illustration for *The Dreaming Boys*

tors, and performers were matters of immediate concern to a large section of the population. A major source of controversy involved the works and views of Richard Wagner, who spent three years in Vienna, from 1861 to 1864, before he had to flee to escape from debt collectors. The public divided into his ardent defenders and his equally vehement detractors. A strong critic of Wagner and of those who were influ-

Dagobert Peche, fantasy bird, in silver

enced by him, Hanslick found in Brahms a man whose work he could deeply admire and whom he considered the worthy successor of Beethoven.

Johannes Brahms (1833–1897) was born in Hamburg,

Maria Likarz, fashion design, color lithograph poster

where, even though the family was poor, he received a solid musical education. He did not move to Vienna until 1862, but there he found both employment and appreciation. Composed in the tradition of Beethoven and Haydn, his works were mainly instrumental, including four symphonies, but he also wrote songs and choral music, of which the best known is *Ein deutsches Requiem* (A German Requiem, 1869). Although he received wide recognition, enjoying a good income and an international reputation during his lifetime, his neoclassical style was attacked by the pro-Wagner factions.

Anton Bruckner (1824–1896) had a more difficult life. Born in a village near Linz, he studied and then had his first major appointment as a teacher and organist at the Abbey of St. Florian. In 1855 he became cathedral organist at Linz and only in 1867 moved to Vienna. There he became court organist and continued giving concerts, teaching, and composing. A devout Catholic, he composed in the great tradition of Austrian church music. His works include nine symphonies and a large body of religious choral music. Because of his admiration for Wagner he faced the steady opposition of the influential Hanslick. During this time he received only limited recognition, and he faced financial difficulties. Finally, at the end of his life, when he was in bad health and without adequate means, he was given a free apartment in a cottage on the grounds of Belvedere palace.

Hugo Wolf (1860–1903) was similarly a member of the Wagner camp. Born in Windisch-Graz (Slovenigradec) in Carniola, he subsequently moved to Vienna. In 1884 he became the music critic for the weekly review *Wiener Salonblatt* (Vienna Salon Newspaper), in whose pages he wrote strong defenses of Bruckner's works and launched bitter attacks against Brahms. In his own work he is best known as a composer of Lieder. In his over three hundred songs, using the poems of Goethe, Lenau, Heine, Eichendorff, and others, his intention was to reflect the mood or dramatic spirit of the poem. Although often strongly criticized in Vienna, his work achieved wide recognition in Germany in his lifetime.

Gustav Mahler (1860–1911) was similarly influenced by Wagner. Born in Bohemia in a Jewish family, he came to Vienna at the age of fifteen to study in the conservatory. He then turned to teaching and conducting, where his rise was swift. Following engagements in Budapest and Hamburg, he became in 1897 the artistic director of the Vienna opera at the age of thirty-seven. After ten years in this position, he resigned because of ill health and his desire to devote more time to his own compositions. Thereafter he spent about half of every year in the United States, where he was the conductor of the New York Philharmonic Orchestra. His reputation rests on his nine completed symphonies, his symphonic work *Das Lied von der Erde* (Song of the Earth, 1908), and his Lieder, such as the song cycles *Lieder eines fahrenden Gesellen* (Songs of a Wayfarer, 1883–1885) and *Des Knaben Wunderhorn* (The Youth's Magic Horn, 1888–1896). In Vienna he was associated with the Secession artists.

A new direction in European music was inaugurated by Arnold Schönberg (1874–1951). Born in Vienna in a Jewish family, he had the opportunity to acquire a good musical education. He started composing as a child; in 1897 his work, not yet in an innovative style, was first performed. In 1899 he began to change his music; the first new composition, *Verklärte Nacht* (Transfigured Night, 1899), was not well received by the public or the critics. In 1901 he went for two years to Berlin, where he worked for a cabaret and won the support of Richard Strauss. Returning to Vienna in 1903, he continued his composing and became a friend of Mahler. With his song cycle, *Das Buch der hängenden Gärten* (The Book of the Hanging Gardens, 1909), using poems by Stefan George,

Schönberg brought to a logical conclusion the "liberation of dissonance" that had commenced in the nineteenth century. In place of traditional harmony, with its restriction to keys, based on tonic triads, he gave equal value to all notes, and all combinations of notes, in the chromatic (half-tone or twelve-tone) scale. His atonal or, as he preferred to call it, pan-tonal music encountered outright hostility from Vienna's music-loving public. Unable to earn an adequate living in Austria, he returned to Berlin in 1911, where he remained until he was recalled for war service in 1915. During this period Schönberg and his pupils continued to have difficulty in winning popular understanding of their work. In 1925 Schönberg was invited back to Berlin, and he remained there until the Nazi political victory of 1933, after which he emigrated to the United States.

Schönberg's two famous pupils, Alban Berg (1885–1935) and Anton Webern (1883–1945), continued his work. The Viennese-born Berg, like Webern, did his most important work in the interwar years. His opera *Wozzeck* opened in Berlin in December 1925, but it met with a negative reception. He was the most "lyrical" member of the Schönberg school, as is reflected in his instrumental music and another opera, *Lulu*, which was not completed before his death. Webern was also born in Vienna, the son of a successful mining engineer. After receiving a doctorate from the University of Vienna and studying with Schönberg as a private pupil, Webern became a member of the Socialist Party's workers' symphony and a proofreader for a music publisher. Although he was not politically active himself, he was deeply affected by current events. After the German annexation of Austria in 1938, he was unable to publish his work, which did not meet the approval of the Nazi authorities. In September 1945 he was accidentally shot by a U.S. soldier during the occupation. He is best known for his songs and his chamber music.

124

Important literary works also appeared at this time. Arthur Schnitzler (1862–1931) is perhaps the most representative writer for the period. Born in Vienna in a Jewish family, he became a physician and came to know in close detail the society about which he wrote. In numerous novels, novellas, short stories, and plays he dealt with the experiences and inner life of his contemporaries, as reflected in their experiences of love, hatred, happiness, sorrow, life, death, and suicide. Among his best known works are *Leutnant Gustl* (Lieutenant Gustl, 1901), a story that employs interior monologue and stream-of-consciousness techniques; the plays *Liebelei* (Light of Love, 1895) and *Reigen* (La Ronde, 1903), which portray sexual escapades, disillusionment, and heartbreak in various classes of Viennese society; and *Professor Bernhardi* (1911), a drama that shows how even a seemingly neutral scientific profession like medicine was wracked by the political struggle among Liberals, German nationalists, and anti-Semites in turn-of-the-century Vienna.

After Grillparzer, Hugo von Hofmannsthal (1874–1929) enjoys the reputation of being the foremost Austrian poet and dramatist. He wrote poems, stories, and dramas, but he is perhaps best remembered for the librettos he wrote for the operas of Richard Strauss, who is not discussed here because he lived primarily in Munich and Switzerland. These librettos, unlike many of their kind, can stand without the accompanying music; they draw on mythic themes, as in *Elektra* (1903) and *Die Frau ohne Schatten* (The Woman without a Shadow, 1916), or provide an elegiac portrayal of Viennese society in ages past, as in *Der Rosenkavalier* (The Rose Cavalier, 1911) and *Arabella* (1929). Hoffmannsthal's attempts to revive the traditions of medieval mystery plays and Baroque theater include *Jedermann* (Everyman, 1911) and *Das Salzburger Grosse Welttheater* (The Salzburg Great Theater of the World, 1922).

Karl Kraus (1874–1936) was a writer of a different type. He was born in Bohemia in a Jewish family that moved to Vienna when he was two years old. In 1899 he founded the review *Die Fackel* (The Torch), which was eventually to run for 992 issues. Until 1911 major writers of the period were among the contributors, but after that year Kraus wrote all the articles himself. His highly popular satirical and critical writings covered all phases of Austrian life. He was particularly concerned with the use of language and the necessity for clear expression. In addition to his work in the review, he is known for his lengthy drama about the First World War, *Die letzten Tage der Menschheit* (The Last Days of Mankind, 1922), which was written to be read rather than performed.

As is evident from the dates listed, these authors published also in the postwar period. After the war other writers, basing their observations at least partially on their prewar education and experience, wrote about the Habsburg period or the first years of the republic. The major question capturing their interest was how the catastrophic events of wartime and the immediate postwar experience could be explained. The most important novel in this regard is *Der Mann ohne Eigenschaften* (The Man without Qualities, 1930–1943), by Robert Musil (1880–1942), which deals with Vienna in 1913–1914. Joseph Roth (1894–1939) similarly wrote about Habsburg themes and the Austria of his childhood, as in his book *Radetzkymarsch* (Radetzky March, 1932). The works of another author, Heimito von Doderer (1896–1966), reflect the problems of the first third of the twentieth century in both the empire and the republic; they include *Die Strudelhofstiege* (The Strudelhof Stairway, 1951), *Die Dämonen* (The Demons, 1956), and *Die Wasserfälle von Slunj* (The Waterfalls of Slunj, 1963).

The great achievements of Vienna in the humanities, the

social sciences, and the natural sciences cannot be adequately dealt with in this general survey, but the work of one man, Sigmund Freud (1856–1939), will be discussed because of his preeminence in modern thought. Born in Moravia in a Jewish family, Freud came to Vienna in 1860, where he was educated, entering the university in 1873. After the completion of his medical studies, he worked in the General Hospital in the neurology section. In 1886 he opened his own office, where he treated patients with mental illnesses. The years from 1895 to 1899 he devoted to his major work *Die Traumdeutung* (The Interpretation of Dreams, 1900). He lectured regularly at the university, becoming a full professor in 1920. Through his studies he developed a theory of human behavior and of the operation of the mind that had implications beyond the field of medicine. He also argued that abnormal behavior and some illnesses could be best treated through psychoanalysis, whose methods and name he originated. His arguments concerning human sexuality, particularly infantile sexuality, and the role of the subconscious in determining behavior, as well as many of his other ideas, met with a mixed reception. Like many of his contemporaries, he had strong defenders and severe critics. Kraus, for instance, wrote: "Psychoanalysis is that mental illness for which it claims to be the treatment."[3] Nevertheless, his work was revolutionary in that it opened new fields of inquiry and presented challenging new attitudes toward the workings of the human mind.

Even in this brief survey the importance of Vienna as the center of a vibrant and creative intellectual life can be appreciated. Moreover, the city at this time had a general European reputation for warmth, light, and gaiety. Many Austri-

[3] Karl Kraus, *Beim Wort genommen* (Munich: Kösel-Verlag, 1974), p. 351.

ans after 1918 were to look back with regret on these times, which could easily be regarded with nostalgia and sentimentality. Although these aspects can be overemphasized, the monarchy in its last years did offer much to its Austrian German citizens, particularly those who lived in Vienna, even with its overcrowded housing. The city included and was surrounded by extensive and well-cared-for parklands; restaurants, inns, wine gardens, and beer halls served a generally prosperous and contented clientele. Popular entertainments, from the amusement park in the Prater to the numerous theaters and concert halls, were available and open to all. Music, as has been emphasized, was an essential part of the life of the city. In addition to the classical music that has been described, the Viennese had a wealth of popular and folk music. The favorite folk quartet of the time was led by Johann Schrammel, whose name was subsequently used to designate this music, which has remained popular in restaurants and beer halls. Viennese citizens not only listened, but also were performers; they sang, danced, played instruments, and joined choruses.

For many Europeans the lively spirit of Vienna was best captured by the waltz, whose popularity swept the Western world. The first waltzes of Josef Lanner (1801–1843) and Johann Strauss the Elder (1804–1849), who were both composers and conductors, enjoyed an immediate success. Elegant and carefree, this music could be appreciated by all; Vienna danced in the ballrooms of the wealthy and the dancehalls open to the general public. Johann Strauss the Younger (1825–1899) surpassed his father in creative ability and popularity. Of his hundreds of waltzes among the best known are "An der schönen blauen Donau" (The Blue Danube, 1867), "Geschichten aus dem Wienerwald" (Tales from the Vienna Woods, 1868), "Wein, Weib, und Gesang" (Wine, Women, and Song, 1869), and "Kaiserwalzer" (Emperor Waltz, 1888), the last written to commemorate the fortieth anniversary of Franz Joseph's reign. Along with his brothers Josef and Eduard, who were also musicians, Strauss enjoyed enormous popularity in Europe and America.

Viennese operetta grew up with the waltz. Johann Strauss led the way here too, writing sixteen operettas, of which the masterpiece is *Die Fledermaus* (The Bat, 1874). This work, combining music, dance, comedy, and spectacle, had enormous appeal for Viennese audiences. Other popular operettas were *Der Zigeunerbaron* (The Gypsy Baron, 1885), by Strauss; *Der Bettelstudent* (The Beggar Student, 1882), by Karl Millöcker; and *Der Vogelhändler* (The Bird Seller, 1891), by Carl Zeller. The most successful composer of operettas after Strauss was, however, the Hungarian Franz Lehár (1870–1948); a particular favorite of the public was his *Die lustige Witwe* (The Merry Widow, 1905), which made fun of Montenegro and European diplomacy.

In conclusion, in this survey, which has dealt only with Austrian German cultural life, certain aspects need emphasis. First, although German was the first language of all those considered, we do not find here a consciously German-national emphasis: the music was addressed to all people; Wagner and Loos designed buildings for modern man, not just Germans; Viennese literature and art were part of general European movements. Most of those whose works have been discussed were Catholic Germans or assimilated Jews, who believed that they were considering universal human problems and addressing issues faced by mankind in general.

Second, although most of this narrative has dealt with the multitude of problems faced by the Habsburg Empire, these themes are not addressed directly in the literature of the time. For instance, the national conflicts, the major disrupting factor in the empire, are seldom reflected in these plays or novels. Authors often chose classical or historical themes, but they used them usually to comment on the general human condition rather than on specific economic, social, or political problems of the century. Some writers, like Schnitzler, wrote penetrating studies of the internal life and the sentiments of their characters, which do indeed cast light on social relations and attitudes, but the major public problems are not considered directly.

Third, although much has been written about death themes in Austrian literature and the high suicide rate in Vienna, Austrian culture was in general optimistic, assertive, and forward-looking. The journal of Secession was called *Sacred Spring*, not winter; the architecture was for the city of the future, not *Weltuntergang* (the end of the world). Although there was indeed a spirit of irresponsibility and cheerful fatalism in the air in 1914, no one was prepared for the impending catastrophe.

WAR AND DISSOLUTION

The immediate origins of the First World War can be traced to the development of the South Slav question in both parts of the Dual Monarchy, and its relationship to the Serbian government. Of the South Slavs, the majority of Slovenes lived in Austria, most of the Croats and Serbs in Hungary. Croats were found primarily in Croatia-Slavonia, which had an autonomous status within the Hungarian kingdom and in Austrian-controlled Dalmatia. Bosnia-Hercegovina was primarily South Slav, with the population division 44 percent Orthodox Serb, 33 percent Muslim, and 21 percent Catholic Croat. With the growth of national self-awareness in the empire and the increasing pressure of magyarization, South Slav political leaders, like the Czech, turned to formulating programs to protect their interests. They too had alternatives. Various plans based on the idea of trialism – that is, that the South Slavs should form a third unit in the monarchy – were considered. Some Croatians called for the joining of Dalmatia, Croatia-Slavonia, and Bosnia-Hercegovina in a large, predominantly Croatian state to be given an autonomous status within the empire. Serbs had other possibilities. They could favor joining with the Croats and Slovenes in a South Slav union within Austria-Hungary, or they could seek union with Serbia, a choice that, of course, would involve a cession of Habsburg territory, if not a breakup of the empire. The entire question of the political orientation of the South Slavs became increasingly acute when in 1903 a military coup brought a new dynasty to power in Belgrade.

After 1878 Serbia, under Milan Obrenović (1868–1889), had become a Habsburg client state. Although the relationship changed under his successor, Alexander (1889–1903), Serbia in these years did not pose a threat to the monarchy. The new regime, under King Peter Karadjordjević (1903–1921), adopted a different course of action. Convinced that both Macedonia and Bosnia-Hercegovina were rightfully Serbian lands, the government embarked on an aggressive course of national expansion that was bound to bring it into conflict with Vienna. This change in the Serbian–Habsburg relationship paralleled the revival of the Eastern Question as a dominant theme in European international relations.

From 1897 to 1906 the Balkans enjoyed a comparative state of peace. The great powers, especially Russia and Austria-Hungary, cooperated to prevent the major issue, the fate of Macedonia, from leading to a European crisis. However, after the defeat by Japan in 1904–1905 halted its further expansion in Asia, Russia once again turned its chief attention to Balkan affairs. At the same time the Habsburg Monarchy and Serbia came into increasing conflict; from 1906 to 1911, during the so-called Pig War, the monarchy applied severe restrictions on Serbian trade. Relations deteriorated even further in 1908. In that year the Young Turk Revolution not only caused a major change in the Ottoman government, but also brought into question the status of Bosnia-Hercegovina, still under Ottoman suzerainty. Acting to meet this problem, after an informal agreement with the Russian foreign minister, Aleksandr Izvolskii, the Habsburg foreign minister, Alois Lexa von Aehrenthal, announced the annexation of the region. His method of carrying through the action caused a severe strain in relations with St. Petersburg and violent protests in Belgrade. In March, 1909, at the height of this crisis, the Habsburg government delivered an ultimatum to Serbia demanding that the annexation be recognized. Since at this time the Serbian leaders did not think they could challenge Austria-Hungary militarily, and since they did not have Russian backing, they accepted the terms of the ultimatum, promising that Serbia would change its policy "toward Austria-Hungary to live henceforth with the latter on a footing of good neighborliness."[4]

In February 1912, after the death of Aehrenthal, Leopold Berchtold became foreign minister. Austria-Hungary was still a member of the Dual Alliance and the Triple Alliance, alignments formed in the 1880s. Changes had occurred, however, in the relationships of the other great powers. Britain in 1904 settled its colonial differences with France and in 1907 made similar arrangements with Russia. The Triple Entente was based on these agreements and on the strong Franco-Russian military alliance of 1894. Although the co-

---

[4] Note of the Serbian government, March 31, 1909, Ludwig Bittner and Hans Uebersberger, eds., *Osterreich-Ungarns Aussenpolitik von der bosnischen Krise 1908 bis zum Kriegsausbruch 1914* (Vienna: Osterreichischer Bundesverlag, 1930), II, 225.

lonial rivalries among all the states continued, it was the Balkan entanglements that were to lead Europe to war.

Despite the efforts of the Young Turk regime to strengthen the state, the Ottoman Empire continued to disintegrate, losing territory in three wars. In 1911 Italy declared war and annexed Tripoli. In 1912 a coalition of Balkan states went to war and in the final peace treaty forced the Ottoman government to surrender all its remaining European lands except Constantinople and a small strip of surrounding territory. In 1913, in the Second Balkan War, the Ottoman Empire joined Serbia, Greece, and Romania in a conflict with Bulgaria. These events also weakened the monarchy's Balkan position. Although the great powers agreed to the Habsburg desire that an Albanian state be established, an action that would limit Serbian gains, the wars resulted in a doubling of Serbian territory and population. This obvious increase in Serbia's strength, together with its connections with the Russian government and certain elements of the Habsburg South Slav population, led some Habsburg statesmen to consider the state a grave danger not only to the monarchy's territorial integrity, but even to its very existence.

In this atmosphere of Balkan tension and domestic national controversy the event occurred that was to lead ultimately to the downfall of the Dual Monarchy. On June 28, 1914, the heir to the throne, Franz Ferdinand, and his wife, Sophie, were assassinated during a state visit to Sarajevo, the capital of Bosnia-Hercegovina. This deed was accomplished by seven young Bosnians who obtained their weapons from the chief of the Serbian army intelligence, Col. Dragutin Dimitrijević, who was also the head of the Serbian conspiratorial organization, Union or Death, called by its opponents the Black Hand. These actions and the subsequent steps by which the European powers were drawn into a suicidal conflict have perhaps caused more controversy and been studied more thoroughly than any other event in modern European history. Suffice it here to say that the Habsburg government, conscious of its South Slav problem and overestimating the Serbian threat to either its internal or its external security, on July 23, 1914, delivered an ultimatum to Belgrade with a forty-eight-hour time limit. The document was drafted with the expectation that it would be rejected. Although the government was in touch with its German ally after the assassination, it did not consult Berlin or Rome about the terms of the ultimatum. When the Serbian reply was deemed unsatisfactory, Austria-Hungary declared war on July 28, again without consulting its allies. The subsequent Russian mobilization led to a series of events that brought both the competing European military plans and the alliance systems into operation. By August 12 Germany and Austria-Hungary were at war with Russia, France, Britain, and Serbia. Italy and Romania, Habsburg allies, did not feel obligated to enter the conflict because of the methods adopted in Vienna to deal with the Serbian crisis, including the failure to consult with them.

Although it was thus a Habsburg action that precipitated the general conflict, the monarchy was not prepared for a great war. In the previous years the military budget had been too low to maintain the prestige, much less the strength, of a great power. The army lacked essential weapons, such as an adequate supply of machine guns, and it did not have a sufficiently strong artillery. Its multinational composition and the problems inherent in the relationship between Vienna and Budapest further weakened its effectiveness and cohesion. Nevertheless, the army held together and the great majority of its soldiers of all nationalities fought loyally until the last months of the war.

The monarchy's record on the battlefield was not, however, glorious. The initial plan had been to defeat Serbia first, thus closing this front and perhaps winning Bulgarian intervention. Not only did the army fail to eliminate Serbia, but a Russian attack in Galicia forced a Habsburg retreat along the northern border. Thereafter, although relying heavily on German support, Habsburg troops played a major part in the great campaigns on the eastern front and in the Balkans. Serbia was defeated and occupied in 1915, but that year also brought Italy into the war in the enemy camp. On that front, however, the Habsburg Army was uniformly successful, because the campaigns here were popular with both the Austrian Germans and South Slavs, who saw their territories threatened by the Italian claims.

Although the Ottoman Empire, in November 1914, and Bulgaria, in October 1915, joined with Austria-Hungary and Germany, their enemies were more successful in winning allies; of particular significance was the entrance of the United States in April 1917. In the camp of the Central Powers the German Army was obviously the main source of strength. During the war German units and financial aid had to be dispatched to the assistance of the weaker ally. Under these circumstances Germany became the predominant partner, but the monarchy was never in anything like a vassal relationship. As in all such circumstances, the allies often disagreed on policy; they had, for example, different programs for the Polish lands. The alliance nevertheless held together until the final defeat on the battlefield. For both powers the failure of the German Army to win a decisive victory on the western front was the major determinant of their future history.

At the beginning of the war there were no major domestic problems connected with the military effort. As in all of the belligerent countries, the outbreak of hostilities had been greeted with considerable patriotic enthusiasm. The Reichsrat was prorogued in March 1914 and not called back into session until May 1917. Karl von Stürgkh, as minister-president of Austria, hesitated to convene an assembly in which there were so many Slavic delegates. As in previous difficult situations, the government ruled through the use of Article 14. Civilian officials at this time had frequent clashes with the military, which could exert a great deal of authority under wartime conditions. Many in the army, as well as in the government, had doubts about the loyalty of the Czechs and South Slavs. In the regions directly involved in the fighting, which were under military control, some officers acted as if they represented an occupying power in an enemy territory.

Despite the tension caused by such an attitude and the existing national antagonisms, the majority of the population in all national groups supported the Habsburg military effort. Nevertheless, at the beginning of the war some politicians emigrated to the Entente countries, where they argued for a change in the political status of their nationalities. These men were self-appointed spokesmen and represented no party or official organization. The activities of Thomas G. Masaryk for the Czechs and Ante Trumbić and Frano Supilo for the Croats were to be the most damaging to the monarchy. In the same manner, Polish leaders from Galicia were in touch with their colleagues in the German- and Russian-controlled Polish lands, who together used their influence with the Entente governments. The émigré politicians were, in general, in favor of the radical program of breaking up the Habsburg Empire into its national components. Until the spring of 1918, however, none of the Allied governments adopted the dissolution of the monarchy as a serious war aim. The national committees were, nevertheless, useful cards in their own game. They could be used against the Central Powers much as the German government employed the Ukrainian question against tsarist Russia. Certainly there was little idealism in Allied wartime negotiations. In the Treaty of London of 1915, which brought Italy into the war, not only Austrian German territories, but also South Slav lands in Dalmatia and Istria, were promised to Rome.

A major weakness of the Habsburg position, certainly in regard to its own population, was its lack of major war aims. The government had blundered into a world conflict because its responsible leaders thought that Serbia represented a deadly danger. With the defeat of that state in 1915, the major objective had been achieved. Very little else remained by which to justify the huge sacrifices that continued to be demanded of the population. Because of the position of the Hungarian government, which had accepted the war with Serbia only on the assurance that no territory would be annexed, and which steadfastly insisted that the relationship established by the Ausgleich would not be changed, Habsburg public opinion could not be calmed with promises of a victor's peace and large acquisitions of land. After two years of bitter fighting, and with no alternate program to hold off popular discontent, some officials felt that at least assurances should be given concerning postwar domestic reforms.

The situation became worse when on November 21, 1916, Franz Joseph died at the age of eighty-six. The great burdens of a wartime government then fell on the shoulders of his grand-nephew Charles. Weak but well-meaning, the twenty-nine-year-old emperor had neither the training nor the temperament for the position. Franz Joseph, despite his advanced age, had remained an active head of state until his death. Moreover, he had the respect and even affection of his people, the majority of whom had known no other ruler. Charles could not command the same loyalty. The son of Franz Ferdinand's brother Otto, he had not expected until after the assassination to be the heir to the throne. In 1911 he had married Princess Zita of Bourbon-Parma; her sentiments were bound closely to France and Italy, not to the German powers.

Despite his difficult position, Charles did take certain steps; it is to his credit that he recognized that the interests of the monarchy demanded an early end to the war, but he handled the matter badly. In the spring of 1917 he attempted to begin a discussion of peace terms with the Allies by using his brothers-in-law, the princes Sixtus and Xavier of Parma, who were officers in the Belgian Army. He did not fully inform his foreign minister, Ottokar Czernin, or his German ally. These negotiations, which never really got started, were to cause him extreme embarrassment when they were revealed by the French government in 1918.

Charles's attempts to improve the domestic situation were equally unsuccessful. With the increasing deterioration of internal conditions, Charles, against the advice of Heinrich von Clam-Martinitz, the Austrian minister-president, decided to reconvene the Reichsrat, an action that was bound to bring the national controversies again into the open. Charles was, however, in no position to deal with them. Also against his Austrian ministers' wishes, he had succumbed to the arguments of István Tisza that he should be crowned king of Hungary. This act involved an oath and the obligation to defend the Hungarian constitution and the territorial integrity of the lands of the kingdom. This action meant that the Hungarian government, determined to defend its special position, had another weapon with which to block basic reform in the empire, even in the Austrian lands. The debates in the parliament, which reopened in May 1917, clearly demonstrated the determination of the Czechs and South Slavs to present their demands for reforms that would benefit their nationalities.

In November 1916 the various Czech parties had been joined together in the National Committee as well as in the

National Union, a parliamentary club. The major Croatian activities were carried out within the Hungarian kingdom, but Croatian and Slovenian representatives in the Reichsrat cooperated with the Czech delegates in demanding reforms. On May 30, 1917, the Slovenian representative, Anton Korošec, declared: "On the basis of the principle of nationality and of Croat state rights, we demand the unification of all of the lands inhabited by the Slovenes, Croats, and Serbs of the monarchy in one autonomous state, free from all foreign domination, ruled in a democratic manner and under the sceptre of the Habsburg dynasty."[5]

Ukrainian and Polish representatives similarly used the parliament to present their demands. These national declarations faced the Austrian government with another dilemma. Quite obviously wartime conditions made immediate major reform impossible, but it could not even give assurances for the future. Not only was the Ausgleich involved, but the Czech, South Slav, Polish, German, Hungarian, and Ruthenian national programs overlapped and conflicted. The government could not satisfy one set of claims without enraging other parties in the disputes.

During the war, these national controversies dominated domestic politics. Social and economic problems were also, of course, aggravated by the privations of wartime. The Bolshevik revolution of November 1917 introduced yet another element into the picture. Not only had the tsarist government been overthrown by a revolutionary party, but its call for an immediate peace with no annexations and no indemnities had wide appeal in war-weary Central Europe. The Social Democrats had by this time adopted the same basic program of a peace without victory. At the beginning

[5] Z. A. B. Zeman, *The Break-Up of the Habsburg Empire, 1914–1918* (London: Oxford University Press, 1961), p. 128.

of the war, like the other parties, the Austrian German Socialists had supported the government and had regarded autocratic, tsarist Russia as the principal enemy. About the only important opposition to this stand had come from Friedrich Adler, the son of the party leader, and a small group associated with him. In October 1916 he went so far as to assassinate Stürgkh. Viktor Adler and Karl Renner retained their headship of the party, but by late 1917 a strong leftist faction had emerged, with Otto Bauer as its most prominent member. This group pressed for a peace based on the principle of no annexations and no indemnities; Bauer had also come to the conviction that the monarchy would inevitably break into its national components. The leftist peace program was soon accepted by the entire party, and at the end of the war Bauer held the predominant influence. There was no split in the organization; the unity, which had been so important to many Socialist leaders, such as Viktor Adler, was thus maintained.

Although no revolutionary acts like those which had taken place in Russia occurred in Vienna, the dissatisfaction of the workers was shown in a series of strikes at the beginning of 1918. The winter of 1917–1918 was extremely difficult. On January 14 the ration of flour was cut substantially. Almost immediately 10,000 workers at the Daimler plant in Wiener Neustadt went on strike, and others quickly followed their example; at the height of the action 153,000 had left their jobs in Lower Austria, 113,000 in Vienna, and 40,000 in Styria. There were also strikes in Hungary, but relatively few in the Bohemian lands. The actions were in protest against the shortages of food and fuel and in support of peace. On February 1 the Habsburg Fifth Fleet, stationed at Cattaro (Kotor), mutinied over the conditions of service. Both the strikes and the mutiny were suppressed with little difficulty.

The inability to deal with the major national demands

demonstrated another Habsburg weakness. By this time the Western Allies had adopted peace programs that contained compelling propaganda appeals. After the tsarist government fell, the Western leaders were able to claim that the war was an ideological struggle of the forces of freedom and democracy against those of oppression and autocracy. The Bolshevik program of a peace without victory was paralleled by Woodrow Wilson's emphasis on self-determination. Point 10 of his Fourteen Points called for the reorganization, but not the dissolution, of the Habsburg Empire: "The peoples of Austria-Hungary, whose place among the nations we wish to see safeguarded and assured, should be accorded the freest opportunity for autonomous development." The exile committees could make excellent use of this material. Engaged in a campaign to convince Western opinion that the monarchy was a "prison of its people," the émigré leaders called for its destruction. The Habsburg government had no program that it could use to combat the charges; it could not offer the nationalities a hope of autonomy or of radical reform in the Hungarian kingdom, where it was really needed.

In this situation it was obvious by the last year of the war that the fate of the empire would be decided on the battlefield. And indeed, until the late summer of 1918 victory seemed a possibility. In March 1918 the Treaty of Brest-Litovsk was concluded with the Bolshevik government, and in April Romania too signed a separate peace. The Austrian population expected that as a result of these agreements food supplies from the East would alleviate the near starvation conditions in some areas and that soldiers would be released to serve on other fronts. Habsburg and German hopes, however, were soon crushed. In March 1918 the German army launched a series of unsuccessful assaults on the western front; by August it was clear that the tide had turned in the Allied favor. At the same time, Allied armies encamped in Thessaloniki started a great offensive up the Balkan peninsula; Bulgaria and the Ottoman Empire surrendered in September and October. The Habsburg southeastern frontiers were now open to attack.

By this time the process of dissolution had commenced. In the spring of 1918 the Allied governments had come to accept a breakup of the monarchy. They thus recognized the Czechoslovak National Council in Paris as the representative of the Czech and Slovak people, whose national lands were, of course, a central and integral part of the Habsburg Empire. Within the monarchy national committees formed during the war began in October to take control of their regions. In Prague the local national committee assumed the functions of an independent government; in Agram (Zagreb) the National Council of Slovenes, Croats, and Serbs acted similarly. Among the German parties only the Social Democrats were adequately prepared to meet the situation. They were willing to accept the principle of self-determination for the monarchy's nationalities, but they claimed the same right for the Germans, declaring on October 3: "We demand that all German territories in Austria be unified in a *German Austrian state,* which would regulate its relations to the other nations of Austria and to the German Empire according to its own needs."[6] This program was subsequently accepted by the other German parties.

The end to over six centuries of Habsburg rule came quickly. On October 16 Charles, in a desperate attempt to save the situation, issued a manifesto designed to turn Austria into a federal state. On that same day Hungary ended the Ausgleich; on October 21 a provisional German administration was organized in Vienna. On November 3 the imperial au-

[6] Otto Bauer, *Die Osterreichische Revolution* (Vienna: Wiener Volksbuchhandlung, 1923), p. 74.

thorities in their last major act signed an armistice. On November 11 Charles, faced with the dissolution of the monarchy, stepped down, but he did not abdicate. As can be seen, the empire fell into its national divisions even before the fighting had ended. Separate governments were indeed established, but the truly difficult problem, that of assigning the territorial divisions, had yet to be resolved.

Conclusion

AUSTRIAN GERMANS IN 1918

I N this account of Habsburg history the emphasis has been placed on the Austrian Germans and on the relations of the monarchy with the rest of German Central Europe. In the immediate prewar years, as we have seen, the German-speaking people still held the strongest political, economic, and social position in the monarchy, but at the same time, their national movement in most respects had not developed as far as those of other nationalities – for instance, the Hungarians, Poles, and Czechs. Here, first, the special German position is reviewed, and second, a brief estimate of Austrian German attitudes toward themselves and united Germany is given.

By 1914 Austrian Germans, including assimilated families whether Slavic, Jewish, Irish, Spanish, or other, did indeed as a group enjoy a privileged status. They spoke the major language, which was that of the Austrian parliament, the ministries in Vienna, the joint ministry with Hungary, the Austrian supreme court, the army and navy, the Austrian Catholic church hierarchy, and the higher educational institutions. It was similarly the language of business and industry, as well as of the predominant culture, that of Vienna. Germans also held the top positions in the bureaucracy, the military, the professions, the higher church hierarchy, industry, finance, business, culture, and higher education. Most

Austrian Germans accepted this situation as natural; it seemed to show that among the Habsburg nationalities they worked harder, were smarter, and had a more highly developed civilization. It must also be remembered that Austrian German superiority was not class-based. The aristocracy, middle class, peasantry, artisans, and industrial working class all tended to be better off than their counterparts among the other nationalities.

Having held this position for so long, and feeling usually comfortable, safe, and self-righteous, the Germans had no need to establish organizations to defend their own nationality or to challenge others. Moreover, as long as national identity was a matter of culture and language alone, the Germans did not feel endangered. Only in the nineteenth century, with the development of ideas of popular sovereignty and – even more – the concept that nationality should form the basis of the state, did serious problems begin to arise. Self-determination, a fine principle for most of the monarchy's nationalities, was a destructive force for the Germans, who were not compelled to consider its implications until after 1871, or perhaps even until after the Badeni decrees of 1897.

As we have seen, no specifically German-national party of significance emerged. The two great mass parties, the Social Democrats and the Christian Socials, were indeed chiefly German in membership, but they had official programs designed to appeal to class rather than to national interests. There were, of course, smaller German-based provincial political organizations, but here again they were concerned primarily with local national controversies or with the question of their relationship with the central administration in Vienna. In addition, the development of German or Austrian German national feeling was to a degree inhibited by the question of the appropriate relationship of the Austrian German to the German Empire: should he look to Vienna or to Berlin as his national capital?

In the first part of the nineteenth century such problems of divided loyalty were minimal. The Habsburg monarch was until 1806 the Holy Roman Emperor; thereafter, Austria held the presidency of the German Confederation. In 1848 Austrian German representatives at the Frankfurt parliament could argue for German unification on a grossdeutsch basis. There was thus as yet no great conflict between the interests of the Austrian Germans and those of the citizens of the other German states. Moreover, until 1866, or even 1871, the possibility always existed that Austria might head a reorganized and strengthened German Confederation. The unification of Germany came as a shock to many, since now the Protestant Prussian Hohenzollerns rather than the Catholic Austrian Habsburgs were German emperors, presiding over a united Germany. Individual Austrians might indeed, like Grillparzer, ask: "I am born a German, am I one still?"

By the time the war came in 1914 there was no common Austrian German consensus about the future. The majority were undoubtedly most concerned about maintaining their position intact, and they supported the dynasty and the empire. Only a small minority wanted to break up the monarchy, with the German regions, including Bohemia, joining Germany. Some provinces, in particular Vorarlberg, Tirol, and Salzburg, were drawn economically, geographically, and even culturally to southern Germany, but even here no strong group stood for annexation. It should be noted that although other national groups had plans for the territorial organization of the future autonomous or independent administrations, the Austrian German mass parties did not formulate similarly detailed plans. The Christian Socials wanted to keep things as they were; the Social Democrats stood for the federal solution, but they were deeply aware of problems of drawing boundaries. Other German-based parties concentrated on defending the status quo against the attempts of other nationalities to improve their positions.

Of course, in 1914 the Austrian Germans did not expect to lose the war; even the most pessimistic could not have foreseen the extent of the catastrophe occurring four years later. Germany was an ally; its government had backed the Habsburg decision to attack Serbia. Although there were many disagreements during the war, about both the conduct of campaigns and the possible postwar settlements, the two states fought together until the end. Neither before the war nor during the fighting did anything happen to prepare the Austrian Germans for the formation of an Austrian state. Some remained primarily loyal to the dynasty and empire and others to their German nationality or their province – but there was little if any "Austrian" sentiment.

PART II

THE REPUBLIC OF AUSTRIA

3

THE FIRST REPUBLIC, 1918–1932

T HE manifesto issued by Charles on October 16, despite its intent, accelerated the process of dissolution. Faced with a military catastrophe and the actions of the various national committees to assume authority in their regions, the German parties too had to act and form their own organizations. Thus on October 21, 1918, the provisional National Assembly of the "independent state of German-Austria" was called to meet in the hall of the provincial assembly of Lower Austria in Vienna. This body was composed of the delegates of the German parties who had been elected to the 1911 Reichsrat, whose terms had been extended to December 31, 1918. Since five of these men had died, the assembly was now composed of 72 Christian Socials, 42 Social Democrats, and 102 members of German-national and liberal parties organized in the Nationalverband (National Association). To head this assembly three presidents were elected, one each for the principal party groupings, along with a Council of State of twenty members. On October 30 a provisional government was formed, with Social Democrats holding leading positions: Karl Renner was appointed as chancellor and Viktor Adler as foreign minister; Social Democrats also held the important ministries of interior and war. When Adler died on November 11, he was replaced by Otto Bauer as party leader and foreign minister. The Social Demo-

151

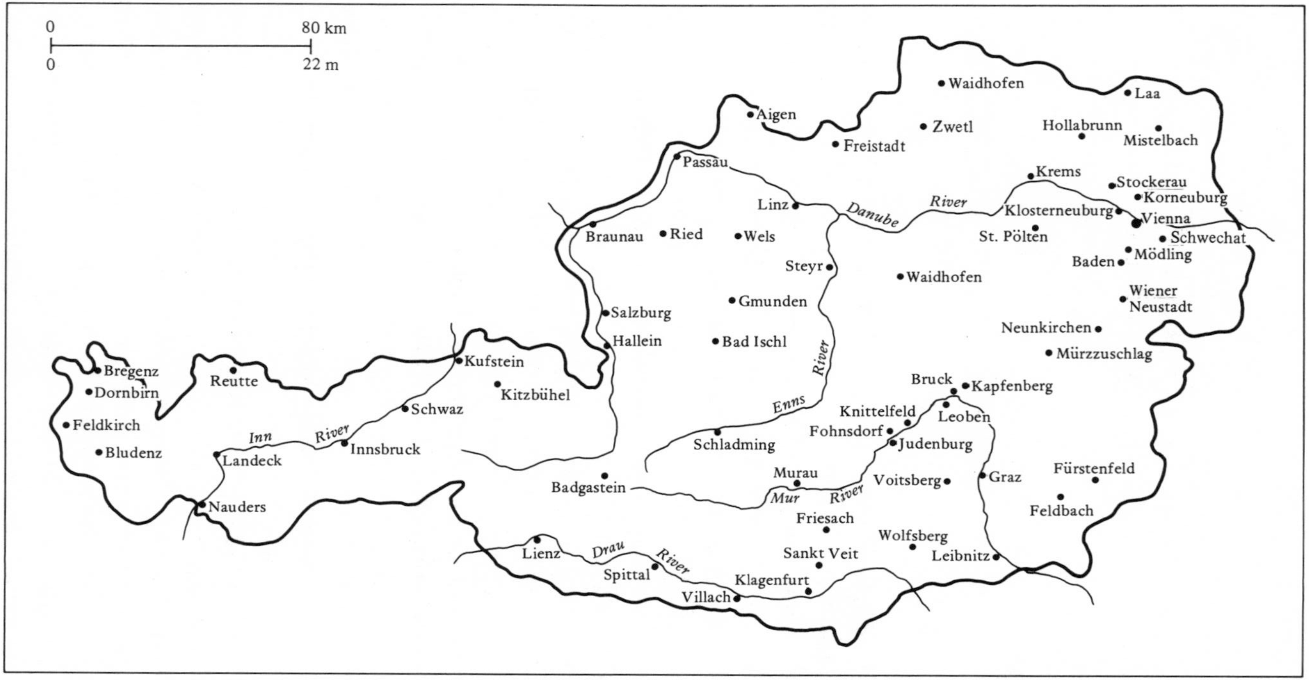

Map 5. Modern Austria

cratic strength reflected the position of the party at this time. Although it had hitherto refused to join a "bourgeois" government, this attitude was abandoned under the circumstances and in return for ministerial positions. The party had the enormous advantage of being the one most easily able to adjust to the revolutionary atmosphere at the end of the war. In view of the violent political upheavals that were occurring throughout Central and Eastern Europe, it seemed almost inevitable that the Austrian government too would have to move to the left. Equally obvious was the mood of unrest and discontent among the defeated people.

The establishment of the new German-Austrian regime was paralleled by the disintegration of the old imperial structure. For a while the two governments existed side by side. On October 27 the government of Max von Hussarek was replaced by what was to be the last imperial cabinet. Formed by Professor Heinrich Lammasch, a known pacifist, it included among its numbers Ignaz Seipel for social welfare and Josef Redlich for finance. The main task of this government was to seek a separate peace, a goal most difficult for those with German-national inclinations.

The fate of the emperor and his officials was strongly influenced by events in Germany. There William II abdicated on November 9 and a government under Social Democratic leadership took control. The Austrian Socialists wished Charles also to abdicate. Instead, on November 11 he issued a statement, drafted by Seipel, which included the words "I renounce all participation in state affairs." He in fact never formally abdicated. Thereafter, the imperial family withdrew first to Schloss Eckartsau, outside Vienna, and then in March 1919 to Switzerland. In April the assembly passed measures aimed at confiscating Habsburg property.

The transfer of power and authority from the imperial officials to the provisional government proceeded peacefully.

Similar changes were put into effect in the provinces, where local assemblies took over control from the appointed governors. Little effective support was shown for the maintenance of a monarchy. Peasants and workers alike were disillusioned by the defeat. Although most Christian Social leaders would probably have preferred, at least in theory, a constitutional monarchy, they too allowed themselves to be influenced by the spirit of the time to accept what was in fact a compromise solution. On November 12, after Charles's withdrawal, the provisional assembly took the decisive step. Austria was declared to be a republic and, in what was to be a highly controversial decision, "a constituent part of the German Republic." The German-national sentiments of both the Social Democrats and the German parties were thus expressed. The Babenberg colors – red, white, and red – became those of the flag and the republic.

In February 1919 elections were held in those areas which were not under foreign occupation to choose representatives for the National Assembly that would frame the constitution. Seventy-two Social Democrats, sixty-nine Christian Socials, and twenty-six German-national representatives, together with three others, were elected. In March a coalition government was formed of the two major parties, with Renner as chancellor and the Christian Social Jodok Fink as vice-chancellor. Otto Bauer remained foreign minister until July, when the difficulties arising in connection with the negotiation of the peace treaty led Renner to assume this position. The principal tasks of this assembly were the consideration of the peace terms and the formulation of the constitution.

The government faced almost insurmountable difficulties. The internal conditions were indescribable; as Renner wrote: "Der neue Staat hat ein Trümmerfeld übernommen" (The new state had taken over a field of ruins). Moreover, the extremely disturbed political conditions in the entire Central European area were bound to affect Austria. The great impact of the Bolshevik revolution in Russia was soon to be seen in parallel actions in the neighboring lands of Hungary and Bavaria. Within the state both of the coalition partners found their own ranks divided over the political form of the state. In 1919, however, two main problems overshadowed all of the rest – negotiating a peace treaty and meeting the challenge that came from radical Socialist and Communist agitation. In addition, the government had to deal with the shattered economy, whose disastrous state was due not only to the war, but also to the fact that the Austrian lands were no longer part of a great empire.

THE TREATY OF ST. GERMAIN

As could be expected, the Austrian government wished to negotiate a peace treaty as soon as possible. Without a clear knowledge of the boundaries of the state, a regular administrative system could not be established. Matters were delayed by the fact that the victorious Allies were far more interested in the German question. Meanwhile, an Austrian delegation with Renner at the head was appointed; on May 7 it received a list of instructions drawn up by the executive committee of the assembly. On May 12 the delegation departed for St. Germain, a suburb of Paris, where it was kept waiting for three weeks in conditions of virtual internment. The instructions from the assembly were to be useless; the Austrians did not negotiate a peace treaty – they were handed the terms. Although the general outlines of the settlement were given to them in June, more complete stipulations were not delivered until September 2. The delegation was allowed to make written objections, but the final document reflected changes in only inconsequential details. The Austrian sur-

155

render in November 1918, unlike the German, had been unconditional. Although the terms thus violated no previous agreement, they were far harsher than expected. Despite the extreme shock that the treaty caused in Vienna, the government had no choice but to accept it. After the National Assembly approved the terms by a vote of ninety-seven to twenty-three, the treaty was signed on September 10.

Because in a very real sense the treaty shaped the history of the First Austrian Republic, and in fact laid the basis for its subsequent downfall, a careful examination of its terms, particularly the territorial provisions, is necessary. At the peace conference perhaps the basic issue was the question of the exact status of the Austrian government: that is, was it the heir of the Habsburg Empire, or was it, like the other succession states, a new creation? If the latter, it had not been a participant in the war and thus could not conclude a peace treaty. Nor, of course, could it be burdened by any penalties connected with the lost war. Such an interpretation, however, did not suit Allied, especially French, policy. In the treaties both Austria and Hungary were designated as the heirs of the defunct empire. As such, Austria had to accept a "war guilt" clause and was made liable for reparations, with the amount to be settled in the future. In the same manner the Austrian Army was limited to thirty thousand professional soldiers. Having refused to concede the substance of the issue, the Allies quite illogically were willing to accept the form. In the end the Austrian representatives concluded a *state* treaty and not a *peace* treaty, implying a political agreement between the signatory powers rather than a settlement after a war.

It will be remembered that at the time of the proclamation of the republic, Austria was also declared a "constituent part of the German Republic." The clearly expressed desire to join Germany, although meeting with some sympathy among the

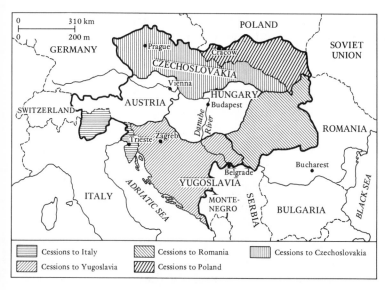

Map 6. The breakup of the Habsburg Empire after World War I

Americans and British, was violently opposed by the French and Italian governments. France in particular was strongly against allowing Germany any gains. In addition, France was also concerned about Czechoslovak and Yugoslav security should a strong German bloc be formed in Central Europe. Article 88 of the Treaty of St. Germain expressly forbade the joining of the two German states unless the consent of the Council of the League of Nations was given, an unlikely event because of the composition of that body. A similar provision was included in the Treaty of Versailles. At the same time the Allies, again on French initiative, compelled the change of the name of the state from German-Austria to Austria.

More significant than these peace conditions, most of which were to be changed in the next twenty years, were the boundaries assigned, which were to be retained even in the agreements of 1945 (see Map 6). Within the Austrian part of the Habsburg Empire, Germans lived in compact groups in the provinces of Upper and Lower Austria, Styria, Carinthia, Tirol, Salzburg, and Vorarlberg. Three million Germans were also to be found in Bohemia, Moravia, and Silesia, but not always in areas contiguous to those previously mentioned. At first, there was some hope that the principle of self-determination would be applied to these latter people, who were later to be known collectively as the Sudeten Germans. The Czechoslovak government rejected this idea, of course, since it was continuing the policy, adopted under the old empire, of claiming historic boundaries against Vienna, but national borders against Budapest. Attempts of local German groups to agitate for autonomous rights were put down by force; the Czechoslovak government regarded these actions as traitorous. Although the drawing of the boundary in areas bordering on Germany can be understood from strategic considerations, the assignment of over 350,000 Germans of Upper and Lower Austria to Prague can less easily be justified. The new Czechoslovak state was thus composed of 3.1 million Germans along with 8.7 million Czechs and Slovaks. Of course, this multinational character was not unusual in the succession states of the Habsburg Empire. The peace treaties in no sense solved the national problems; they simply redistributed them and set up new lines of discontent.

Second to the national losses to Czechoslovakia were those in Tirol. Here the declared intentions of the victorious powers were, in fact, contradictory. In the Treaty of London the Italians had been promised the strategic frontier of the Brenner Pass, but, in contrast, Point 9 of Wilson's Fourteen Points had spoken only of a northern Italian frontier drawn "along clearly recognizable lines of nationality." At the end of the war Italian troops were in occupation of South Tirol. Moreover, in the peace negotiations Wilson was willing to accept

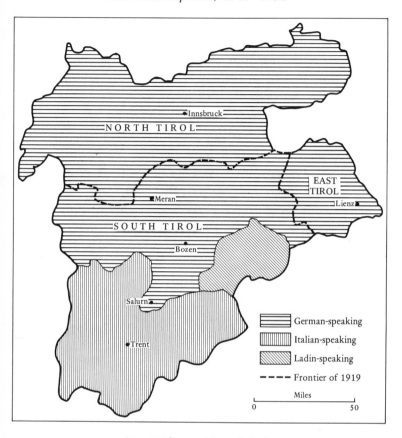

Map 7. The partition of Tirol

the Italian claims against Austria in the interest of Yugoslav gains elsewhere. In the final settlement the Brenner frontier was given to Italy, and thus 220,000 outraged and militant Tiroleans passed under Italian rule (see Map 7).

The question of South Tirol henceforth remained a major block to good relations between Austria and Italy. The inhabitants of the Tirol maintained their strong provincial sentiments and their resentment of the partition. In May 1919,

159

in the hope that the action would aid in preventing dismemberment, Tirol declared itself an independent state; in April 1921, 98.6 percent of the population voted to join Germany. As will be shown in subsequent sections, this problem has never been satisfactorily settled.

Despite its severe defeats on the two questions of South Tirol and the Czech borderlands, the new state had a greater success in maintaining its national frontiers in other areas. Even after the armistice local fighting continued in two regions – Carinthia and Western Hungary. An area of mixed Slovene and German population, Carinthia was also an object of interest to the Slovene national government, with its center in Ljubljana, (Laibach) which in December 1918 joined the Kingdom of the Serbs, Croats, and Slovenes. The majority of the local Carinthian population, however, backed the provincial government in Klagenfurt and stood behind its position that the entire province should go to Austria. When South Slav troops from across the frontier entered the area, local armed units, the Home Guard (Heimwehr), quickly formed to repel the invader. Fighting lasted over a prolonged period; in May 1919 Yugoslav troops were able to take Klagenfurt.

In the question of Carinthia the Austrians enjoyed the support of a victor power. At this time Italy was interested in containing the influence of the new Yugoslav state, so its government backed the Austrian position. At the peace conference it was finally decided that a plebiscite would be held in two stages. The first was to cover the southern section of the province, known as zone A, which was primarily inhabited by Slovenes. The second, zone B, included Klagenfurt and was a German area. In October 1920 the majority of the inhabitants of zone A voted to join Austria, a decision that made a plebiscite in zone B unnecessary. The Austrian success here was partially offset, however, by the parallel loss

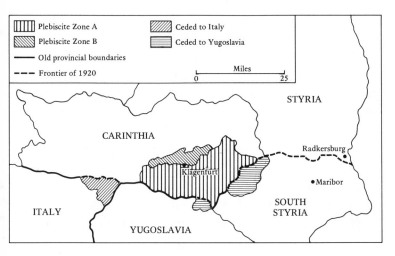

Map 8. The Slovene question

to the South Slav state of the Maribor (Marburg) area of Styria (see Map 8).

All of the regions so far discussed had been part of Cisleithania. Austria now laid claim to a small area, known as Western Hungary, that had formerly been under the control of Budapest, but that was primarily inhabited by Germans. It was also of economic importance in that it was the market area for Vienna. This question too took long to solve and was to lay the basis for much bad feeling in Hungary. The problem was complicated by the fact that the Czechoslovak government expressed an interest in annexing the land to provide a corridor to Yugoslavia. Although the region did have a Croatian minority, Belgrade showed no great enthusiasm for the idea. After a long period of negotiation, the Allies included in the Treaty of Trianon of June 1920, which dealt with the Hungarian lands, a provision that gave the territory to Austria. As had been the case with the Heimwehr in Carinthia, similar Hungarian bands resisted the change.

161

Finally, in 1921, the Italian government mediated the dispute. A plebiscite – generally considered an unfair one, as the Hungarian army was in control – was held in December in the city of Odenburg (Sopron) and the surrounding district. The Austrian government lost the city but retained the rest of the area, which entered the state as the province of Burgenland.

To conclude the question of the territorial composition of the Austrian republic, a word should be said about Vorarlberg. Like Tirol, this province in the months after the war showed no great enthusiasm about joining the Austrian state. In May 1919, 80 percent of the population voted in a plebiscite to join Switzerland. Later this region became a center for the support of union with Germany. Geography apart, the population thought that joining either of the other neighbors would serve its economic and political future better than attaching itself to Austria. Again, the refusal of the Allies combined with the strong opposition of Vienna prevented this action.

THE COMMUNIST QUESTION

In addition to the problems connected with the peace, the Austrian government was faced with the issues raised in the country by the victory of the Bolshevik revolution in Russia and the influence of this event on its population. In 1918 and 1919 the attraction of Bolshevik doctrines was actual and immediate in the defeated states, in particular in Germany and Austria, where Marxist parties were strong. In the winter of 1918–1919 this question caused the Social Democratic government in Berlin to call upon the army for support against Communist and left-wing Socialist attempts to advance the revolution there one step further. The resultant split in the German labor movement was to have disastrous consequences. In Austria also it was not clear after the war whether the parties of the left would try to undo the compromise that the republic actually represented. At this time, it must be remembered, the Bolshevik government in Russia expected a spread of world revolution.

In November 1918 a Communist Party was organized in Austria with the aim of capturing the state by revolutionary action and of introducing a dictatorship of the proletariat along Leninist lines. This group had in its military auxiliary, the Rote Garde (Red Guard), an armed force that was to play an important role in subsequent political actions. The party as a whole was to remain small. In February 1919 delegates representing a mere three thousand members attended the first party meeting. In subsequent elections only a relatively few Austrians voted Communist. The party never presented a clear program, and even more important, it never had a leader of distinction. Nonetheless, the existence of the group caused great concern to the Austrian government and to the leadership of the Social Democratic Party, which saw in Communist activities a challenge to its own domination of the workers' votes.

As members of the governing coalition, the Social Democrats were also faced with criticism from their own left-wing members along the lines of earlier party controversies. In the winter of 1918–1919 the immediate political problem was the status of the Workers' Councils, which had already been formed in connection with the strike of January 1918. At the end of the war they were joined by Soldiers' Councils, composed of bitter and disillusioned veterans. Although at first there were no connections between the two groups, a central organization for both was set up that represented a political rival to the official government. The question thus arose whether the councils, like their Soviet counterparts in Russia, would become effective centers of power. The Austrian Communists, like their Russian colleagues, used the slogan "All power to the councils." They also did not choose to run candidates for the elections to the National Assembly.

The pressure from the left became even stronger when on March 21, 1919, a Communist government under Béla Kun was established in Budapest and when in April and May a similar regime appeared in Bavaria. The Hungarian government immediately appealed for aid from the Austrian workers, and the Hungarian embassy in Vienna became a center for the organization of assistance and for propaganda. The Social Democratic Party met this challenge to its own position and to the state by clever tactics. The party encouraged its followers to join the Workers' Councils and then to dominate their decisions by majority vote. They thus controlled the radical left through a democratic process.

A similar tactic was adopted to deal with the army, which was also subject to Communist influence. With the disintegration of the Habsburg Army, the republic was left without a military force. To remedy this situation Julius Deutsch, the Social Democratic head of the defense ministry, organized the Volkswehr (People's Army). A professional army with salaried soldiers, this force was strongly influenced by the Soldiers' Councils and other left-wing elements. The Communists, who were also members of the Red Guard, were concentrated by the army command in the Forty-first Battalion, where the Social Democratic leaders could watch them. At first a question existed whether the Volkswehr could be used to defend the government against Communist activity. The army was to be tested twice, in April and again in June.

On April 17, under Communist leadership, demonstrations took place in front of the parliament. The police were not able to control the crowd, which proceeded to set the building on fire. In subsequent street fighting the fire engines

164

were not able to penetrate the crowd, and members of the Forty-first Battalion joined to fight the police. Five policemen and a woman were killed in these clashes. Order was restored when the other units of the Volkswehr and Social Democratic leaders took control. This incident clearly demonstrated that the army as a whole would support the legal government against revolutionary challenges.

A further action was then planned by the Communists for June 15. Through their domination of the Workers' Councils the Social Democrats were again able to frustrate the attempted rebellion. On the night of June 14–15 the chief of police of Vienna, Johann Schober, arrested over a hundred Communist leaders. Nevertheless, on June 15 crowds under Communist leadership assembled and incidents occurred leading to an estimated twenty deaths. Without adequate leadership and with the Volkswehr again proving its reliability, the Communist agitation failed to shake the government. Thereafter, the Communist threat diminished rapidly. In July 1919 the Kun regime in Budapest fell, to be replaced by a strongly rightist government; the Bavarian revolt, which had lasted scarcely six weeks, was similarly repressed. In August the Forty-first Battalion was disbanded. At the same time the Workers' Councils declined sharply in influence. These episodes thus ended in a victory primarily for the Social Democratic Party. Subsequently, no real challenge was to arise to its control of the workers' votes. As long as free elections were held, its position on the left was secure.

THE CONSTITUTION: THE FIRST GOVERNMENTS

Although peace was thus made and the Communist challenge neutralized, the coalition government faced increasing difficulties. The two parties, with their widely differing views of politics and life, had come together in an emergency, but neither trusted the other. As the immediate problems receded, the pressure for cooperation lessened. Within the Social Democratic organization questions were again raised about the wisdom of associating with a bourgeois regime. Leading Socialists, including Otto Bauer, continued to believe that the party should use the opportunity to strengthen itself so that it could exploit any new revolutionary situation that might arise; others opposed this stand along the classical lines of Marxist debate. Among the Christian Socials, many saw all Socialists as Bolsheviks – as too red to make acceptable alliance partners.

The coalition finally broke up on June 10, 1920, over a number of relatively minor issues. Renner would have preferred to continue it, but by this time both Otto Bauer and Ignaz Seipel, who was emerging as the most significant Christian Social leader, were willing to end the partnership. To replace the coalition ministry a Proportional Cabinet (Proporzkabinet) was formed representing the Social Democrats, the Christian Socials, and the German-national parties that had not been in the previous government. Appointments were given in strict proportion to the representation in the assembly, and there was no real cooperation among the parties. The ministry was headed by the Tirolean Christian Social Michael Mayr, who was the state secretary for constitutional and administrative reform. The chief task of the government was to run the state until new elections in October indicated the actual strength of the parties. At this time also the new constitution was approved.

The principal controversies surrounding this document concerned the question of a federal as against a centralized form of organization and issues connected with the political power of the two major parties. As was natural, the provinces wished to retain as much authority as possible. To their inhabitants their home regions had far more political reality and historical significance than the new concept of the Austrian state. Their loyalties often lay primarily in their provincial capitals, particularly after the destruction of the empire. As we have seen, Tirol and Vorarlberg in plebiscites expressed the desire to form other associations. Since the strength of their party lay in the provinces, the Christian Socials backed a federal organization. In contrast, the majority party, the Social Democrats, fully expecting to continue to hold power in the future, preferred a centralized government. They also feared that their interests and that of the workers would suffer in a federal state. Although the final document was a compromise, the man chiefly responsible for its drafting, Hans Kelsen, was nearer to the Social Democrats in sympathy. The constitution reflected this fact and demonstrated the strong position that the party held in the first years of the republic.

The document, approved by the assembly in October, remained in effect until 1933. The final form provided for a two-house parliament, but with power concentrated in the Nationalrat (National Assembly), which was to be elected on the basis of universal suffrage. The second house, the Bundesrat (Federal Assembly), represented the interests of the provinces, and its members were chosen indirectly. This body had only a suspensive veto. The president of the republic, who was to be chosen by a special National Assembly consisting of the two houses meeting together, was allowed chiefly representational powers; his method of election and his weak position were reflections of the Social Democratic desires. The composition of the Nationalrat was to be determined by proportional representation. Changes could be made in the constitution only with the approval of two-thirds of the members. With the approval of the consti-

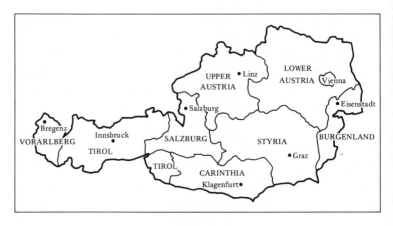

Map 9. Austria: the provinces

tution, and after the city of Vienna was separated in 1922 from Lower Austria to form a ninth province, the basic political pattern of the republic was set (see Map 9).

On October 17, 1920, the first regular elections were held. Before this time, however, the leaders of the factions that constituted the German-national camp had come to recognize that they would need a stronger organization. After negotiations among seventeen of these groups, in September the Grossdeutsche Volkspartei (Greater German People's Party) was formed. It stood, as could be expected, for the strongest possible relationship with Germany and attracted in particular the support of students, teachers, and bureaucrats. In the elections the former Social Democratic advantage was lost. Instead, the Christian Socials, with eighty-five representatives, were the strongest single party. The Social Democrat representation fell to sixty-nine; the Greater Germans won twenty representatives and the Bauernbund (Peasants' League) eight. The Communist Party, with only twenty-seven thousand votes, had no representation. Since the Greater Germans would not join the Christian Socials in

168

a coalition government, a cabinet was formed of Christian Socials and neutral officials under Michael Mayr. At the same time Michael Hainisch, a nonpolitical candidate, became the president of the republic.

The first government had to face the enormous problems of political discontent, economic dislocation, and then the possible financial collapse of the new state. The precariousness and uncertainty of the entire situation were shown in the plebiscites not only in Tirol, but also in Salzburg, where in May 1921, 99.3 percent of the voters showed their preference for Germany. The Mayr government lasted only until June 21, 1921, when it was replaced by a cabinet under the leadership of Schober, the police chief of Vienna, who had acquired a reputation of strength on the basis of his handling of the riots and demonstrations. He faced the same problems as his predecessor. Inflation increased in severity and the general economic condition of the country continued to decline. Loans and other financial assistance from abroad were difficult to attract as long as this situation existed and reparations were at least in theory still owed.

In foreign affairs problems were also encountered. Former Emperor Charles attempted twice, once in the spring of 1921 and again in October, to regain power in Hungary. Although he failed and was subsequently exiled to Madeira, where he died in April 1922 at the age of thirty-five, his actions caused repercussions in both internal and foreign policy. At this time also Austria was forced to allow Italy to mediate the Burgenland question, a procedure that led, as we have seen, to the failure to acquire Odenburg.

The Schober government did, however, have to its credit one positive action in foreign relations, although a highly controversial one. In the summer of 1921 President Hainisch and Schober met with Masaryk and Eduard Beneš to discuss common problems. In December 1921 the Treaty of Lana was signed between the two states. Basically a treaty of trade and friendship, the document nevertheless called upon Austria to recognize the existing borders and thus in effect to give up all claims in relation to the Germans in Czechoslovakia. In addition, each state agreed to remain neutral should the other be attacked by another power and to allow no organizations on its territory that threatened the security of the other. All conflicts between them were to be mediated. In return, Czechoslovakia granted a loan of 500 million gold kronen, to be used for the purchase of coal and sugar. As could be expected, this agreement was intensely unpopular with the Greater Germans, who, with others, saw it as the first step in the formation of a Danube Confederation under Czechoslovak, and thus really French, leadership. With his political position weakened, Schober was forced to resign. He was replaced in May 1922 by Ignaz Seipel, the most influential man in the Christian Social Party, who was to dominate the Austrian political scene until his death in 1932.

By 1922, when Seipel became chancellor, an Austrian republic, with definite boundaries and a constitution, was thus in existence. It was, however, gravely handicapped by the conditions under which it had been founded and by the terms of the peace treaty. As has been shown, the republic itself was the result of a compromise between the views of the two major parties. Its form was the first choice of neither. The Christian Socials had been happy under the empire; if a change were necessary, they would have preferred a constitutional monarchy organized on a highly conservative basis. The Social Democrats openly acknowledged that the republic was only a brief stopping point on the road to the establishment of a socialist system. The German-national groups of all varieties did not want an Austrian state at all, but a union with Germany.

The issue of Austrian patriotism dominated the entire history of the First Republic. Under the empire, as we have seen, the inhabitants of the German-speaking areas had been in varying degrees, and depending on the individual, loyal to the empire, their provinces, or the wider concept of a German nation. No one had fought for, or believed in, a specifically Austrian idea – apart from the empire. Like the republic, the Austrian state was a second choice for all concerned. In this account the entire question of an *Anschluss* with Germany will be covered in connection with the events of 1938, when this alternative became a possible and practical policy. Throughout the 1920s the repeated discussions of the problem were largely academic; the conditions of the time made it absolutely impossible, no matter what the feelings of the inhabitants were, for such an action to be accomplished. This issue, along with the other stipulations of the Treaty of St. Germain, was dependent on French postwar policy.

This state, primarily concerned with the difficulties of defending itself against a Germany of potentially far greater strength, placed its reliance for the future on the building of what were largely artificial barriers against its rival. Such a policy precluded any increase of German power such as that which would have been brought about by an Anschluss. The imposition of unequal and punitive economic and military conditions on the defeated states was a part of this program, as were the building up of the succession states of Poland, Yugoslavia, Romania, and Czechoslovakia and their inclusion in a French alliance system. The French policy, although understandable from a narrow French standpoint, placed on the shoulders of the Austrian republic a heavy burden, from both the political and the economic standpoint, and one under which it finally collapsed. Georges Clemenceau, the chief author of the French view, did not help matters by commenting, in words that are repeated in almost every Austrian book on this period: "L'Autriche, c'est ce qui reste" (Austria, that is what is left over).

Although the political conditions in the state were difficult, it was the economic situation that was truly catastrophic. Through the centuries the lands of the Habsburg Monarchy had developed an economic interrelationship. With the gaining of separate statehood, the German-Austrian lands consisted of a capital city containing a third of the population, an industry highly dependent on outside resources, in particular coal, and a great deal of very beautiful scenery. Although Austria potentially did have the resources for a sound economy that could provide an acceptable standard of living for the population, these were not developed, nor did the country have the capital to invest in necessary new enterprises. Most disastrous was the inability of Austrian food production, given the technology available, to cover the needs of the people; only 17.8 percent of the land was arable. Moreover, normal economic relationships had been interrupted. The city of Vienna had obtained most of its foodstuffs from neighboring Hungarian territory; the coal for the Austrian industry came from what were now Czechoslovak lands. In the postwar years none of the successor states was interested in reestablishing the old relationships; instead, each erected tariff walls around its own lands. Only the Czechs, who inherited 80 percent of the industrial equipment of the old monarchy, were not harmed by this condition.

Equally disastrous was the financial picture of the new state. Burdened with the debts of the war and the liquidation of the empire, the republic also had to face the possibility of reparation payments. The value of the currency at once began to fall. With expenses far above revenues, the state tried to solve the problem with the printing presses. The resulting inflation made the krone virtually valueless by the time of Seipel's administration. The stabilization of the currency became the first task in the rehabilitation of the economy of the country.

The effect of these conditions on the population was devastating materially and psychologically. Throughout the existence of the First Republic unemployment remained high, a situation whose terrible political consequences will be shown in later sections of this account. Taxes and prices similarly reached high levels. The obvious economic and political weakness of the state made many question its basic viability (*Lebensfähigkeit*). Some of those who argued for union with Germany were influenced by the sincere belief that the country could never stand on its own feet. This attitude affected the leadership of all of the parties. Bauer, for instance, was convinced that the state could not survive economically. And, indeed, during the period of the First Republic Austria was not a truly viable unit. Repeated international loans, each involving a considerable degree of foreign control over internal affairs, alone kept the government from collapsing. The first task of the Seipel government was to try to meet the problem of the basic financial instability.

THE SEIPEL ERA

Ignaz Seipel, the leading Austrian political figure for the decade 1922–1932, came from a lower-middle-class background (his father was a cab driver). Born in 1876, Seipel became a priest in 1899 and, subsequently, a professor of moral theology at the Universities of Salzburg and Vienna. He was, as we have seen, a member of the last imperial cabinet. Under the republic he soon rose to occupy the leading position in the Christian Social Party. Assuming the office of chancellor in May 1922, he had to deal immediately with the obvious major problem, the terrible economic condition of the country, in particular the spiraling inflation. To stabi-

Ignaz Seipel

lize the currency and to rebuild state finances, it was clear to Seipel that foreign loans were necessary. The Social Democratic Party at the time was arguing for a program of self-help, but with the failure to gain the cooperation of foreign-

174

controlled Austrian banks, such a policy could not succeed.

In the summer of 1922 Seipel traveled extensively to try to impress on foreign governments the seriousness of the Austrian financial crisis and the importance for the European equilibrium of maintaining the Austrian state. Finally, in October, with support from the League of Nations, he was able to acquire the necessary financial aid. In the Geneva Protocol, signed on October 4 by Britain, France, Italy, and Czechoslovakia, Austria received a guarantee for a loan of 650 million gold kronen. The political cost of this agreement was, however, high. The Austrian government had to promise that the question of Anschluss would be postponed for twenty years, that a League of Nations commission would supervise Austrian finance, and that an immediate reform of the state expenditures would be undertaken so that the budget would be balanced in two years. The state tobacco monopoly and the customs revenues were to guarantee the loan.

The agreement met with immediate opposition in Austria. As could be expected, the Greater Germans strongly objected to the limitation on the Anschluss, but they finally accepted the agreement. The sharpest criticism came from the Social Democrats, who attacked the provisions allowing for foreign interference as well as the limitation on the union with Germany. Despite these objections, the loan and the accompanying reform measures were to be successful from an economic point of view.

Viktor Kienböck, the finance minister, was a close friend and associate of Seipel. Under his management the budget was balanced and the currency stabilized, although at a high social cost. Under strong outside pressure the government made great efforts to reduce its expenditures. The first action was the firing or pensioning of about eighty-five thousand civil servants, a move that hit hard at the Greater German

Party, many of whose members were government employees. Taxes also were raised and social service benefits curtailed. These measures were accompanied by an increase in unemployment; by 1926 the figure had risen to over 240,000. Inflation, however, was halted. In December 1924 a new currency, the schilling, was introduced, and the old kronen were exchanged at a rate of ten thousand to one. The reforms introduced at this time concerned state finances, of course, and not the general economic condition of the country, whose basic problems were in no way solved.

In October 1923 elections were again held. Despite Seipel's hopes for an absolute majority, the Christian Socials elected only eighty-two representatives; the Social Democrats had sixty-eight and the Greater Germans ten. At this time also the Agrarian League (Landbund) appeared on the political scene, with five representatives. This party, a successor to the former German Peasant Party, had its center in Upper Austria, Carinthia, and Styria and was composed of those peasant-farmers who did not belong to the coalition associated with the Christian Socials. It adopted in general a realistic and practical attitude toward political problems and was to play a significant role henceforth in Austrian politics. Seipel's failure to win a majority despite the success of his financial program can be attributed to the fact that his measures had caused great hardship to the middle-class backers of his party. Moreover, the issue of the continuance of rent controls, which Seipel opposed, was of major importance in the election campaign in Vienna. The failure of the League of Nations to withdraw its commission from Vienna at the end of two years, as originally agreed, also injured the Christian Socials.

In November 1924 Seipel left office, and his choice, Rudolf Ramek, became chancellor, to remain in office for two years. Heading a weak administration, based on a coalition

with the Greater Germans, Ramek had to deal with continual economic problems as well as scandals resulting from
involvement of members of the government in shady financial transactions. Two major banks, the Central Bank of the
German Savings Bank and the Postal Savings Bank, failed.
On the positive side, the League commissioner left and the
accompanying controls were removed.

Returning to office in October 1926, Seipel remained
chancellor for two and a half years. Elections in April 1927
again did not go as he wished; rent control in Vienna remained a major issue. Running together on a single list, the
Christian Socials and the Greater Germans won eighty-five
seats, a loss of nine representatives; the Social Democrats,
commanding 42 percent of the vote, their largest plurality in
the First Republic, won three additional places, with a total
of seventy-one representatives. The Agrarian League received nine seats. Although a government was formed from
a coalition of the Christian Socials, the Greater Germans,
and the Agrarian League, the margin of control was small.
It was estimated that if the Social Democrats won some three
hundred thousand more votes in the next election, they would
have the 51 percent absolute majority that they sought. With
the hardening of ideological lines that took place in the 1920s,
this possibility was deeply disturbing to the middle-class
parties.

THE IDEOLOGICAL FRONTS: THE HEIMWEHR

Although the Seipel years did witness the financial stabilization of the state and limited economic progress, the general political picture was not bright. Most apparent was the
sharpening of differences between the two major political
parties and the formation of private armies to back the position of the rival political camps. The chief problem in Aus-

trian politics in the 1920s was the obvious fact that the Christian Socials and the Social Democrats were divided by far more than their disagreements over state policy. As under the empire, each party represented a view of life and held a set of principles that could not be easily compromised in the interest of interparty harmony. As the decade advanced, these differences became more acute and the personal disagreements of the party leaders increasingly bitter. Particularly evident was the open rivalry between Seipel and Bauer, each standing at the head of his own party and each finding policies of compromise ever more difficult to accept.

The left in Austrian politics was composed of the Social Democratic and the Communist parties. As we have seen, the Communists had been largely contained by their Socialist competitors. They were not able to win a single seat in the parliament or a place on the Vienna communal council. Throughout the 1920s the Social Democrats were able to hold their control of the workers' votes and to expand their influence to win some middle-class support. Ideologically Marxist, Social Democratic newspapers and orators spoke often in strong terms of class warfare and of the capture of the state by force. In fact, the party remained moderate and revisionist in practice. As we have seen, it joined in a coalition in the first year of the republic; thereafter it continued to participate in the regular political life of the state. Moreover, Austrian Socialist doctrine adapted itself to the realities of the Austrian scene, particularly in regard to the peasant question. The leaders recognized that a purely Socialist regime was possible only in Vienna, not in the predominantly peasant provinces. The party also accepted the existence of peasant property, which was theoretically acquired by work and not by exploitation, and agreed that should its socialist system be adopted, the peasants would remain the free owners of their land.

In the question of religion also adjustments were made,

owing to the fact that most peasants and many workers were sincere, believing Catholics. In opposition to the Communist and Socialist line of thought that regarded religion as an "opium for the people" and called for a campaign against it, the Austrian Socialist party emphasized that religion was a private matter. Thus it did not oppose Catholicism as such, but only the church organizations and societies that did not support the interests of the workers. The Socialist program, calling for the sharp separation of church and state and civil control of education, nevertheless contradicted the Catholic viewpoint expressed by the Christian Social Party.

Even though Austrian Socialism was in practice revisionist, and though it had made important theoretical compromises, many Austrians were deeply fearful of what would occur should the party win power through the elections or through a revolutionary seizure of power. The great issues in European Socialism had been and still were those of the use of revolutionary tactics and the establishment of a "dictatorship of the proletariat" should the party gain control of the government. On the question of violence, Socialist spokesmen such as Otto Bauer had repeatedly argued that forceful methods should be used only when no other means existed and then only in a defensive manner. The most controversial declaration on this subject was made in November 1926 at a meeting of the party in Linz. Here the usual debates had taken place over the question of democracy and the dictatorship of the proletariat. The final party statement issued here reemphasized the necessity of winning power by democratic means: only if the bourgeois forces organized a counterrevolution against a Socialist government should force be used and a dictatorship established.

If, however, the bourgeoisie should resist the social revolutionary change, which will be the task of the power of the state of the working class, through systematic restriction of economic life, through forceful insurrection, through conspiracy with foreign counter-revolutionary powers, then the working class would be compelled to break the resistance of the bourgeoisie by the instrument of dictatorship.[7]

Despite the revisionist nature of the Socialist program, the party rhetoric caused continued concern. People were afraid of what might happen should the Social Democrats win over 50 percent of the vote and thus control the government. Many property owners, Catholics, and others lived in dread that once Socialists held the principal state offices, they would introduce a dictatorship and end the democratic system. ◆

Although the Social Democratic Party formed part of a governing coalition for only a short time, its influence on Austrian life was tremendous. In the period from 1918 to 1921 it succeeded in introducing much social welfare legislation, reforms associated with the work of Ferdinand Hanusch, the minister for social administration. The eight-hour day was made standard, and regulations were issued concerning vacations, social insurance, and the employment of women and children. Similarly, the Socialist administration of Vienna, which lasted until 1934, followed pre-1914 patterns and adopted an ambitious program, including the construction of hospitals, kindergartens, public baths, parks, and, most important, large apartment complexes to provide low-cost housing for the poor, a major problem dating from the previous century. It similarly organized such amusements as sports contests, Alpine expeditions, and theater and concert presentations. The Social Democratic worker could thus live in a world organized by his party. He was a member of a Socialist union; his housing, recreation, and newspapers and other reading matter could all originate with and reflect the

[7] Charles A. Gulick, *Austria: From Habsburg to Hitler* (Berkeley: University of California Press, 1948), II, 1390.

opinion of this very ideologically oriented political organization. With its emphasis on environment, education, and cultural activities, this party aimed at providing a better life and a new mental outlook for its working-class constituents.

The Christian Socials, composed of different elements from the middle class and the peasantry, could never have the cohesion in interest and ideology of their Socialist opponent. As a party they had previously been loyal to the dynasty and to the monarchy. At the time of the revolution many of their members had been distrustful of the democratic forms introduced. In the succeeding years the party members, including the middle-class artisans, white-collar workers, shopkeepers, professional men, and peasant farmers had been greatly hurt by the economic disasters. Most important was the strong Catholic tie that all of the members of this party shared. They had previously fought strongly the Socialist and Liberal attempts to separate church and state, particularly the laws concerning education and family matters, such as marriage. The members of this party were also extremely disturbed by the revolutionary vocabulary and the Marxist slogans of the Social Democrats. As the years advanced it became more evident that many in this party had no basic devotion to, or conviction about, the principles of parliamentary and democratic government. In the face of an apparent threat to their religion and the possibility that a Socialist victory might lead to a dictatorship, many were willing to accept the destruction of the republic.

The evolution in this direction can be seen in Seipel's views. In 1918 he had, as we have seen, supported the republic; in 1925 he declared: "There can be no contradiction between a *correctly conceived democracy* and the conviction, shared by all religious people, that all power comes from God."[8] By

[8] Alfred Diamant, *Austrian Catholics and the First Republic* (Princeton, N.J.: Princeton University Press, 1960), p. 108.

1928 his views had shifted, perhaps under the influence of the repeated failures of his party to win a majority in the elections. He began more often to attack "Godless socialism," which had ended respect for "piety and authority" and to talk about "correctly conceived" or "true" democracy, a term that became finally close to dictatorship in his usage. Although his knowledge of Marxism was "no more than fragmentary and second hand,"[9] he increasingly attacked the Socialist party and in particular Otto Bauer. In 1924 he was severely wounded by a fanatic, an action that he appears to have believed was Socialist-instigated.

Most dangerous for the state was not only this cleavage in ideology between the two major groups, but also the fact that the political parties acquired private armies. Of particular significance was to be the Heimwehr, also called the Heimatschutz. During the last years of the war and the first years of the peace the disintegration and chaos in the monarchy had brought into existence small local bands formed to maintain order and also, as in Carinthia, to defend the state boundaries. These groups were always well armed, since plenty of guns were left over from the war. Both the police and the army were also weak at this time. As we have seen, the Volkswehr had been initially a Socialist and radical center, and as such it had won much distrust. The Heimwehr organizations were regarded by many as a needed supplement to the insufficient state forces. Seipel saw them as a reserve behind the army.

At first there were few links among the various groups. Most were based on individual provinces, and each had its own leaders. Particularly significant for the future were the Heimwehr organizations of Walter Pfrimer in Styria, Richard

---

[9] Klemens von Klemperer, *Ignaz Seipel: Christian Statesman in a Time of Crisis* (Princeton, N.J.: Princeton University Press, 1972), pp. 231, 258.

Steidle, backed by Major Waldemar Pabst, in the Tirol, Ernst Rüdiger Starhemberg in Upper Austria, Julius Raab in Lower Austria, and Major Emil Fey in Vienna. Before 1927 these bands did not represent an effective political force. Although all were anti-Marxist, they had no single ideology or common policy. Later, Catholic elements were to conflict with the Fascist-indoctrinated groups linked to Italy. Other armed groups on the right also existed, particularly veterans' organizations. The National Socialists did not become of similar importance until the victory of their party in Germany.

The Social Democrats, on their side, adopted similar tactics. In 1922 a regular Austrian Army, removed from direct political interference, was established under the direction of Karl Vaugoin. Since it was organized on conservative lines and with an emphasis on imperial traditions, the Socialists lost the military arm that they had held in the now-defunct Volkswehr. In 1923 they therefore formed the Republican Defense League (Republikanischer Schutzbund) under the leadership of Julius Deutsch. This group was trained as a regular army and acquired an impressive arsenal of weapons; its membership in the 1930s was estimated at about eighty thousand.

The existence of two armed forces, backing opposing political views, created a dangerous situation. A policy of disarmament by both the right and the left was clearly indicated. Although the Social Democrats did propose such action, neither the government nor the right trusted their sincerity. With both sides armed, an incident was bound to occur. An event of January 1927 was to have a great influence on the subsequent course of Austrian history. At that time in the village of Schattendorf in Burgenland a veterans' group and the Schutzbund clashed, an act that led to the killing of a veteran and a child by right-wing elements. The accused were freed by a citizens' jury after a trial six months later. In protest a massive demonstration took place on the Ringstrasse in Vienna on July 15–16. The crowd could not be controlled either.by the police or by the Social Democratic leaders on the scene. After the demonstrators set fire to the justice building and refused to let the fire engines through, the police intervened and fired on the crowd, causing a loss of some ninety lives. Under Social Democratic sponsorship a general strike of one day and a transportation strike of two days were called. Both actions were unsuccessful. The government forces were able to control the situation in Vienna; in the provinces the Heimwehr joined in the suppression of the strikers. The episode in the end was a Seipel victory. In retaliation, the Social Democrats urged their members to leave the church. This confrontation was to be the last of this kind until 1934, although in October 1928 a dangerous situation arose in Wiener Neustadt when both the Heimwehr and the Schutzbund scheduled marches. Police and army intervention kept the two groups apart.

In internal political matters Seipel continued to face the usual problems of a coalition government. In December 1928 Wilhelm Miklas, a Christian Social, was elected president. Suddenly, in April 1929, Seipel resigned. The unexpectedness of the action at first caused considerable confusion. Although his reasons were not clear, it has been suggested that Seipel was concerned over the decline of membership in the church. He was also a sick man; he was a diabetic, and his health had deteriorated after an assassination attempt. Although Seipel left office, his influence remained paramount in the Christian Social Party and thus in the government. As will be seen, he continued to take an active part in Austrian political life.

CHRISTIAN SOCIAL MINISTRIES: THE GREAT DEPRESSION

After the departure of Seipel, a successor of similar stature was hard to find. For a short period, from May to September 1929, Ernst Streeruwitz, a former staff officer in the imperial army, headed the government. He was followed by Schober, who formed a ministry composed half of officials and half of party men. It included Vaugoin as vice-chancellor and war minister, as well as the former president Hainisch, the future cardinal of Vienna Theodor Innitzer, and the historian Heinrich von Srbik. The composition of the government was designed to win public confidence. Schober was still considered a strong man: the property-owning middle class looked on him as a defender of its interests, whereas the industrialists saw him as a block to the Socialist threat. However, his political position was weak. The Heimwehr, finding that it would not have the influence in this government that it expected, opposed him, as did the Social Democrats.

The ministry of Schober was dominated by two main problems: the renewal of the economic crisis and the actions of the Heimwehr. In the years following Seipel's reform of state finances the Austrian economy had improved, although it remained as before greatly dependent on foreign investment, and the production costs of industry were still too high. The currency was sound, but Austrian goods were expensive. In October 1929 the event that heralded the beginning of the Great Depression, the crash of the New York Stock Market, took place. Shortly thereafter the Boden-Creditanstalt, one of the great banks of Vienna, closed. In what was to prove an unwise move, Schober supplied some state funds, but also compelled the Creditanstalt, a bank owned largely by the Rothschild family, to absorb the responsibilities of the other institution. These events were followed by the beginning of the great economic crisis lasting from 1929 to 1937. By June 1931 there were over 350,000 unemployed, a figure that was to rise to 480,000 in 1938; of those with jobs many did not work full time. The political implications of this disaster were soon to undermine the democratic basis of the First Republic.

The growing internal instability brought about a constitutional change that Seipel had also considered during his ministry. In December 1929 the constitution was amended to strengthen the position of the president in relation to parliament. He was to be chosen by direct election; he was given the important powers of being able to dissolve the assembly and of issuing emergency proclamations; and he was in command of the army.

Meanwhile, the Heimwehr was clearly increasing in strength and moving further right in political ideology. In May 1930 some members announced a political program similar to that of the Italian Fascists. In this declaration, known as the Korneuburg Oath, parliamentary democracy and the capitalist economic system were denounced, and the intention to seize power was openly declared. The statement ended with the words "Let every comrade realize and proclaim that he is the bearer of the German national outlook: let him be prepared to offer his possessions and his blood, and may he recognize the three forces: faith in God, his own unbending will, the command of his leaders."[10] This declaration served to sharpen the political conflicts in the state and to divide the population further.

The issue of the Heimwehr split the center parties. Although the Greater Germans had no single outlook, the Landbund opposed the Heimwehr and organized its own private army, the Bauernwehr (Peasant Guard). Schober

[10] Ibid., p. 374.

personally was against the Heimwehr because it had become a serious threat to the maintenance of order in the state, with its continual parades, demonstrations, and militant declarations. He would have liked to disarm all of the private organizations. As a first step he expelled the chief of staff, Major Pabst, who was a German citizen, an action that won him the open enmity of the Heimwehr.

Although Schober was thus beset with domestic difficulties, he did win some limited successes in foreign policy. Recognizing the necessity of securing further foreign loans for internal development, he conducted negotiations in The Hague that resulted in January 1930 in the lifting of reparations and the end of the claims of the successor states. He also concluded treaties of friendship and commerce with Italy and Germany. Nevertheless, his position became increasingly weaker; Seipel, always a dominant figure, intrigued against him.

In September 1930 the Schober government was replaced by a ministry under Vaugoin that lasted barely sixty days. Seipel entered as foreign minister, and most significant, Starhemberg, now the commander of the Heimwehr, became minister of interior. The Ministry of Justice went to another Heimwehr leader, Franz Hueber, a brother-in-law of the prominent German Nazi leader Hermann Göring. Since the Greater Germans and Landbund would not cooperate, this was a minority government. Its chief task was to hold new elections. Although the attempt was made to form an anti-Marxist coalition, the elections on November 9, the last to be held for parliament in the First Republic, were a disaster for the Christian Socials. The Social Democrats emerged as the strongest party, with seventy-two seats, while the right split into factions. The Christian Socials, with sixty-six seats, thus lost seven. This number was gained by the Heimatblock (Home Bloc), the political arm of the Heimwehr, which won a total of eight places. Nineteen representatives were elected by the National Economic Bloc, a new organization combining the Greater Germans and the Landbund under the leadership of Schober. The Austrian National Socialists won over 110,000 votes, but received no representatives; the Communists polled a small 20,000. In a previous election in Germany the Nazi Party had won 107 of the 575 seats in the Reichstag and thus emerged behind the Social Democrats as the second strongest party there.

After the elections a government based on the Christian Socials and the Schober faction was formed, headed by Otto Ender, with Schober as foreign minister, Vaugoin as war minister, and Engelbert Dollfuss as minister of agriculture. It then took steps that were to bring a severe setback in foreign policy and to lead to a major economic crisis. In both Austria and Germany a dangerous internal situation and the rise to prominence of extremist groups threatened the prestige and position of the parliamentary governments. Each needed a success to bolster its domestic standing. In this critical time Schober, in March 1931, met with the German foreign minister, Julius Curtius, to discuss plans for an Austrian–German customs union, a measure that would win wide approval in both countries. Unfortunately, neither the Italian dictator, Benito Mussolini, nor the French premier, Aristide Briand, was informed beforehand of the negotiations. Thus, when the Austro-German plan was announced, the European powers were not prepared for it. France, Italy, and Austria's neighbors, Yugoslavia, Czechoslovakia, and Romania, joined in the Little Entente, objected that the agreement was a step toward the forbidden Anschluss. The League eventually placed the matter before the Hague tribunal, which decided by an eight-to-seven vote that the action was in opposition not to the Treaty of St. Germain, but to the Geneva Protocol.

Meanwhile, however, the French government had acted. Although the entire world was affected by the economic crisis of the time, France was in a relatively strong position, and it thus had a financial weapon that it could use for foreign policy goals. At this time the French government withdrew the substantial funds that it had on deposit in the Austrian Creditanstalt, thus contributing to the collapse of that institution in June 1931. The greatest of the Austrian banks, this organization had most savings banks and a large part of Austrian industry dependent on it. The city of Vienna and the successor states were also financially involved. The Austrian government did not have the economic means to stand behind the bank's losses. The British were able to extend short-term credit for 150 million schillings, but French money was needed. In a form of political blackmail France was able to insist on the end of the customs union and, in addition, the imposition of outside controls on the Austrian banks and state finances. In the face of French pressure the Austrian government in September abandoned the union, but not before the Creditanstalt had folded.

During this crisis the Ender government fell and Seipel once again stepped into a leading political position. In negotiations with the Social Democrats he attempted to find a basis for the establishment of a national government. Although a Seipel–Bauer coalition had much in its favor, the basic strong differences between the two party programs and the mutual distrust of their leaders hindered such an action. In June Karl Buresch, the governor of Lower Austria, was able to form a government with Christian Socials, Greater Germans, and the Landbund as the base. Schober became vice-chancellor and foreign minister. This basically weak ministry had to deal with the first serious Heimwehr action. In September 1931 Walter Pfrimer, at the head of the Styrian organization, attempted a remarkably badly organized coup.

Since he received no support from outside his province, his forces were easily quelled by the army. However, after a trial he and his followers were freed. Pfrimer belonged to the radical wing; thereafter conservatives and legitimists, with Starhemberg at the head, were to control the movement.

In January 1932 Buresch reorganized his government. Most significant was the fact that he could no longer count on the support of the Greater Germans. The coalition partnership that had enabled the Christian Socials to stay in power since 1922 was thus at an end; the ministry represented only a minority in parliament. At this time two men, Dollfuss, who remained as minister of agriculture, and the Tirolean lawyer Kurt Schuschnigg, the new minister of justice, were to emerge to prominence and to inherit the Seipel position in Austrian politics. In April 1932 local elections were held in Vienna, Lower Austria, Salzburg, Styria, and Carinthia. In all of these the Nazi gains were impressive, but particularly in Vienna. Here this party won fifteen seats on the communal council. Particularly hard hit were the Christian Socials, since many members of the middle class, officials, and young people went over to the rising Nazi Party. From this time on the Greater Germans, the Landbund, and the Heimatblock saw their electoral strength decline. In the future three mass parties were to dominate Austrian politics: the Social Democrats, the Christian Socials, and the National Socialists. This balance was to determine the fate of the Austrian republic.

When the Buresch ministry fell on a vote of confidence in May 1932, few Austrians realized that their political system was about to face a major crisis or that their parliamentary democracy was about to come to an end. However, up to this time the history of the republic had certainly not been a particularly happy one. After the war the state had been given an independence that no party particularly sought and a republican form of government that had no large group of committed supporters behind it. Of the two great parties, the Social Democrats looked forward to a future socialist society; the Christian Socials would have preferred a conservative constitutional monarchy with a strong Catholic orientation. The German-national parties, whose sentiments were shared by others, did not want an Austria at all.

The attitude of the European powers who created the state was also anything but helpful. Of the Western democracies, France by its economic policies directly contributed to the weakness of the democratic government and the fragility of the state's independent status. As Italy's influence grew stronger, its government, although at first supporting independence, pressed for a Fascist system. With the growing strength of National Socialism in Germany and the rise of that party in Austria, both the republican form of government and independence were to be placed in jeopardy.

4

AUSTROFASCISM, ANSCHLUSS, AND WAR, 1932–1945

DOLLFUSS AND AUSTROFASCISM

Engelbert Dollfuss, who replaced Buresch as chancellor on May 20, 1932, was anything but a typical Austrian statesman. Born on October 4, 1892, an illegitimate child from a peasant background, he grew to only four feet eleven inches in height. After receiving a good education in Catholic establishments, he served on the Italian front during the First World War, where he won repeated decorations for bravery. Returning to Vienna, he specialized in agricultural questions. During a period of study in Berlin, he married a German girl of Prussian extraction. As we have seen, he was minister for agriculture and forestries in the previous cabinet.

As head of the government, Dollfuss faced a very difficult situation. In a coalition with the Landbund and the Heimatblock he had only a one-vote majority, and he could not rely on it with certainty. He was also compelled to allot the Heimatblock the important Ministries of Trade, Interior, and Education. At first, he did not try to put through a set program, but concentrated on the dangerous economic situation. The extreme financial problems of the state made it necessary once again to turn to the League of Nations for help. In July Austria was able to obtain 300 million schil-

Engelbert Dollfuss

lings, but as was the case with the Geneva Protocol, the conditions were harsh, including a renewal of the ban on an Anschluss. Since the agreement, the Lausanne Pact, called for repayment over a period of twenty years, this stipulation added ten years to the limit already in effect. Strict economic controls with foreign supervision were again to be imposed. Both the Greater Germans and the Social Democrats opposed the agreement, arguing that Austria could get along without outside help and, of course, objecting to the Anschluss limitation. The weakness of the Dollfuss position was shown in this question: the pact was approved in two separate votes – in one the government majority was one; in a second, two.

Since Dollfuss could not count on a majority in the assembly, he had to look for other ways to run the country. Both the National Socialists and the Social Democrats pressed for new elections. Foreseeing another Christian Social defeat, Dollfuss instead moved toward authoritarian rule. His actions were to make him more dependent on Heimwehr support and to make his relations with the left even more strained. Emil Fey became state secretary for security in October. The antagonism felt toward the Social Democrats was increased when their newspaper, *Arbeiter-Zeitung*, in January 1933 disclosed that Italy was illegally sending to Austria weapons intended to be transshipped to Hungary. This apparent violation of the Treaty of St. Germain called forth strong protests from the Western powers and the Little Entente.

A chance occurrence in the parliament allowed Dollfuss to rid himself of its controls. On March 4, in the course of a disagreement over electoral procedure, the first of three presidents of the assembly, Karl Renner, resigned his position so that he could vote; the Christian Social president, Rudolf Ramek, then followed his example for the same reason. In the confusion, the third president, the Greater German, Sepp Straffner, acted in a similar manner. Since there was now no presiding officer, there was no means of either ending the session or calling a new meeting. The state president, Miklas, could have used his power to dissolve the parliament and call for new elections, but he did not act.

This event served to end parliamentary democracy in the First Republic. Using the opportunity presented to him, Dollfuss on March 7 issued a proclamation that effectively brought parliamentary government in Austria to a close. On March 15 Straffner and Renner attempted to call a meeting of the assembly. The police blocked the entrance to the building, but some Social Democrat and Greater German representatives had arrived previously. A meeting of a half hour, which was without practical results, was held. In April in a speech in Villach, Dollfuss gave his judgment on the events: "And so Austria's Parliament has destroyed itself; and nobody can say when it will be allowed to take up its dubious activities again."[11] In a final step away from legality, the Austrian highest court, the Verfassungsgerichtshof (Constitutional Court), was made powerless by the withdrawal of its Christian Social members.

Dollfuss's assumption of full power in the state was accompanied by a curbing of civil liberties, including freedom of speech, assembly, and the press. With the approval of his party he henceforth governed on the basis of the Economic Empowering Act, a measure that had been passed in 1917 to enable the wartime government to deal with its economic problems, in particular to regulate the distribution of the basic necessities of life. His two major opponents remained the Social Democrats and the National Socialists, two parties with little else in common. During the next period he was able to stay in office principally because of his close alliance with and dependence on Fascist Italy and his control of the chief

---

[11] Gordon Brook-Shepherd, *Dollfuss* (London: Macmillan Press, 1961), p. 102.

military forces in the state: the army, the police, and the Heimwehr. In this period both the National Socialists and the Social Democrats pressed for the holding of elections, but the fact that both Italy and the Heimwehr supported the introduction of an authoritarian political system made it apparent that Austria would not soon return to the road of parliamentary democracy. The influence of the National Socialists was to become much greater when in January 1933 Hitler became the German chancellor.

In the National Socialist Party and Adolf Hitler, the Austrians had a movement and a leader of native origin. Hitler was born in Braunau in April 1889; his early education there and his experiences in Vienna, where he lived from 1907 to 1913, shaped his outlook on life and politics. The National Socialist German Workers' Party of the 1920s was a descendant of the prewar Austrian German Workers' Party, an organization that in 1920 affiliated with the National Socialists of Bohemia and Bavaria. In Austria its leader was Walter Riehl; this party gave to the German branch both its name and its symbol, the swastika. In its early years the party split into two factions, one wishing to follow a revolutionary, the other an evolutionary, course. There was also disagreement on whether Riehl or Hitler, who became the Munich leader, should hold the highest position. With Hitler's increasing success in Germany, the Austrian party became more dependent on the German organization. Austrian Nazis swore allegiance to Hitler, and they accepted his political program. Like Germany, Austria was divided into regions or *Gaue,* each under a *Gauleiter.* In the next years Austria too had the Nazi organizations of the SS (Schutzstaffel: Nazi elite guard), the SA (Sturmabteilung: Storm Troops), and the Hitler Youth. Although after the failure of the Munich *Putsch* of 1923 Hitler decided on a legal course of action, the Austrian party tended to be violent and revolutionary in its program.

Throughout the 1920s the party remained obscure and small; in June 1928 it had only forty-four hundred members. The elections of 1930, which gave the German Nazi Party a significant victory, contributed to the position of the Austrian branch. By January 1933 its numbers had risen to over forty-three thousand. Even more important were the events of 1933, when Hitler first became chancellor and then gained dictatorial powers. Germany was thereafter ruled by a man who had gained German citizenship only in 1932 and one who had a frank and open pan-German program. Where previously the Austrians had shown more relative enthusiasm for an Anschluss than the Germans, the impetus was now to be from the other direction. No action could, of course, be immediately expected. Not only had Hitler still to overcome significant internal opposition, but other steps, such as the breaking of the military restrictions of the Treaty of Versailles, of necessity had to have first priority. Because of these limitations and world conditions, the German objective was at first not a union of the two states, but a *Gleichschaltung* (political coordination) of the governmental systems. The methods used to put pressure on Dollfuss included acts of terror and a massive propaganda attack. The leader of the Austrian Nazis in 1932 was Theo Habicht, the inspector general for Austria. An appointment of Hitler's and a Reich German, he was able to bring unity to the Austrian party and suppress regional feuding.

The party was, however, adversely affected by the worsening Austro-German relations. In May 1933, when Hans Frank, the German minister of justice, made an open propaganda visit to Austria, he was immediately expelled by the Austrian government. In retaliation Germany put a one-thousand-mark tax on German visitors to Austria, a move that just about ruined the tourist industry. With the continuation of the terror acts, the Austrian government finally in

197

June outlawed the party, and severe measures were taken against its members. Detention camps were set up, particularly at Wöllersdorf near Wiener Neustadt, which held at first Nazis and then all opponents of the Dollfuss regime. Many escaped over the borders into Germany, where some joined the Austrian Legion, an armed body whose numbers by 1934 came to reach around ten thousand. Habicht and other leaders moved to Germany and subsequently directed party activities from Munich.

The Dollfuss government simultaneously moved against the Social Democrats. The ability of the regime to control the relatively weak Nazi Party can be easily understood. What cannot so readily be explained is the political collapse of the Socialists, the strongest single Austrian party, which in 1930 commanded over 41 percent of the vote and had an armed force at its disposal. During the destruction of the republic the Socialist leaders had followed a very cautious policy. Not only had they allowed the elimination of parliament, but they had accepted repeated limitations on their activities. At this time they saw projected meetings and parades forbidden; their main newspaper, the *Arbeiter-Zeitung*, repeatedly censored; strikes interfered with; and finally, in March 1933 their armed force, the Schutzbund, outlawed. Against these moves they used neither their weapon of the general strike nor their armed power. This paralysis can best be explained by the general world situation and the internal balance of forces. With Fascist and authoritarian governments in office in Germany, Italy, and Hungary, and with Nazi power rising within Austria, most Socialist leaders apparently felt that resistance would be suicide. The government had behind it the police, the army, the Heimwehr, and as a last resort, Mussolini; the National Socialists had potential German support. The Social Democrats had only their own forces. Although the Schutzbund was illegal, its organization and membership remained basically intact; it simply went underground. When in May the Communist Party was similarly outlawed, it followed the same course. The Nazi Party was, as we have seen, made illegal in June. Thereafter, these parties, representing the majority of the Austrian electorate, were to continue most of their activities outside the legal structure of the authoritarian state.

In October 1933 Social Democratic and trade union leaders held a meeting to discuss the situation. Here they decided upon the four conditions that they would not tolerate: first, the dissolution of the party; second, the closing of the Socialist trade unions; third, the occupation of the Vienna City Hall; and fourth, the imposition of a Fascist constitution. During this period members of the party remained in constant touch with government representatives. The Social Democratic Party was certainly, in the majority, anything but a revolutionary party. Owning huge properties in Vienna, it had a large economic stake in the existing society. Its ability to deal with the situation was also severely hampered by the deep divisions in the party over both theory and practice. Its weakening appeal to the electorate was shown in the decline in its membership from 773,000 in 1927 to 480,000 in September 1933.

The Dollfuss policy of resistance to Nazi pressure, on the one hand, and the failure to come to any understanding with the left, on the other, left the chancellor increasingly dependent upon Italy. This situation in turn meant that he had to accept a great deal of interference in Austrian affairs from Rome. By this time the Italian government had established a close relationship with Austria. After the advent to power of Benito Mussolini in October 1922, Italy had embarked upon an ambitious foreign policy designed to establish its preeminent position in the Mediterranean, the Danubian region, and the Balkans. Identifying France as the chief opponent, Mussolini wished to organize Austria, Hungary, and Bulgaria, all of which were dissatisfied with the peace settlement, into a front against the French-dominated Little Entente. He, of course, encouraged these states to emulate the Italian Fascist system. Although Dollfuss had done away with the parliament, Mussolini was not satisfied. In meetings with Dollfuss in Rome in April 1933 and in Riccione in August, the Italian dictator pressed for further political changes. In the second meeting he did indeed promise support against Germany, but the price was high. He demanded that radical reforms be made in the Austrian political structure along Fascist lines, that decisive actions be taken against the Socialists, and that the Heimwehr be given a stronger position in the government. After his return from this visit Dollfuss showed his willingness to cooperate. In a speech in September in the Trabrennplatz he called for a "social, Christian, German Austria, on a corporative basis and under strong authoritarian leadership."[12]

A move had already been made in this direction. In May 1933 Dollfuss announced the formation of the Fatherland Front. Its purpose was to join together those who supported his program, including that of an independent Austria, and to make political parties unnecessary. Like the Christian Social Party, it had strong ties with the Catholic church. The organization had, like other Fascist groups, a symbol, the *Kruckenkreuz* (crutched cross), and a slogan, "Osterreich erwache!" (Austria awake!). The Fatherland Front did not prove to be a political success. Those parties or factions which did join, including the Christian Socials and the Heimwehr, fought each other for the control of the organization. It certainly did

[12] Diamant, *Austrian Catholics,* p. 194.

not become a strong front of patriotic citizens determined to resist foreign intervention.

Cooperation with Mussolini involved not just changes in the Austrian political structure, but the destruction of the left. In January 1934 Fulvio Suvich, the Italian under secretary of state for foreign affairs, came to Vienna with a direct demand for the elimination of the Social Democrats. Pressure in this direction was also coming from the Heimwehr, whose political activities were intensifying. Constant provocative actions against the Socialists were undertaken; searches for Schutzbund arms depots were carried on throughout the country. In addition, the police began arresting provincial Schutzbund leaders; Fey and Starhemberg delivered aggressive, inflammatory speeches. It was clear that both the Heimwehr and the government were preparing to act. The incident that led to the final clash came, however, on a Socialist initiative, but one that did not have official party backing.

On February 12, 1934, the Linz Schutzbund leader Richard Bernaschek decided to resist a police search for weapons, an action that was taken against the advice of the Socialist leadership in Vienna. When the police came, they were met with machine-gun fire. At the same time the Schutzbund mobilized and a general strike was announced. The entire action proved to be a miserable failure. The Socialist forces were severely hampered by the fact that many of their leaders had been previously imprisoned; they thus lacked a strong effective central leadership. Electricity was cut off, the streetcars were stopped for a short time, but almost everything else functioned normally. The post, telegraph, phones, and railroads, the major communication links, continued in operation. The great majority of the workers went to their jobs. Schutzbund forces did fight in Vienna, Graz, Linz, Steyr, and certain other centers, but they were easily subdued by the police and army. The Social Democratic membership in general let its armed force fight, but it did not join in the struggle as a group. Dollfuss at this time also adopted the very dubious plan of allowing the army to use artillery against a housing project, the Karl Marx Hof, which was a Socialist center of resistance. After four days the fighting ended throughout the country. The casualties were low when consideration is taken of the significance of the act: 196 were killed from the Socialist and 118 from the government forces; 10 of the leaders of the revolt were later executed.

The Social Democrats had not really been prepared for resistance. They did not have support in the army or the police, and their own forces were too weak. Moreover, even if they had won, they could not have maintained themselves in power with Hitler and Mussolini in control in neighboring states. The situation foreseen in the Linz declaration in 1926 had indeed come to pass; the opposition had left the democratic basis of the state, but the Socialists could do nothing. The party was outlawed; the Vienna municipal and provincial councils, which were dominated by Socialists, were reorganized; Socialist property was confiscated. Mass arrests followed, but some leaders, including Bauer and Julius Deutsch, who left on February 13, were able to flee to Czechoslovakia. Although most of the Socialist organizations were dissolved, the Free Trade Unions, which included most Austrian workers, were not. In the next years the Christian Social and Heimwehr unions competed, largely unsuccessfully, for their members. The government also tried to set up a nonparty Trades Union Federation.

Meanwhile, under the direction of Otto Ender, a new constitution was drafted, which was issued in May 1934. The preamble stated: "In the name of God the Almighty, who is the source of justice and law, the Austrian people receive this constitution for a Christian, German, federal state on a corporative basis."[13] Although the document clearly reflected Italian Fascist influence, its main tone was in line with conservative Catholic Austrian traditions. Particularly important in its formulation had been the papal encyclical *Quadragesimo Anno,* issued by Pius IX in May 1931, on the fortieth anniversary of *Rerum Novarum,* which had concerned labor conditions. This declaration attacked both liberal and socialist ideas and gave support to corporative principles. Its main thrust was against Marxist doctrines: "It is impossible to be at the same time a good Catholic and a real Socialist."[14]

On the basis of these principles the political organization introduced at this time was designed to replace the political parties with professional organizations, the corporations, which were to have an advisory role in the preparation of legislation. The seven groups of corporations were agriculture and forestry, public service, industry, manufacturing, commerce and transport, banking and insurance, and the free professions. Both employers and employees were members of the same corporation, and they were supposed to settle their disagreements within its structure. Individual Austrian citizens were thus to be represented according to their economic and social functions rather than their political convictions or geographic distribution.

The May Constitution introduced an exceedingly complex form of government and one that was never in fact put into full operation. A legislature of five chambers was created, including the Council of State of forty to fifty members, appointed by the president from among outstanding citizens; the Federal Cultural Council of thirty to forty persons representing culture, science, education, and religious institu-

[13] Ibid., p. 264.
[14] Brook-Shepherd, *Dollfuss,* p. 172.

tions; the Federal Economic Council, based on the corporative idea, of seventy to eighty members drawn from professional and occupational groupings; and the Provincial Council of the eight governors and the mayor of Vienna. All of these were merely consultative bodies, which could only consider laws submitted to them by the government. These groups also elected the Federal Diet of fifty-nine of their members, which had the power to accept or reject laws, but only those put before them. The president was to be chosen by the mayors of all of the Austrian municipalities. The constitution was submitted for ratification to a rump parliament consisting of 76 of the former 165 members. Of these, 74 accepted it. At the same time a new temporary constitutional law replaced the Economic Empowering Act as the basis on which Dollfuss continued to govern. In May also a concordat was signed with the Vatican; the Austrian church was now fully behind the new order.

The basic pattern for a totalitarian regime had thus been set; Austrofascism was established. The system had the support of the Christian Socials, the Catholic church, and the army, police, and bureaucracy. The backing of Fascist Italy was also crucial to its maintenance. The constitution gave Dollfuss the position of a dictator. The parties were replaced by the Fatherland Front. The Social Democratic, Communist, and Nazi organizations were illegal; even the Christian Socials could not function as a party. Basic civil rights were ignored, and leading opposition politicians were in jail or in exile. However, despite an appearance of calm, the situation was not stable. To a large extent the old political groupings continued to function, and the former controversies were not stilled. Right up to the entrance of the German army in 1938, conversations were held among representatives of all the political viewpoints. Intrigues and conspiracies also abounded. Even within the groups that supported the gov-

ernment, there was little harmony. The Christian Socials and
the Heimwehr differed constantly; the Heimwehr was split
by the Fey–Starhemberg feud. Most dangerous was the
increasing strength of Germany in Europe and the attraction
of its rise in power for the nationally minded in Austria. In
Austrian politics, it must be remembered, the term *national*
denoted German, not Austrian, sympathies.

Throughout this period Dollfuss's ability to resist Nazi
pressure continued to lie in the willingness of Mussolini to
back this stand. After the suppression of the Social Democrats these assurances were again forthcoming. In March 1934
Austria signed the Rome Protocols with Italy and Hungary.
These were economic agreements and a mutual consultation
pact. Mussolini thus again showed his desire to pursue a
Danubian policy aimed at making Italy the predominant great
power in the area. In June Hitler and Mussolini met for the
first time at Spa. Here Hitler declared that he did not want
to annex Austria, but did wish Dollfuss replaced by a non-
party man and Nazis taken into the government. This statement reflected his belief that Nazi control could be established from within and that the immediate aim should be
Gleichschaltung and not Anschluss. At this meeting Mussolini defended the Dollfuss policies.

Although Hitler realized that the moment had not come
for an annexation, and, in fact, in March 1934 ordered an
end to direct attacks on the Austrian government, he could
not always control the activities of the Austrian Nazis, who
proceeded nevertheless to organize an attempt to seize control of the government. The endeavor was an Austrian party
affair under the leadership of Theo Habicht, apparently
planned and executed without Hitler's knowledge. The aim
of the conspiracy was to seize the president of the republic
and the entire government and to force the formation of a
Nazi-controlled regime under the chancellorship of Anton

von Rintelen, a former Christian Social who had played an active, if not always reputable, role in the political life of the republic. The putsch was to be carried out by the organization of the SS *Standarte* 89, a group composed principally of Nazis who had been discharged from the Austrian Army for their political convictions. It was planned that 154 men dressed in Austrian army and police uniforms would seize the government officials.

The revolt, put into effect on July 25, 1934, was marked by confusion and mismanagement on all sides. The government authorities were informed beforehand; some of the men involved in the conspiracy had talked openly. Little was done, nevertheless, to protect the members of the government, and in fact the first stages of the conspiracy were accomplished with success. The Vienna radio station was occupied and also the building where it was believed the government was meeting. The plan failed because the conspirators had acted on false assumptions. They had chosen a time when they thought the members of the government would be together. The ministers did meet, but Fey, who had heard of the plot some two and a half hours earlier, had informed Dollfuss of the impending danger. The chancellor had then dismissed all of the ministers except for Fey; the state secretary for security, Karl Karwinsky; and Gen. Wilhelm Zehner, the defense minister. Fey's motives at this time are not clear. He evidently acted in the hope that the police and Heimwehr forces under his control could handle the revolt and that he would gain political advantage from this success. When the conspirators seized the building, they did not achieve their objective of taking the government intact. During the action, however, Dollfuss was shot; over two and a half hours later he died without the presence of a priest or a doctor, whom the conspirators refused to summon.

The ministers meanwhile had assembled at the Austrian Defense Ministry. They were able to get in touch at Velden with President Miklas, who had escaped capture. Schuschnigg, at this time minister of education, took charge of the government, and Rintelen was jailed. Negotiations were then commenced with the conspirators, who agreed to leave the occupied building in return for an assurance of safe passage to the German border. This condition was subsequently broken when the government learned of Dollfuss's death; instead the men were jailed. The revolt was similarly crushed in the rest of the country. After the radio station was seized, the conspirators had announced that a new government under Rintelen was being formed. Upon hearing this news Nazi bands in Carinthia, Salzburg, Tirol, Styria, and Upper Austria had acted. The Austrian Legion crossed the border, only to return quickly to Germany. These local revolts were easily handled by the authorities. Over a thousand Nazis fled over the border to Yugoslavia, where they were interned and later allowed to leave for Germany.

The attempted putsch brought a strong international reaction. Mussolini concentrated his troops at the Brenner frontier and thus made his opposition to German intervention clear. The dangers in the situation were obvious to Hitler, who reacted with anger. The Austrian people had responded just as negatively to a move from the right as they had in the previous February to the Socialist revolt. The army and the Heimwehr had remained loyal to the government. The Italian position had also been strong. In face of this reaction Hitler was forced to act to control the Austrian Nazis: Habicht was dismissed, the Munich Austrian center was disbanded, the activities of the Austrian Legion were limited, and the Nazi Party in Austria was instructed to restrict its actions. Franz von Papen, a conservative, Catholic, highly experienced diplomat, was sent to Vienna to calm the situation down. The attempt to gain power by revolution from within was abandoned.

THE SCHUSCHNIGG GOVERNMENT: THE ANSCHLUSS

The government that was appointed after the death of Dollfuss represented a division of power between the new chancellor and the Heimwehr, which now reached the peak of its influence. Starhemberg took the office of vice-chancellor and head of the Fatherland Front. In his foreign policy Schuschnigg continued the Dollfuss line of maintaining Austrian independence against Germany, but of leaning strongly on Italy for support. In August 1934 he met with Mussolini in Florence. There were also indications of continued European concern for Austrian survival after the failure of the putsch. In September Italy, France, and Britain repeated their assurances of support for the maintenance of Austrian independence. Similar statements were issued at the Stresa Conference of April 11–14, 1935. In a speech of May 1935 Hitler emphasized his intention not to interfere in the internal affairs of Austria or to seek an Anschluss.

In internal policy Schuschnigg did introduce a new element. With the death of Charles in Madeira in 1922, the question of a Habsburg restoration had for the moment subsided. Meanwhile, the heir, Otto, was growing up. More than any of his predecessors as chancellor Schuschnigg was sympathetic to the Habsburg cause. During his period in office he was in constant consultation with Otto, whom he kept fully informed on government business. In July 1935 the anti-Habsburg laws were repealed and much of the Habsburg property returned. Monarchist sentiment was also increasing, as is shown by the fact that more than a thousand

Austrian municipalities gave Otto, who was living in Belgium, honorary citizenship. Schuschnigg, arguing that it was an internal matter, consistently maintained the Austrian right to decide the question, but he personally recognized the practical impossibility of a restoration. Although Schuschnigg's feelings were clear, it is hard to judge how many of his compatriots shared his sentiments, apart from some former officers and officials and members of the aristocracy who looked back on the prewar days with regret. Certainly a restoration would have been almost impossible. Hitler was violently anti-Habsburg; Italy also opposed Otto's return. The strongest reaction came from the Little Entente, whose members apparently were more willing to accept an Austrian union with Germany than a Habsburg restoration. The Yugoslav government stated flatly that it would declare war to prevent such an event.

Within the country the basic problem remained that of finding a firm political alignment on which to govern. The left had been eliminated; the right was severely split. The government rested on the dual support of Schuschnigg's followers and the Heimwehr, but that organization remained divided between the opposing leaders, Fey and Starhemberg. Schuschnigg also by this time had his private armed forces, which he had personally organized. In the ranks of the right-wing organizations there were continuing bitter disagreements between Catholics and Fascists on political and, even more important, on educational questions. Schuschnigg was able to use these conflicts to eliminate his two rivals. In October 1935 he reorganized his cabinet without Fey. Starhemberg, still commander of the Heimwehr, remained in the government and pressed also for control of the army. By May 1936 Schuschnigg was strong enough to remove Starhemberg as vice-chancellor and leader of the Fatherland Front, leaving him with only minor influence in the government. The chancellor personally took the Ministries of Foreign Affairs and Defense as well as the headship of the Fatherland Front, so that he had the clearly predominant role in state affairs. In October 1936 he was able to disband the Heimwehr. This action was made easier by the fact that in April Austria had reintroduced universal military service in violation of the peace treaty. This and other actions taken to strengthen the state appeared to make the private armies unnecessary. It will be noted that this move, like the suppression of the Social Democrats and the Nazis, caused no popular reaction, despite the wide participation in Heimwehr activities in the previous years.

Although the internal political problems remained acute, Schuschnigg's main difficulties involved his relations with his two totalitarian neighbors. The Austrian ability to resist German pressure was clearly tied to Italian fortunes and to Mussolini's determination to continue a Danubian policy that included an independent Austria. The basic assumptions for an Italian course in foreign policy were brought into question when Italy in October 1935 started a war in Ethiopia. This event caused Austria great difficulties and also embittered its relations with the Western powers. When the League imposed economic sanctions on Italy, Austria could not join against its ally. Along with Hungary and Albania, Austria thus voted in opposition to fifty-two other League members. This situation naturally disturbed Austria's ability to obtain credit from the Western states. Austria, however, was compelled to remain tied to Italian policy. In March 1936 the Rome Protocols were widened, and the signatories were obligated to take no steps in foreign policy without mutual consultation.

This agreement marked the final step in the Austrian–Italian relationship. In fact, the Italian course had already altered. After 1934 German foreign policy had been increasingly active. In March 1935 the disarmament clauses of the Versailles Treaty were denounced, and a year later the Rhineland was reoccupied. This latter act severely limited the military actions that the Western powers could take in case of a crisis in Eastern Europe. In 1935 also Germany and Italy began to improve their relations; the Rome–Berlin Axis was formally established in October 1936. The shift in Italian interests was already apparent at the time of the negotiations concerning the Rome Protocols in March 1936. The Austrians were then told to come to an agreement with Berlin even at the cost of concessions. When Schuschnigg visited Mussolini at Rocca della Caminate in June 1936, he received the same advice.

Similar urgings for an understanding were also coming from the German and Austrian Nazi side. After the failure of the putsch the Austrian Nazis, as instructed, did restrict their activities. As before, the party was rent with controversy and divided between those who wished revolutionary action and their opponents, who wanted to negotiate with the aim of introducing Nazi and German-national members into the government and the Fatherland Front. This latter aim was strongly seconded by Franz von Papen after he arrived in Vienna in August 1934. He worked to reduce the differences between Austria and Germany to the level of a "family" affair and, specifically, to have members of the national opposition added to the government. Amnesty for imprisoned Nazis was also a German objective. Negotiations on these questions were carried on between Papen and Schuschnigg; Schuschnigg sought primarily a clear German recognition of Austrian independence, and he was willing to make concessions to obtain this objective. In the agreement, signed on July 11, 1936, he did gain a German recognition of Austrian sovereignty. Both countries stated that the internal politics of the other were a domestic affair. Nevertheless, Austria agreed to conduct its foreign policy in conformity with the principle that "Austria acknowledges herself to be a German State."[15] Other matters were regulated in a further document, which was not published. The most important concession here was Schuschnigg's agreement to take into his government representatives of the national opposition, a stipulation that incidentally conflicted with the "nonintervention" section of the published pact. In addition, amnesty was to be granted to Nazi prisoners, the one-thousand-mark tax was lifted, and a truce was called in the press and radio war.

With the signing of this agreement the Austrian government henceforth was pledged to a German course in foreign policy. In internal affairs Schuschnigg brought into the cabinet the Greater German moderate Edmund Glaise-Horstenau, a military historian and director of the Vienna Kriegsarchiv (Military Archive), as minister without portfolio. Schuschnigg, however, hesitated over the second appointment. His naming of Guido Schmidt as foreign minister did not mark a fulfillment of this condition; Schmidt was a friend and confidant. In the next months Schuschnigg concentrated on a policy of attempting to bring together the nationals and the moderate Nazis to divide them from the radicals. In these negotiations an important role was taken by the moderate Arthur Seyss-Inquart, a Viennese lawyer. In 1937 a special section was formed within the Fatherland Front to represent these interests.

Despite these negotiations the Austrian government continued to fear violent and illegal acts from the Austrian Nazis. The agreement had confused many of the radicals, who often acted on their own initiative. In May 1937 the police

[15] Text of German-Austrian Communiqué, July 11, 1936, *Documents on German Foreign Policy, 1918–1945* (Washington, D.C.: U.S. Government Printing Office, 1949), Series D, I, 281–282.

raided an illegal Nazi headquarters in Vienna, where they found evidence of continued conspiracy and of the receipt of German money. Again in January 1938, in a similar move against offices on Tienfaltstrasse, they discovered papers concerning preparations for another armed action, the so-called Tavs Plan. Here again the objective was to establish Nazi control of the government. Although such activities were at that time not a part of official German policy, the Austrian government could not judge this to be the case from the evidence.

Although the July agreement obligated Austria to conduct its foreign policy as the "second German power," the government made efforts to find other sources of support. Not only were they hard to find, but even Italian backing was rapidly weakening. The Rome–Berlin Axis agreement of 1936 had included an understanding on spheres of influence, which allotted Central Europe, including Austria, to Germany and the Mediterranean region to Italy. In April 1937 Hitler removed a possible source of conflict by indicating his lack of interest in Tirol. When Schuschnigg met Mussolini in Venice in April 1937, the loss of Italian support was apparent. At the meeting of the Rome Protocol powers in January 1938, Italy advised Austria to follow the Axis out of the League of Nations and to join the Anti-Comintern Pact, an agreement signed in 1937 linking Japan, Germany, and Italy. With the line to Rome apparently rendered useless, Schuschnigg tried to approach the Little Entente as well as other powers. Yugoslavia, however, after 1937 was increasingly shifting toward a German policy; the other states had their own difficult problems and could not be expected to provide assistance to maintain Austrian independence. Austria was in fact by January 1938 fully isolated diplomatically.

The general European situation was thus favorable for the

event whose achievement had been a major source of debate since the establishment of the republic, the Anschluss. Throughout this account the community of history between the Habsburg Empire and the German states has been stressed. It has been seen that in this relationship the Habsburg Monarchy had retained over the wide span of history the first position. Only in 1871 did it become clear that this leadership had been permanently lost. With the dissolution of the monarchy in 1918, most Austrians had wanted to join the German state. They felt not only that this union would be a logical expression of the principle of self-determination, but also that an Austrian state could not stand alone. In November 1918 the provisional assembly unanimously declared German-Austria a part of the German Republic; plebiscites held in Tirol and Salzburg reflected similar sympathies. The repeated actions of the Allied powers to prevent an Anschluss, of course, gave further prestige to the idea.

Throughout most of the postwar period the major political parties had stood for union, although with varying degrees of enthusiasm. The Greater German Party's attitude was clear; equally convinced were the Social Democrats. After the Social Democratic victory in Germany in 1918, this party could only see its position strengthened by union with Berlin, a conviction that was kept until Hitler came to power, when it was at least for a time shelved. The Socialists were also deeply concerned about the economic viability of their small state. Although the Christian Socials were also for union, they had some reservations. Basically Catholic conservatives, some of its members did not look with complete favor on joining a predominantly Protestant country. At this time, Catholics formed 32 percent and Protestants 64 percent of the German population. The attitude of the most prominent Austrian Catholic leader, Seipel, was perhaps typical. Although he stood by the policy of no foreign agreements without Germany, his stand was in fact complex. He talked a great deal about the question, but stood neither for nor against it.

The rise of National Socialism and the victory of Hitler in January 1933 altered the situation. Although Hitler was an Austrian by birth and, in fact, had a political program whose basis reflected ideas he had picked up as a poor student in Vienna, his party came to represent many of those qualities which the Austrians admired least in the northern Germans. For the Social Democrats, whose political brothers in Germany were in jail, the choice should have been easy; in 1933 the party program did indeed drop the former support of Anschluss. Moreover, despite the fact that Austria too became an authoritarian state, Austrofascism was not in practice the equivalent of National Socialism. Nevertheless, the basic problem remained. Although Dollfuss strongly emphasized Austrian and Catholic tradition, in his speeches he constantly recalled the German character of the Austrian state. Schuschnigg was if anything more German-oriented. He too stood for Austrian independence, but as a "second German state." Moreover, vocal and important elements in Austria always called for German union. The influence of the idea was particularly strong in exactly those circles that had contributed to the rise of national feeling among other nationalities in the Habsburg Empire – the teachers, historians, writers, and youth of the country. When it was apparent that no foreign power would fight to prevent a union, the inner tension became stronger. It should also be emphasized that most Austrians who followed this course did not favor a straight annexation of their country by Germany. What they wished was better expressed by the word *Zusammenschluss;* that is, the two countries would come together, but Austria would essentially remain an autonomous section within the framework of the larger state.

Although the annexation of Austria was one of his immediate plans, Hitler's decision to carry through this act in March 1938 came as a result of a chain of events and was in fact hastily taken. Papen, as we have seen, constantly pressed for an agreement between the Austrian government and the Nazis. Schuschnigg's policy closely paralleled this aim. He continued to wish to bring together the moderate nationalists and the Nazis and to establish Seyss-Inquart, rather than the Nazi Party leaders, as the middleman in his relations with Germany. Negotiations were carried on between Seyss-Inquart and Guido Zernatto, a close confidant of Schuschnigg's and general secretary of the Fatherland Front, for the inclusion of the Nazis in that organization.

The idea of a personal meeting between Hitler and Schuschnigg arose early in 1938 when Papen extended a preliminary invitation that was at once accepted. In January and February a series of dramatic events took place in Germany. In a confrontation with the German Army Hitler removed the top officers and made himself the supreme commander of the German armed forces. He then purged the Foreign Ministry and replaced Konstantin von Neurath with Joachim von Ribbentrop. On February 5 Papen was also summoned to Germany, where he met with Hitler. There he was able to protect his position, and he returned in two days to Vienna with an invitation to Schuschnigg to come to Berchtesgaden. Schuschnigg at first hesitated, but Papen assured him that the meeting would "in no case be to the disadvantage of the Austrian government nor will it entail any aggravation of Austro-German relations."[16]

In previous negotiations with Seyss-Inquart, Schuschnigg had already formulated the concessions that he was willing

---

[16] Kurt von Schuschnigg, *Austrian Requiem* (New York: G. P. Putnam's Sons, 1946), pp. 10–11.

to make to the Nazi and national demands. These, like all other Austrian governmental matters, had been leaked to Germany. In his visit with Hitler, Schuschnigg expected to be able to negotiate. On February 12 the chancellor, accompanied by Guido Schmidt, arrived in Berchtesgaden, where they were witnesses to a fine theatrical performance. Hitler had summoned a number of the top German generals to give the appearance that a military action might back the German demands. Hitler himself delivered a tirade on Austrian history:

> The whole history of Austria is just one uninterrupted act of high treason. That was so in the past and is no better today. This historical paradox must now reach its long overdue end. . . . Every national idea was sabotaged by Austria throughout history; and indeed, all this sabotage was the chief activity of the Habsburgs and the Catholic church.

On his own role Hitler declared:

> I have a historic mission; and this mission I will fulfill because Providence has destined me to do so. I thoroughly believe in this mission; it is my life. . . . I have chosen the most difficult road any German ever took; I have made the greatest achievement in the history of Germany, greater than any other German. . . . I have achieved everything that I set out to do and have thus become perhaps the greatest German of all history.[17]

After being subjected to this monologue, Schuschnigg was presented with the German demands, which were set out in ten points. The basic objective was to strengthen the position of the Nazis and the national opposition in the Austrian gov-

[17] Written by Schuschnigg from his memory of the meeting. Ibid., pp. 12–19. The German protocol of the conference is in *Documents on German Foreign Policy*, D, I, 513–514.

ernment. Members of the Nazi Party were to be free to support their program openly, and as individuals they were to be admitted into the Fatherland Front, but the party itself was to remain illegal. Seyss-Inquart was to be made a minister with control over the police. Full amnesty was to be granted to Nazis, including those who had participated in the assassination of Dollfuss. In conclusion, the agreement of July 1936 was reaffirmed; Germany again was to recognize Austria's sovereignty and independence and not interfere in its internal affairs, a declaration quite strange in view of the other demands presented. Schuschnigg was able to change a few small details of the German terms, but none of their essential implications. Under extreme pressure he and Schmidt signed the agreement.

When Schuschnigg returned to Vienna, he presented the document to Miklas, whose signature was also necessary. The Austrian president did not like the terms, but he accepted them. The relations between the two top officials in the Austrian government had long been strained. In the subsequent rebuilding of the cabinet Seyss-Inquart became minister of interior, but he had associated with him Michael Skubl, the head of the Vienna police, who was regarded as loyal to Schuschnigg and his government. Schuschnigg's policy at this time was the full implementation of the agreement. The Austrian representatives in other countries were not informed of the tone of the Berchtesgaden meeting; no attempt was made to obtain outside aid. Schuschnigg had returned from Berchtesgaden convinced that the German army would march if needed. His basic policy was to remain, "Never again a war against Germany as in 1866, and never a civil war."[18]

In Germany Hitler took measures to maintain the Aus-

[18] Schuschnigg, *Austrian Requiem*, p. 44.

trian fears. He discussed with his generals actions that might be taken to give the appearance that Germany was poised to march, although no such plans existed. At the same time some efforts were made to put the Berchtesgaden agreement into effect. On February 16 instructions were issued that German Nazis should not meddle in Austrian affairs. However, at the same time Hitler took some other actions that were very disturbing to the Austrian government. In a speech on February 20 he referred to ten million Germans "subjected to continuous suffering" because of their sympathy with the Nazi cause. Austrians were obviously included in this number. He also appointed the Carinthian Maj. Franz Klausner as the head of the illegal Austrian Nazi Party. Although this action seemed like interference in internal affairs to the Austrians, it was taken within the framework of the Berchtesgaden policy. Klausner was instructed to act legally, and his predecessor, the radical Josef Leopold, was scolded for his actions. However, no matter what the German intentions were, the situation in Austria could not be controlled completely from Berlin. With the publication of the news of the agreement, Nazi sympathizers throughout the country came more and more into the open. Nazi salutes and symbols appeared everywhere. The danger existed that Schuschnigg might lose control of the situation.

Although, as we have seen, Schuschnigg at first adopted a passive and compliant attitude toward the German demands, these new events forced him to take decisive action. His defiance was publicly proclaimed in a speech to the parliament on February 24. Here he emphasized Austrian patriotism and ended with the declaration, "Until death red-white-red! Austria!"[19] On March 6 preparations for a plebiscite on

---

[19] Norbert Schausberger, "Der Anschluss," in Erika Weinzierl and Kurt Skalnik, *Österreich 1918–1938* (Graz: Verlag Styria, 1983), I. 530.

the question of continued Austrian independence commenced; the public announcement of the event, which was to be held on March 13, was made on March 9.

At the same time negotiations continued with the Socialists. Their support was necessary should a policy of resistance be adopted, but the terms for cooperation remained the same. The Social Democrats wished to be able to resume their activities freely and openly, although not necessarily as a political party. They were willing to enter into the government trade union organization, but only if they could elect their own representatives. They also wished an assurance of a government program of social legislation. Schuschnigg was, however, faced with the dilemma that he would have to allow the Nazis anything that he gave another group. At the last minute an understanding was reached in which the government agreed that workers' organizations with elected officials could function within the Fatherland Front. Schuschnigg could thus apparently count on Socialist support in a crisis. In this critical time he also, on February 17, received a message from Otto. The pretender suggested that Schuschnigg should resign and that he should become chancellor. Schuschnigg recognized the total impossibility of such an act, which would have brought about an immediate German, Italian, and Little Entente reaction and possibly an intervention.

Meanwhile, preparations for a plebiscite continued despite the advice that came from all sides against it, including from Mussolini, who expressed his strong opposition. The entire action rested on very dubious grounds. Once the conditions for voting were announced, it was apparent that there were no assurances that it would indeed be free or secret or that it would accurately reflect majority Austrian opinion. No list of voters was prepared; no one under twenty-four, the legal age, was to participate, an act that excluded a large number of Nazi sympathizers. The wording of the proposition was also questionable. The Austrians were to be asked to vote on a statement that was designed to win the approval of as many as possible: "For a free and German, independent and social, for a Christian and united Austria, for peace and work and the equality of all who declare themselves for Nation and Fatherland."[20] Only yes ballots were to be provided; voters who were against the proposition had to supply their own.

The news of the plebiscite, which Hitler heard on March 9 a few hours before its public announcement, determined his final decision. Until this time he had formally adopted a moderate position aiming at the fulfillment of the Berchtesgaden agreement. Under the strong influence of Hermann Göring he now began to swing to a different policy. Efforts were to be made to gain a postponement of the plebiscite, but more important, the question of a military occupation of Austria was seriously considered. Until this time no plans for such an action had been made. Relations with Austria had been primarily a Nazi Party, not a military, concern. The army did, however, have a contingency plan, Operation Otto, which had been prepared in case a restoration of the Habsburgs was attempted. This was not a detailed plan, but rather a study paper. On March 10, however, it was taken out; on March 11 Instruction No. 1 was issued for its implementation. The German Army was given about a day to prepare for action. At the same time Hitler wrote a letter to Mussolini, requesting his approval. Until the last minute he was not certain how his Axis partner would react.

With the closing of the German border and the reports of troop movements, the seriousness of the situation became

---

[20] Walter Goldinger, *Geschichte der Republik Österreich* (Vienna: Verlag für Geschichte und Politik, 1962), p. 244.

clear to Vienna. The German demand for the postponement of the voting for two weeks to allow it to be organized on the lines of the previous Saar plebiscite was presented to Schuschnigg by Glaise-Horstenau and Seyss-Inquart. The chancellor rejected this idea, but agreed to call the plebiscite off. He was then met by a further demand: Göring telephoned Seyss-Inquart and instructed him to ask for the resignation of Schuschnigg and the formation of a cabinet under Seyss's direction. Although Schuschnigg agreed to resign, Miklas refused to appoint Seyss-Inquart. Attempts were made unsuccessfully to find another man who would form a government. Göring by telephone instructed Seyss to threaten Miklas with a German invasion should he not comply, but the president remained firm.

On the evening of March 11 the Austrian radio announced the cancellation of the plebiscite and the resignation of the Schuschnigg government, with the exception of Seyss-Inquart. Throughout the country Nazis began to take over the provincial administrations. Schuschnigg also spoke on the radio and concluded with "God protect Austria!" Until this time Hitler had not yet finally decided on a military occupation. After the broadcast and under strong pressure from Göring, Hitler came to a decision. Very important to his plans also was his receipt of Mussolini's approval, which drew from the German dictator a very emotional response: "I shall never forget him for this . . . never, never, never, whatever happens."[21] Meanwhile the decision had been taken in Austria that no resistance would be made and that the army would be instructed not to oppose the entrance of German troops. It had been estimated that the Austrian Army could fight for only two days. Seyss-Inquart then proceeded to try

---

[21] Joachim C. Fest, *Hitler,* trans. Richard and Clara Winston (New York: Harcourt Brace Jovanovich, 1974), pp. 547–548.

Hitler in Vienna in 1938

to form a ministry of moderate Nazis and nationals. At the same time, he attempted to stop the German invasion from taking place. Hitler had, however, made up his mind.

On March 12 the German Army crossed the border. No resistance, political or military, was apparent. Hitler at first, and in contrast to Göring, had favored not an immediate Anschluss, but something like a personal union on the Zusammenschluss lines, with Austria retaining a measure of autonomy. His wildly enthusiastic reception in his birthplace of Braunau, in Linz, and all along the route to Vienna appears to have changed his mind. Everywhere the German entrance and Hitler's appearance were greeted by huge hysterical crowds. President Miklas, refusing to accept the union, resigned, and Seyss-Inquart as head of state signed the law joining Austria to Germany. Article 1 declared that Austria

223

was a province of the German Reich, a stipulation reminiscent of Article 2 of the November 1918 declaration. A plebiscite was announced for April 10.

Once in occupation of Austria, the German leaders made preparations to win the plebiscite. The secret police moved at once; about seventy thousand men who had shown themselves opposed to a Nazi, German-national course were arrested. At the same time efforts were made to win the Catholics and the moderate Socialists. The Catholic church had already made conciliatory moves; church bells rang as Hitler entered Vienna. In a meeting arranged by Papen with Cardinal Innitzer, Hitler gave the assurances on questions of education and other matters that the church wished. Karl Renner also agreed to give his support. In a press interview on April 3 he declared that he would vote yes. With wide approval thus assured, the plebiscite took place as planned; 99.73 percent voted for the Anschluss. Almost all observers agreed that the verdict reflected Austrian opinion, but that if the vote had been held in freer circumstances, the percentage would not have been so high.

AFTER THE ANSCHLUSS: THE WAR

After the formal incorporation of Austria into Germany a little more than a year was to pass before Europe entered the second great conflict of the century. By that time the moves to amalgamate the Austrian political and economic life into that of the larger framework had almost been completed. The basic pattern was largely determined by the ideas of Adolf Hitler, although, as we have seen, soon after his entrance into Austria, he had altered his original conception of establishing some sort of dual administration under his personal leadership. With the Anschluss the Austrian state thus fell under the control of one of its own former citizens; a native son came home in triumph. Hitler himself repeatedly spoke of Austria as "his own country" and his "homeland." His early years as an Austrian resident had determined his future political convictions. It was perhaps only in the prewar Habsburg capital that such a combination of irrational and nationalistic concepts could have been acquired.

The first task of internal administration was that of coordinating the political systems of Germany and Austria. The question of exploiting the Austrian economic assets and bringing them into the German war planning was also important. To administer the new arrangements three separate and usually competing groups vied for control of the state offices. Quite naturally both party and government officials from Germany proper sought high positions in Vienna. Within the country local nationalists like Seyss-Inquart competed for appointments with the members of the formerly illegal Nazi organization, who in turn fought with each other. At first, to prepare for the plebiscite, Hitler brought from the Rhineland Josef Bürckel, who had organized the highly successful Saar plebiscite of 1936 in which 90 percent of the population had voted to join Germany. On April 23 he became Reichskommissar for the Reunification of Austria with the Reich. At the same time Seyss headed a separate Austrian provincial government. A year later, in April 1939, the administrative reorganization was complete. Austria was now organized into seven regions (Gaue), and the diets were abolished. Some boundary changes were introduced: Burgenland was divided between Lower Austria and Styria; East Tirol became part of Carinthia; the area of Ausseer Land was joined to Upper Austria. After the conquest of Yugoslavia and Czechoslovakia some territory from these states was added to the adjoining regions.

As can be seen, even with these changes the basic structure of the historic provinces remained intact. Hitler's intention was not to diminish provincial loyalty, but instead to strengthen it at the expense of Viennese centralism. Along with his extremely hostile attitude toward the Habsburg dynasty, Hitler had acquired in his youth a dislike of Vienna and a conviction that the city differed in attitude sharply from the provinces. During the war he commented: "As regards Austria, it was the proper solution to destroy the centralized State, to the detriment of Vienna, and re-establish the provinces. In this way innumerable points of friction were removed. Each of the *Gaue* is happy to be its own master." Vienna was, in his opinion, the focal point of ideas of Austrian separate patriotism: "That's why . . . I divided my Austrian homeland into several *Gaue,* in order to remove it from separatist tendencies and incorporate it more easily in the Germanic Reich."[22]

Not only was Burgenland abolished, but the interests of one of the most significant areas historically, Tirol, were sacrificed. The Italian friendship was vital to Nazi interests at the time. To avoid a possible source of friction over South Tirol, Hitler simply accepted the Italian view and a population transfer. In June 1939 an agreement was signed which provided that by the end of the year the German inhabitants had to decide whether to stay in the province and accept full Italian citizenship or to migrate into German territory. At this time, under official pressure, 81 percent decided to leave. Those who preferred to stay were principally peasants who were closely attached to their land. In fact, because of the wartime disruptions, comparatively few transfers were actually completed.

With the administrative restructuring the attempt was then made to eliminate the name Austria from the official desig-

---

[22] Adolf Hitler, *Hitler's Table Talk, 1941–1944,* trans. Norman Cameron and R. H. Stevens (London: Weidenfeld and Nicolson, 1953), pp. 27, 402.

nations. In 1939 Land Osterreich became Ostmark, a name that in the nineteenth century had been associated with the Carolingian administration of the region, and in 1940 it was changed to the Reichsgaue of Ostmark. In 1942 Hitler substituted the even more neutral Alpen und Donau Reichsgaue (Alpine and Danubian Gaue).

In the distribution of central administrative posts, both Reich Germans and Austrians received positions. The influx of men from the north and their acquisition of central appointments naturally caused friction with native applicants for similar positions and with those over whom they held control. In the provinces the reorganization meant an amalgamation of party and political posts; the tasks of the *Landeshauptmann* (provincial governor) were assumed by the Gauleiter. Although some Germans held these posts, the majority were Austrians. Both Bürckel and Seyss soon were transferred from their central positions in Vienna to more important duties elsewhere. In August 1940 the highly influential position of Gauleiter and head of government in Vienna was given to the Reich German Baldur von Schirach, the former Hitler Youth leader. Seyss-Inquart first received positions in Poland, and then, after the conquest of the Netherlands, he became the *Reichskommissar* there. The highest position achieved by an Austrian, however, was that held by Ernst Kaltenbrunner of the former illegal party. After the assassination of Reinhard Heydrich, he became in 1942 the chief of the German security services. Other members of the Austrian Nazi Party were not so successful. Of the original party, Josef Leopold joined Hitler's staff after the Anschluss; Leopold Tavs remained in the relatively modest position of a party *Kreisleiter* (district leader).

In addition to the administrative *Gleichschaltung* (coordination), the amalgamation of the economic systems, including the railroads and the postal and banking systems, was carried through. Since Austria joined an economy becoming increasingly geared for war, the initial effects were favorable. The war industries absorbed all the labor available, so the great nightmare of the First Republic, massive unemployment, was not a problem. Some changes, however, caused difficulties. The conversion of the Austrian currency at a ratio of three schillings to two marks was not favorable to the schilling. The introduction of German taxation in January 1940 also brought increased payments. In the same manner the disappearance of consumer goods caused discontent. When the first German soldiers, and then other Reich Germans, came to Austria, they immediately bought up not only luxury goods but also clothes, textiles, and leather products, which were not available in Germany itself. Although the small merchants made quick profits, their stocks could not easily be replaced.

Of great importance for the future was the development of Austrian industry and natural resources in the interest of the general war preparations. German investment was already high. In March 1938 it has been estimated at 10 percent of Austrian large industry, that is, 160 million marks of a total of 1.6 billion. German involvement was greatest in the mining and metallurgy enterprises, where it was 25 percent, including 57 percent of Alpine Montan. After the Anschluss the Berlin direction was primarily interested in developing those Austrian assets which were needed for the military and which were also in short supply in the rest of Germany. Oil, nitrogen, and aluminum production was emphasized. Attempts were also made to develop the Austrian hydroelectric potential. The industrialization of new Austrian regions, which was to have such important postwar effects, was also accelerated.

The reaction of the Austrian population to the Anschluss, the Nazi regime, and the subsequent alterations in the government and daily life is difficult to assess. The literature on the subject is often not balanced and is certainly colored by the fact that Germany lost the war. Quite possibly many of those who subsequently proclaimed that they had never supported the Anschluss and the war effort would have been equally vehement on the opposite side had German arms been victorious. It is certainly true that in 1938 there was much enthusiasm for the Anschluss. The initial fervor was undoubtedly dampened to some extent by the obvious fact that the German state was playing a very dangerous diplomatic game. The threat of war was constant from the spring of 1938 onward. The population of Austria, like that of Germany, Britain, France, and every other state, did not want war in 1939. However, once the conflict began, no significant opposition group arose until the war was clearly lost. Before 1945 the only effective partisan activity on Austrian soil was the Communist-led movement in Carinthia, which had a strong Slovenian imprint.

The question of attitude is, of course, made more difficult to answer by the fact that the Nazi authorities had full control of the outlets for the expression of opinion – that is, the press and the radio – and also of the security forces. The Schuschnigg government, an authoritarian regime, had already compiled police records on possible enemies. The Austrian Nazi Party also well knew who had been its previous opponents. The officials thus had complete information on who should be arrested and who should be watched. Moreover, much of the potential opposition to their rule had been previously dealt with. Former Socialist leaders were in exile, in jail, or intimidated. Among the loyal members of the Fatherland Front, many, including Schuschnigg, were arrested and spent the war in internment. The Austrian Army was thoroughly purged, as the Germany Army had been previously. Of the officers, 17 percent, 2,555 men, were retired;

another 18 percent were transferred to administrative positions. Those who remained, like the soldiers themselves, were never a part of strictly Austrian units, but were dispersed throughout the German Army. The police were likewise dominated by Nazis and Nazi sympathizers. With this formidable backing, ably aided by what appears to have been a multitude of Austrian informers, organized opposition movements had little chance.

Despite the Nazi domination of the security forces, the apparent lack of a serious opposition appears more interesting if we consider that the Nazi theories struck directly at the ideological basis of the two forces that had been previously the strongest in Austrian political life – the Socialist party and the Catholic church. Quite apart from the national question, a real Gleichschaltung between basic Nazi doctrine and either Socialism or Catholicism was not within the range of the possible. The strength of these two forces had certainly not been underestimated by the German authorities at the time of the Anschluss. We have already seen how both Karl Renner and Cardinal Innitzer were induced to support the Anschluss openly before the plebiscite. Thereafter the activities of these two divergent political strands were carefully watched.

Much of the task of repressing the Social Democratic Party and the Socialist-led labor movement had, as we have seen, already been accomplished by Dollfuss and Schuschnigg under conservative and Catholic influences. The top leadership had gone either underground or into exile. Soon after the Anschluss the police continued the work of the previous regime and picked up what was left, especially of the leadership of the Revolutionary Socialists, an underground organization of militants formed in 1934, some of whom subsequently joined the Communist Party. Thereafter political activity by the Socialists remained strictly limited to underground actions, such as the formation of circles of friends who met together, but who were not in touch with other groups. Efforts were made to avoid the establishment of anything resembling a network of organizations that could be broken by the police. The Socialists were also hampered by their basic attitude toward the Anschluss. With their vision of an eventual great German revolution, the leadership had consistently stood for a Greater Germany, but, of course, not under Nazi leadership. The general attitude did not change until 1943, when a German victory appeared less probable.

In contrast, Communist opposition was more active at least until August 1939, when the Nazi–Soviet pact was signed, and after June 1941, when Germany attacked the Soviet Union. Limited by the smallness of their numbers, the Communists' efforts were also hindered by the fact that they had a tight organization. The defection of one member could thus lead to the apprehension of many others.

One of the main weaknesses of the leftist political movements remained what we have seen before – the lack of militancy or a revolutionary attitude among Austrian workers. Despite the immense advantages that had come their way with the Socialist administration of Vienna, most workers had stayed home in 1934. Moreover, from a Socialist ideological point of view the shift in 1938 was from one authoritarian regime to another, albeit to a far more fanatical one, and certainly the Anschluss did bring some apparent immediate advantages to the workers, whose services were now in demand. The official organs of control were also stronger: all workers were brought into the German Labor Front, an organization that embraced both employers and employees. The swift onset of war, preceded by months of crisis, worked against the translation of individual grievances into a political opposition.

Like the left, the conservative Catholics had difficulties in accepting important aspects of the new authority. Although at first the Nazi regime tried to appease the church, the incompatibility between the two was soon apparent. October 1938 saw a violent incident take place: members of the Hitler Youth organization and the SA stormed the residence of the archbishop in Vienna. Despite its original assurances, the Nazi movement challenged the church on exactly those issues which had previously been the most sensitive in the Austrian republic – the questions of education and the family. As a result of the effort made to induce people to leave the church, it has been estimated that about three hundred thousand did follow this path and that 50 percent of the Catholic students did not attend religious instruction. Nevertheless, despite the formidable attacks launched against it, the Catholic church, like the other religious organizations, did not become a center of opposition to the regime. As in every country, the German religious institutions enforced the conception of loyalty to the flag and the citizen's duty of obedience to the government in power.

Although both Socialists and Catholics, as well as many other Austrian citizens, suffered hardships under Nazi rule, the worst fate was reserved for the Jews, whose major role, particularly in Viennese cultural and economic life, has been discussed previously. The Nazi Party's strongly anti-Semitic program and its extreme racial doctrines were introduced into Austria soon after the Anschluss. Jews not only had their property confiscated and their jobs taken away, but they also suffered great personal privation and public humiliation. Pressure was put on those who could to emigrate. In 1938 there were approximately 220,000 Jews in Austria; by May 1939 the number had dropped to 121,000, largely because of emigration. Of those who remained after the war started, the great majority were deported to Poland, where they died in concentration camps, although some were able to escape to Allied or other safe lands. Many Austrians shared in the plundering of Jewish property, and there was no apparent open outburst of popular indignation at these measures.

By late 1938 there was, however, little that any individual in Greater Germany could do to fetter the actions of the regime. With firm domination of all sources of information and the armed forces, the Nazi leadership proceeded with the implementation of a national program that was bound to secure the enthusiastic support of any German nationalist, particularly if it could be carried through by diplomatic means. Until the outbreak of the war, it must be remembered, in his public declarations Hitler appeared as the fervent supporter of the principle of self-determination. Whether the regime in Berlin intended only to follow in the footsteps of Bismarck and complete the unification of all Germans or whether the goal was the acquisition of the wider empire of *Mein Kampf* and other Nazi declarations was not all that clear. Statesmen in Paris and London were certainly also divided in their opinions.

After the Anschluss the German attention was turned to a problem that was bound to awaken Austrian sympathies – the fate of the Sudeten Germans, that is, of the German inhabitants of the defunct Habsburg Empire who had been incorporated into Czechoslovakia. These areas were ceded to Germany at the Munich Conference of September 1938 after an intense international crisis. In March 1939 Hitler stepped over the bounds of German national unification and dismembered the rest of Czechoslovakia. An independent Slovak state was established; the Czech lands were organized as the Protectorate of Bohemia and Moravia and placed under direct German control. At the same time Poland and Hungary joined in the partition and took the lands that they claimed. The next state up for partition was Poland. In the early spring of 1939 the German government, again using the national issue, centered its attention on the German population in Poland. In March the British government, fearful of a repetition of the events that led to the destruction of Czechoslovakia, issued a guarantee to Poland. In May Germany and Italy concluded a firm military alliance, the Pact of Steel.

Throughout the summer of 1939 the Polish crisis mounted in intensity. For both sides the crucial question was the stand that the Soviet Union would take should war break out. The answer was given on August 23, when Viacheslav M. Molotov, the Soviet foreign minister, and Ribbentrop signed a nonaggression pact with a secret annex providing for the partition of Poland and other Eastern European territories. In this agreement Soviet domination was recognized over the former tsarist territories of the Baltic states and Bessarabia. For its part the German government gained Soviet acceptance of its control over more than half of Poland and, even more important, the assurance that should war come, the German Army would not have to fight on two fronts. An economic agreement was also concluded. On September 1 Germany attacked Poland; on September 3 France and Britain declared war on Germany.

WORLD WAR II

The first years of the war were marked by spectacular German victories, in which, of course, Austrian forces participated. Poland was conquered within three weeks. The spring of 1940 brought even greater triumphs. Norway and Denmark were taken in April; Holland, Belgium, and France fell in May and June. The British forces on the Continent were forced to make a quick retreat across the channel. When it became clear that France would be defeated, Italy in June 1940 joined its Axis partner in the war.

Although the military situation in the West was highly favorable, conditions on the German eastern front deteriorated. Throughout the campaigns in Scandinavia and France, the Soviet government made no move to disturb the relationship with Germany. In June 1940, to balance the Nazi victories in the West, the Soviet Union took possession of the Baltic States, Bessarabia, and part of Bukovina. In October Mussolini, in an ill-considered action and without consulting his German ally, launched an attack on Greece from Albania. The successful Greek defense opened the entire Balkan region to possible British action. By December 1940 Hitler had decided to attack the Soviet Union; the political allegiance of the Balkan states was thus important. In March 1941 Bulgaria joined Romania, Slovakia, and Hungary in the Axis alliance system; in April the German Army invaded both Yugoslavia and Greece. In June, with the Balkans secure, the German Army launched its massive and ill-fated invasion of the Soviet Union.

This time the German Army did not attain its immediate objective of the swift and complete crushing of the opposition. Although December found German troops outside Moscow, they were not able to take the capital or to deal a crippling blow to the Soviet forces. The German soldiers were also not outfitted for a winter campaign, nor were their vehicles equipped for fighting under severe weather conditions. The turning point in the war was not, however, to come until the next winter. The German defeat at Stalingrad in February 1943, combined with the failure of the German spring offensive of 1943, signified that the Axis powers would not triumph. The entrance of the United States into the war in December 1941 brought its enormous resources in manpower and supplies into the military balance. In September

1943 Italy surrendered, although fighting continued there until 1945. By the beginning of 1944 it was clear that Germany, with ever-decreasing reserves of men and war matériel, could at best fight only a difficult, defensive war.

Under these conditions, scarcely five years after the Anschluss, the fate of Austria became again a matter of international diplomacy. With the impending defeat of the German armies the future of the country was to be decided by three powers whose concepts of the future of Europe were radically divergent. The information available on planning for the postwar world of course comes completely from the Western side; Russian aims can only be deduced. Since the Soviet Union was able so successfully to increase its power in Eastern Europe, the temptation exists to explain this result as a product of careful planning, when in fact it may have been merely a policy of improvisation that brought in the end maximum rewards. From the Western side, in retrospect, the policy toward Austria, as toward the entire Central and Eastern European area, appears one of confusion and contradiction. To all of the Allied powers the Austrian problem was only a part, and a minor part at that, of the general German question.

Not only was there no agreement between the Western states and the Soviet Union on a future peace settlement, but there were also significant divisions between the United States and Britain. Concerned chiefly with winning a military victory over Germany and then with securing Soviet assistance against Japan, the U.S. government was reluctant to assume obligations in regard to Central and Eastern Europe or to face future problems realistically. In contrast, the British leaders, Winston Churchill in particular, followed the traditional policy of seeking to assure the maintenance of the balance of power on the Continent. It was soon obvious that Germany would not succeed in its bid to control Europe, but the danger was very real that the Soviet Union might achieve this objective. To block this possibility Churchill repeatedly urged that the Western armies plan their campaigns so as to arrive in Central Europe before the Soviet Army, and he wished to provide for some sort of federal organization of the region to serve as a counterweight against possible Soviet domination. Practical as this attitude was, the British government could do little without American support.

In addition to the lack of agreement on basic wartime policies, the Allies also had no clear understanding about the status of Austria, that is, whether it constituted a separate state that had indeed been "conquered" by Germany or whether it was an enemy power, indistinguishable from the rest of the German regions. In a speech in November 1939 Churchill counted Austria among the nations taken forcefully by Germany. This declaration, however, did not represent a British conviction. Both the British Foreign Office and Churchill personally believed that the state had been an artificial creation, established in 1919 primarily for strategic reasons. The fate of the area was discussed after June 1941 by the British government and the Soviet Union, and after December also by the United States, who became, of course, a belligerent in that month. In the conversations the British government put forward the idea of a confederate solution to the problem, suggesting two types of organization, with one involving the partition of Germany proper and the association of Austria with Bavaria and the Rhineland, and the other entailing the formation of a Danubian federation with Vienna as the capital. In December 1941 the British foreign secretary, Anthony Eden, discussed with Stalin the Austrian and German questions. Stalin at this time supported a restored Austria and the separation from Germany of Bavaria and the Rhineland. He opposed a Danubian federation, which he rightly judged would be anti-Soviet.

The most important declaration affecting Austria made during the war was issued at a meeting of Allied foreign ministers in Moscow in November 1943. Here the signatories stated:

> Austria, the first free country to fall a victim to Hitlerite aggression, shall be liberated from German domination.
>
> They regard the annexation imposed on Austria by Germany on March 15, 1938, as null and void. They consider themselves as in no way bound by any changes effected in Austria since that date. They declare that they wish to see re-established a free and independent Austria and thereby to open the way for the Austrian people themselves as well as those neighboring states which will be faced with similar problems, to find that political and economic security which is the only basis of lasting peace.
>
> Austria is reminded, however, that she has a responsibility, which she cannot evade, for participation in the war at the side of Hitlerite Germany, and that in the final settlement account will inevitably be taken of her own contribution to her liberation.[23]

The clear contradiction between the first paragraph, which pictured Austria as "victim," and the last, which made the country a Germany ally, pervaded most subsequent thought. Although the wording represented a compromise with the Soviet Union, which wanted to make the country liable for reparations, Austria was in practical planning treated as an enemy state. With no Austrian government-in-exile and with little information available in the West on what was actually occurring in the country, the Allies, particularly the United States, expected that the political reconstitution of an independent Austrian state would take time. The Moscow meet-

[23] The Moscow Declaration, in *Foreign Relations of the United States: Diplomatic Papers, 1945* (Washington, D.C.: U.S. Government Printing Office, 1968), III, 40.

ing also established the European Advisory Committee, which henceforth met in London. This body was to decide the zones of occupation in Austria and its immediate postwar administration.

Until the last days of the war the British government continued to press for actions to impede Soviet domination. Churchill repeatedly made proposals for some sort of federation. In November 1943, at the Teheran Conference, he suggested an association of Bavaria, Austria, Hungary, and the Rhineland, ideas he reiterated in a meeting in Moscow with Stalin in October 1944 and again at the Yalta Conference in February 1944. He also pressed the United States toward military action. In June 1944 the British proposed that the Western armies move north in Italy, cross through Trieste and the Ljubljana gap, and arrive in Vienna before the Soviet forces. The events of the war and the American attitude, however, worked against the British proposals.

Meanwhile, in Austria the internal situation reflected the changing fortunes on the battlefield. The civilian population did not suffer from extremely severe food and fuel shortages, as they had in the First World War; this time the great hardships came only after the end of the fighting. Nevertheless, with the obvious German defeats and rising military death figures, which were to reach 247,000, morale declined rapidly. After 1943, when the Allies invaded Italy, the Austrian lands also became the target of large-scale air raids. Both factories and civilian centers were hit. The first significant raid on Vienna occurred in April 1944; in subsequent attacks more than 9,000 Viennese were killed. The industrial centers were also severely damaged. Between 1943 and 1945, for instance, it has been estimated that Wiener Neustadt was 88 percent destroyed.

In the winter of 1944–1945, with the Russian armies advancing from the east and the Allies from the south and the west, it was obvious that plans would have to be made for the future. As has been mentioned, no Austrian government-in-exile had been organized. Outside the country the two most active groups were the extremes, the monarchists on the one side and the Communists on the other. They were united in wishing to reestablish an independent Austria, an issue that continued to divide the majority parties. The activities of the Habsburg pretender, Otto, and his brothers, Robert and Felix, complicated the entire situation. Despite the fact that the governments-in-exile and all the political leaders of the Habsburg successor states were violently against a restoration, Otto in 1940 came out for the establishment of a Danubian confederation, under his rule, of Austria, Hungary, Romania, Bohemia, Moravia, Slovakia, and perhaps Croatia. Despite the ludicrous nature of the proposal, given the history of the area, both Franklin D. Roosevelt and Churchill at least gave consideration to the idea. In 1942 Otto proposed the establishment of an Austrian battalion in the U.S. Army, a concept that drew strong protests from American immigrant circles. At this time the monarchists cooperated with the Communist-dominated Free Austria Movement, which was not supported by either of the two major Austrian parties.

The Communist Party was similarly active, although in fact the majority of the postwar leaders spent these years in the Soviet Union. Communists dominated the only real wartime resistance organization in Austria. In 1942 actions were undertaken particularly by Slovenes and Communists in the Carinthian and Styrian mountain areas. This movement, the Austrian Freedom Front, was backed by the Soviet government, and the Austrian Communist leader Franz Honner was despatched from the Soviet Union to the area. Close cooperation was established with the Yugoslav Partisans, and two Austrian battalions fought with them. At the end of the war the Freedom Front was the only armed political force in the state.

The extent of resistance activities in the rest of Austria is difficult to judge. According to official figures 2,700 were executed and about 16,000 died in prison. Austrians were also connected with the German attempt to get rid of Hitler in July 1944, led by Carl Friedrich Goerdeler and Col. Claus Schenk von Stauffenberg. The Viennese members of the group were able to carry out their part of the plan and to secure the vital government buildings. The Austrian movement failed with the collapse of the conspiracy in Berlin. This action aimed at a destruction of the Nazi leadership and not at ending the Anschluss. The numbers of Austrians either executed or jailed for opposition to the Nazi regime of course pales beside the figures for this period on the fate of Jews, in whose persecution Austrians obviously cooperated. Of the 220,000 Jews in Austria in 1938 only about 5,000 remained in 1946.

With the approach of the Soviet Army in late 1944 it was clear to the political leaders that steps would have to be taken to prepare for the inevitable occupation. In December 1944 representatives of the former political parties in Vienna met together to decide how to handle the situation. At the same time an underground armed movement, known as 05, had come into existence, and some of its representatives sought contact with the Western powers through Switzerland. These actions in the final days of the war were motivated by the desire to spare the country from massive destruction and also by a great fear of an occupation by the Soviet Army, whose troops crossed into Austrian territory on March 20. With the Soviet forces close to Vienna Hitler gave the command that the city should be defended at all costs. In order to avoid needless destruction a group of officers in Wehrkommando XVII (Defense Command XVII), under Maj. Karl Szokoll, decided to try to get in touch with the Soviet Army command to arrange a surrender of the city. A noncommissioned officer, Ferdinand Käs, was able to make his way through the lines and establish contact with the Soviet forces on April 3. He handed over the plans for the defense of the city, and arrangements were made to cooperate with the Soviet occupation. After Käs returned, the plot was discovered and the principal members executed.

As a result, five days of intense fighting preceded the taking of the city on April 13. The Soviet occupation was followed by a period of violence and looting of the type that also characterized the progress of the Soviet forces through other states, including Partisan-dominated Yugoslavia, and embittered relations between even these war allies. These actions, of which Stalin obviously approved, were to be a burden for the future political activities of the Austrian Communist Party and the Russian occupation. As the Soviet forces entered from the east, the rest of the country surrendered to the Western Allies. Usually local party leaders or military units did not resist; in fact, most Austrians hastened to lay down their arms to the British and U.S. troops. There was a general fear of what the Soviet troops would do in the country, particularly in view of the nature of the German actions on Russian soil. By May 7 fighting was over in Austria. On April 30 Hitler committed suicide in Berlin; the German unconditional surrender followed on May 8.

With the peace the long period of internal upheaval and foreign war came to an end. Certainly the years from 1932 to 1945 had been among the most tumultuous in Austrian history. Within the country an authoritarian regime had been established that not only abolished the parliament, but also destroyed the Social Democratic Party; artillery had been used to capture fortified public housing. This event had been followed by the ineptly organized Nazi putsch, which had resulted in the death of Dollfuss. In March 1938 the An-

St. Stephen's Cathedral burning

schluss, long desired by members of all parties, had resulted in a tighter rule, the suppression of all vestiges of a separate administration, and participation in a devastating war. Not since Napoleonic days had Austrian lands witnessed the passage of great destructive armies. At the end of the war Austrians faced a ruined country: homes, buildings, industries, shops, and offices had been leveled either from the air or from ground fighting; in Vienna, for instance, over twenty-one thousand houses had been destroyed or made uninhabitable. The loss of human life was even more devastating: 247,000 members of the armed forces were killed or missing or had died in captivity; and 29,000 civilians also died. At the end of the war over 750,000 men remained in prisoner-of-war camps, with the last returning from the Soviet Union only in 1955. The essentials of life, such as food and fuel, were exhausted, and transportation had broken down everywhere. Obviously the fate of the country lay in the hands of the occupying armies.

5

THE SECOND AUSTRIAN REPUBLIC UNDER FOUR-POWER OCCUPATION, 1945–1955

IN the spring of 1945 the war was over in the Austrian lands, but unlike the situation after the First World War, the entire country was under foreign occupation. Also in contrast to the previous period, military action had taken place on Austrian soil, leaving a great deal of physical destruction that had to be dealt with immediately. The first moves toward the reestablishment of a political authority took place in Vienna and under Soviet auspices. As we shall see, the Western powers were at first reluctant to proceed quickly in this direction. The United States in particular expected that considerable time would pass before a regular Austrian government could be established, and until then the country would be run by an Allied military administration.

THE REPUBLIC IS RESTORED

In December 1944, as we have seen, some of the former leaders of the old parties met and agreed upon a provisional National Committee. After the fighting in Vienna ceased, these men formed a city administration with Gen. Theodor Körner of the Social Democratic Party as mayor. At the same time, under Soviet sponsorship, steps were taken toward the construction of a national government. At the end of the war Karl Renner, the first chancellor of the Austrian republic,

Karl Renner

now seventy-five, was living in Gloggnitz near Semmering. Soon after the Soviet occupation he went to the local commander to protest the actions of the Russian troops. Since he was known to the Soviet authorities, he was passed from level to level until he finally saw Gen. A. Sheltov, the commander of the Russian Army in the area. Previously, Renner's political reputation had not stood high in Moscow. Lenin had called him "one of the most contemptible lackeys of German imperialism" and a "traitor to socialism";[24] in 1943 he had been attacked in the Soviet press because of his pro-Anschluss attitude in 1938. Nevertheless, the Soviet government was willing to work with him. Renner himself felt that he had the authority to act, since he had been a president of the last freely elected Austrian parliament. With great energy he took control of the situation and, with Soviet approval, issued proclamations to deal with the immediate problems. When he came to Vienna on April 20, the local administration under Körner had already been organized. Renner had originally desired to recall the parliament of 1933, but he soon realized that it was impossible. By this time also the former party leadership had reemerged. After consultations, it was decided that it would be best to form a provisional government to hold office until elections could be held.

Of the prewar parties the Socialists were in the best position. The prewar Social Democrats and the Revolutionary Socialists joined to form the Austrian Socialist Party (Sozialistische Partei Osterreichs, SPO). Not only were they free of the burden of Austrofascism, but the leadership had developed a new spirit and desired to end the ideological squabbling. Most of the militants had left the country; Otto Bauer was dead. The new leader, Adolf Schärf, adopted a more

---

[24] Jacques Hannak, *Karl Renner und seine Zeit* (Vienna: Europa Verlag, 1965), p. 670.

practical attitude and proved less interested in doctrinaire controversies. Renner, of course, stood on the right wing of the party. Despite the milder attitude, the party did have a left wing, led by Erwin Scharf, who was to cause problems later.

The Christian Socials also reorganized, under the name Austrian People's Party (Osterreichische Volkspartei, OVP); it remained basically a party of peasant-farmers, white-collar employees, businessmen, and some workers. Like the Socialists, the members of this party found their doctrinal differences no longer so important. Even the Catholic emphasis, so strong previously, was now muted; priests were forbidden to run for office. The new leaders were to be Leopold Figl, Felix Hurdes, and Leopold Kunschak, the Catholic labor organizer.

The Communist Party (Kommunistische Partei Osterreichs, KPO) emerged as a major political force, primarily because of the Soviet occupation. The top leadership – Johann Koplenig, Franz Honner, Ernst Fischer, and Friedl Fürnberg – had spent most of the war in the Soviet Union. The Communists who had remained in Austria had, as we have seen, been active in the resistance, at least after June 1941, and the majority had subsequently been killed by the police. Honner, who had formed an Austrian brigade within the Yugoslav resistance forces in the last part of the war, emerged as the principal Communist leader.

Because the strength of the individual parties could not be accurately judged, the provisional government, established on April 27, gave each an equal position. The Communists were able to gain the two posts they most desired: Honner became minister of interior with control over the police and Fischer received the Ministry of Education. Renner met the objections raised by these appointments by attaching to each minister two undersecretaries from the other parties, who were given "watchdog" functions. In the division of posts in the first cabinet the Socialists received ten, the People's Party nine, and the Communists three, with three given to non-party men.

At the time that this provisional administration was organized, a proclamation was issued announcing the reestablishment of "the democratic republic of Austria" and annulling the Anschluss. The constitution of 1920, as amended in 1929, was taken as the basis of the government. The Austrian state was thus brought back to the political conditions preceding the Dollfuss period. The political parties resumed their previous functions, and their leaders, as in the years of the First Republic, watched carefully over the interests of their members. Although ideological controversies were avoided, state offices were distributed and specific policies adopted only after hard bargaining among the parties.

The new government was not immediately recognized by the Western Allies, nor did its authority extend outside Vienna. Since its organization was the result of a unilateral Soviet decision, the other states at first looked with great suspicion on what they feared was a Russian puppet regime. They thus withheld their recognition for five months, a period during which the Austrian government was solely dependent upon Soviet support. For their part the three Western powers moved in and occupied their assigned zones. The lines of partition were not finally decided upon by the European Advisory Committee until July, when it was agreed that four authorities would be established: the Soviet zone included Lower Austria, Burgenland, and Upper Austria north of the Danube; the American district covered the rest of Upper Austria and Salzburg; Britain received Styria, Carinthia, and East Tirol; and France was responsible for North Tirol and Vorarlberg (see Map 10). The provincial divisions of the pre-Anschluss period were reestablished. The city of Vienna

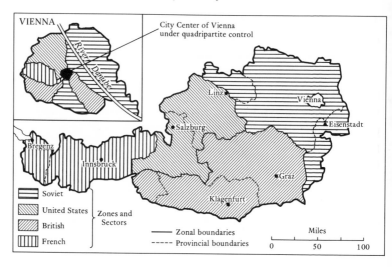

Map 10. The Allied occupation zones and the sectors of Vienna, 1945–1955

was similarly partitioned, but the central portion, which contained the principal government offices, was placed under four-power occupation. To coordinate the administration of the zones, an Allied Council for Austria was established in which each power received the equivalent of a veto right. It will be noticed that despite the previous declarations Austria was in practice treated as an occupied enemy country.

The Western suspicion of the new Austrian regime was shown also in July and August at the Potsdam conference, where Britain, France, and the United States announced their refusal to recognize the Renner government until they had taken control of their zones in Vienna. By this time the Western Allies had established separate provisional governments for the provinces occupied by their troops. It was still a question whether these administrations would accept the authority of the Renner regime. Representatives from these provinces and the central government met first in Salzburg and then in September in Vienna. At this time the Renner government was broadened to include some men from the provinces, notably Karl Gruber from Tirol, who became an undersecretary for foreign affairs. The provisional central government at this time included thirteen representatives from the People's Party, twelve Socialists, ten Communists, and four independents.

Meanwhile, the Western powers occupied their zones in Vienna; the Allied Council held its first meeting in September. Although the U.S. attitude became more favorable, the British remained suspicious of the provisional government. The council did not recognize it as the official government of Austria until October 20. Even then its effective power was severely limited because its actions had to be approved by the council, where each member could exercise a veto. Nevertheless, despite such difficulties, Austria did henceforth, unlike Germany, have a single, central authority whose jurisdiction was recognized in all the zones.

On November 25, 1945, the first free election since 1930 was held. The Socialist and People's parties ran on programs quite similar to their prewar positions. In an attempt to appeal to all classes the Communist Party stood on its resistance record and attacked "fascism," a term that it tended to apply freely to its political opponents. The results were a surprise to many. The People's Party, with almost 50 percent of the vote, won eighty-five seats; the Socialists, with 44.6 percent, had seventy-six seats. The great shock was that received by the Communist Party, with only 5.42 percent and four representatives. The conservative party thus held the majority, and the distribution of votes closely resembled that of the 1920s. Twenty percent fewer votes were cast than in

1930, a figure that reflected not only wartime losses but also the fact that former Nazis could not participate and many Austrians were still in prison camps.

Despite the People's Party's majority, the situation of the country under foreign occupation made necessary the continuance of a coalition regime. In the new government, formed by Figl, the People's Party had six ministries and the Socialists four, and two went to nonparty men. Although the Communist vote had been low, a Ministry of Power and Electrification was created for Karl Altmann so that his party would remain in the government, thus avoiding problems with the Soviet authorities. Schärf became vice-chancellor, and a Socialist held the vital Ministry of Interior. The system of associating undersecretaries with each minister was continued. The coalition system was to last until 1966, although the Communist Party withdrew in 1947 when Altmann left the government. Karl Renner was elected president in December 1945.

The coalition arrangement was accompanied by a system of the proportional distribution not only of the major cabinet posts, but also of other government offices, on the basis of understandings reached between the parties after elections. The close agreement between the two major parties meant that the country did not have a functioning political opposition. The top party leaders determined national policy among themselves; parliament was reduced to the position of approving decisions previously reached outside its confines. The great advantage of the system was that despite its complicated and often cumbersome nature, it gave the nation a strong government in a time of crisis, and it also kept the Communist Party from exploiting divisions within the state. Although the parties quarreled over details of government policy, they maintained a front against the occupying powers. Moreover, the system, based on political cooperation, did much to heal the wounds remaining from the bitter battles of the 1920s and 1930s.

The results of the first election not only jolted the Communist Party, but appear to have similarly surprised the Soviet authorities. They had not interfered in the elections, and they continued to pursue this policy. Hereafter their attitude toward the Austrian government changed; harassment rather than support became characteristic of their actions. However, the Western Allies, in particular the United States, also shifted their opinions. The Austrian government in the future years was increasingly to orient its policy in the direction of the West and to regard the Russian officials and the Communist Party as dangerous opponents.

One of the major political problems that arose at once was that of the position of former Nazi Party members. Under strong Allied pressure and with constant interference, the government passed measures excluding them from holding certain positions and from voting. Some were sent to prison or had fines imposed on them. The measures were very far-reaching. About 524,000 people were affected by the laws, which, if families were included, meant that they involved about two million persons in a population of under seven million. The measures were arbitrarily applied and often with the interference of the occupation authorities in defiance of Austrian law. No measures were taken against those who had occupied similar positions in the Dollfuss and Schuschnigg regimes, which were likewise authoritarian in nature. The effects were largely negative. By the elections of 1949 most of these people were back on voter lists. As a result all of the parties thereafter endeavored to win this important block of votes. In 1945 the Communist Party had run on a strongly anti-Nazi program; it too shifted its line. As the result of the return of this group of voters in February 1949 a new party was formed, the Union of Independents

(Verband der Unabhängigen, VdU), which was based on the former national and Nazi groups.

In the two elections of 1949 and 1953 much the same balance was established as in 1945, except that the Union of Independents took a share of the votes. In 1949 the elections marked a swing to the right. The numbers voting, which included about 482,000 former Nazis, rose by 27 percent. The People's Party won 44 percent of the votes, the Socialists 38 percent, and the Union of Independents 11.67 percent. The People's Party–Socialist coalition continued. In May 1951 the Socialist Körner was elected president. A change in leadership occurred within the People's Party; Julius Raab, who replaced Figl as premier and head of the party, was to be the most important leader in his party for the next eight years. In 1953 the Socialists were able to increase their share of the votes to 42 percent, while the People's Party received 41 percent and the Union of Independents, with its allies, 11 percent. Even though it received a larger number of votes, the Socialist Party remained second in number of delegates. Seats in Austria were distributed on the basis of groups of constituencies based on population, a system that gave conservative rural districts an advantage. In both of these elections the Communist Party and its supporters maintained a steady 5 percent.

Although a stable government was thus established in 1945, the Austrian leaders faced enormous problems. The internal economic conditions remained terrible, and the question of Soviet opposition had always to be faced after the failure of the Communist Party in the elections. The immediate major task was the simple one of avoiding starvation. Although the country had not suffered from a food shortage during the war, with the average consumption maintained at 2,700 calories per day, the postwar conditions were bleak. At first, the normal consumer was reduced to 800 calories on the official ration; in September 1945 this figure rose to 1,550; but in March 1946 it went back to 1,200. In November it returned to 1,550, and finally, in September 1948, it rose to 2,100; rationing ended in that year. The initial low level created not only health problems, similar to the starvation and deficiency diseases after World War I, but also an uncontrollable black market. In addition, as after the previous war, the government had to deal with the problems of getting the economy functioning, of adjusting the question of wages and prices in an inflationary period, and of securing a sound currency.

In a desperate condition, the Austrian state could not have continued to exist without the massive outside aid that the Western powers provided through the first postwar winter. Beginning in spring 1946 direct assistance was given through the UNRRA (United Nations Relief and Rehabilitation Administration) programs and through other private organizations, such as CARE (Cooperative for American Remittances to Europe), on an individual basis. In 1948 the Marshall Plan began to provide even more generous assistance. In the first year Austria received $280 million, of which the most important part went for food; later payments assisted in rebuilding the economy of the country. In all, between 1945 and 1955 the country received $1,585 million in foreign aid from Western sources, with the United States providing 87 percent. The Soviet Union, in contrast, was to adopt policies exceedingly burdensome to the national life.

Although gradually political stability and economic recovery became apparent, general conditions in Europe evolved in a manner that was bound to have an adverse effect in Austria. The growing tension between East and West made of the occupied country a field of battle in the Cold War. The results of the elections of 1945, together with the fact that the state depended on economic assistance from the West, made it clear where Austrian sympathies lay. Under the direction of Karl Gruber, Austrian policy was closely linked with that of the West. Although this position reflected the attitude of the population and certainly the material interests of the state, the ranging of Austria on one side of the Cold War pushed the Soviet Union and the Communist Party into stronger opposition. Because it occupied so much of the country the Soviet Union could do real damage should it choose. To an extent the difficulties that it could cause for the government were lessened by extremely significant changes that took effect in June 1946 in the procedures of the Allied Council. At this time it was agreed that any law passed by the Austrian government would go into effect thirty-one days after it had been sent to the council unless that body made specific objections. In practice, this provision meant that the members had to reject a measure unanimously and that the single-veto right for one power was withdrawn. Laws of a constitutional nature were not covered, but this term was not defined. It was also agreed that the Austrian government could make bilateral arrangements with any occupying power. The division of the members along Cold-War lines hampered the function of the council; after the middle of 1947 few substantive discussions took place. In the minority the Soviet Union made objections to over 550 Austrian laws between 1946 and 1953, but, of course, it lacked the power to block their implementation.

The Soviet government, however, possessed potent weapons that it could use. Most important was the powerful economic lever that was acquired as the result of Western mistakes at the Potsdam conference and of decisions made without adequate thought of the consequences. At the end of the war, as has been mentioned, the Soviet government wished to collect reparations from Austria. The bill was placed at $250 million, to be divided among the victor powers, in addition to deliveries of products. The Western governments regarded this figure and even the idea of assessing reparations as unrealistic, since obviously they could not be collected from Austria; the Western states might end by carrying the burden of the payments themselves. Finally, however, it was agreed in discussions on other sections of the future peace settlement that the Soviet Union could take possession of "German foreign assets in Bulgaria, Finland, Hungary, Rumania and Eastern Austria." A definition of these "German assets" was not given. Thus, although the claim to Austrian reparations was dropped, the Russian government secured a means of extracting in fact far more from the country than the original demand.

Even before the end of the fighting the Soviet authorities had already moved to collect what economic assets they could. As in other countries occupied by their armies, they at once began to dismantle factories and take equipment out of the country under the title of war booty. It has been estimated that the value of the articles removed ranged between $400 million and $1 billion. In September, again in line with their actions elsewhere, the Soviet representatives proposed to the Renner government the establishment of joint companies in which the Soviet contribution would be the former German assets, a proposal that was refused. In July 1946 a further step was taken. In Order No. 17 of that date the Soviet government moved to confiscate what it defined as former German assets, including property that the Austrian government did not believe was properly so considered. The Soviet seizures involved the entire Austrian oil production, mines, industries, and agricultural land. This economic empire was then organized into two major units, the Sowjetische Mineralölverwaltung (SMV, Soviet Mineral Oil Administration) and the Upravlenie Sovetskogo Imushchestva v Avstrii (USIA, Administration of Soviet Property in Austria), which embraced a wide range of concerns. The Soviet authorities also took control over the Danube Steamship Company. Although much of the confiscated property could be defined as legitimate German assets, its ownership by the Soviet Union placed that state in a controlling economic position, and one that could be used for political purposes. In April 1955, 10 percent of those employed in Austrian industry worked either for SMV or for USIA. The Austrian government had no influence over these industries; their products could be sold or exported without state controls. The food produced did not form part of the official rationing system and was distributed in separate Soviet shops. Between 1947 and 1955, 63 percent of the production was sent to the Soviet Union. Many of the items were of vital necessity to the rest of Austria, and replacements had to be imported, usually from and at the expense of the Western states. The Soviet companies enjoyed an extraterritorial status, and they paid no taxes to the government.

Immediately after the Soviet announcement of Order No. 17 the Austrian government acted to try to offset the Soviet action. On July 26, 1946, it moved to nationalize a large section of the economy, including the three largest banks; the coal, iron, copper, lead, and antimony mining companies; the oil and steel industries; the Danube shipping; and a large number of other concerns. The laws were approved by both the conservative People's Party and the Socialists, but strongly opposed by the Communist Party. In the Allied Council the Soviet representatives protested that this measure involved constitutional law, a position that was disputed by the Western representatives. Thus the capitalist West supported wide socialization measures while the Soviet Union and the Communists attempted to block them. In practice, the early nationalization measures did not function well since they were not put into effect in the Soviet zone, which contained 60 percent of the industries involved, many of which were also a part of the Soviet-confiscated property. The Western powers returned to the Austrian government the former German assets, and so this question was not an issue in the Western zones.

As could be expected, this great economic empire gave the Soviet authorities and the Communist Party a strong center of influence. In the more than three hundred USIA concerns, between forty-five and fifty thousand workers were employed. In these, paramilitary organizations called *Werkschutz* (Plant Guards) were formed, numbering about two thousand men, which could and later did play a political role. The Communist Party thus not only enjoyed the support of an occupying power, but had what should have been a favorable position in an important sector of the Austrian economy.

Despite its advantages the Communist Party was unable to win more votes than it had in the First Republic; that is, it continued to be supported by about 5 percent of the electorate. Before the elections of November 1945 the party leadership had undoubtedly been deluded about its potential strength. It had certainly not realized the extent to which its association with the Soviet Union would be a major impediment to electoral success. Quite apart from the question of the acts of violence committed by Soviet troops and the nature of the Communist regime, most Austrians, like other Germans, regarded the Russian occupiers with cold contempt. The close support given by the Austrian Communist leaders to all the shifts and turns of Soviet policy also placed the party in the position of being a Soviet puppet and an apparent agent of a foreign state.

The appeal of the Communist program was also severely damaged by the progress of events in Eastern Europe, where Communist regimes gained power by anything but democratic means. In their program for Austria, however, the Communist leaders did not call for the formation of a united front, as they had elsewhere. Confident of success through their own party organization, they sought only to establish a cooperative relationship with other parties. In the Socialist Party Erwin Scharf, a former Revolutionary Socialist, supported a policy of close ties with the Communists. In July 1945 the Socialist Party leadership agreed to some measures of common action, but they were never implemented. Even after the decisive Communist defeat in the first election, Scharf continued to argue for close cooperation. In 1949 he and his followers were expelled from the Socialist Party. They then formed their own organization and in 1949 campaigned with the Communist Party, a combination that brought advantages to neither.

As the Austrian state and the economy became stronger, both Soviet and Communist influence weakened. A good example of this development is what happened to the police. When the Soviet Army entered Vienna, it attempted at once to ensure Communist control of the security forces. Since their members were under the jurisdiction of the Communist minister of interior, Franz Honner, the initial undertakings were largely successful. At the beginning of May 1945 the majority of the police districts were controlled by Communists, and the chief of police of Vienna also belonged to the party. Honner unsuccessfully attempted to incorporate the entire Austrian Freedom Battalion into the police. The new elections resulted in the replacement of Honner with the Socialist Oskar Helmer as minister of interior. A strong opponent of Communist control, Helmer subsequently concentrated on removing KPO and Soviet influence, and by the fall of 1947 he had succeeded in his goal. Since it no longer held power over the Austrian security forces, the Soviet government concentrated on keeping the police weak and on blocking their rearmament with modern, effective weapons. The Western Allies, of course, with the mounting tensions of the Cold War, had opposite interests. They now came increasingly to favor the building up of a strong and effective gendarmerie that could be used in case of internal political trouble.

The question of the control of the police involved, of course, the issue of who would have the advantage should civil disturbances connected with political movements erupt. Such a situation happened in 1950 when two sets of strikes occurred. Although the economic situation in Austria had improved, particularly with the Marshall Plan, the rising cost of living remained a constant problem. As in other countries, workers in Austria had to face the consequences of inflation and the fact that wages simply did not keep pace with prices. A legitimate source of grievance did exist here and accounted for the fact that strike movements gained much popular support. After the war the workers' interests were represented by the Austrian Federation of Trade Unions (Osterreichischer Gewerkschaftsbund, OGB), established in 1945. This organization was composed of fifteen separate unions, to which two-thirds of the Austrian labor force belonged. Although the body was nonpolitical, the leadership was dominated by the Socialists. By 1950 many of the members had become dissatisfied with the organization and its policies. The strikes that were organized at this time under Communist leadership thus did to some extent reflect the growing discontent with the economic conditions and the OGB's activities. The first set of strikes commenced on September 26 in the USIA factories in Vienna; however, similar actions took place in Linz, Steyr, and other industrial centers in the Western zones. These strikes, which did not have OGB support, were over by September 28. A second wave commenced on October 4, with the center in Vienna and Lower

Austria. Since the OGB and the Socialists stood firmly against the movement, it became clear that unless the Soviet authorities intervened on the side of the strikers, they would again fail. This time the strike lasted only one day. This strike action marked the last time that either the Communist Party or the Soviet authorities attempted to take an initiative in Austrian domestic affairs.

THE STATE TREATY

Although the Austrian government had achieved notable successes and it was apparent that the coalition regime did represent both the interests of the country and the desires of the majority of the population, the chief goal, the signing of a definitive peace treaty and an end to the occupation, had not yet been accomplished by the end of the decade. The country remained in the difficult position of having on its soil the armed forces of great powers who were to become increasingly antagonistic to each other. Moreover, the costs of occupation were enormous. At the end of 1945 about 350,000 Allied troops (200,000 Russian, 65,000 British, 47,000 American, and 40,000 French) were stationed in Austria. They took up scarce housing, and they consumed locally produced food. The occupation costs assigned to the Austrian budget in 1945 involved the payment of 10 million schillings to the three Western powers and 450 million to the Soviet Union. The ending of this difficult situation was the prime objective of successive governments. It will be remembered that bad as it was, the Treaty of St. Germain had been signed a year after the conclusion of the First World War; the Austrian State Treaty ending the second great conflict took ten years to complete. The initial problem faced by the Austrian leaders was that Austria was a secondary matter to all of the great powers concerned. As during the war, the fate of the land remained closely attached to a solution of the German question, which itself hinged on the larger East–West conflict. Throughout this period the Austrians' principal fear was that their small territory, following the German example, would be permanently partitioned. At no time could the government sign a separate peace with the Western powers, as Japan did, because partition would have been the inevitable result.

In the negotiations the Austrian government was, of course, completely dependent on the actions of the great powers. Despite all the Allied declarations and pronouncements, Austria was in fact a defeated enemy nation. At first, the Austrian desire for a quick settlement was favored by the United States and opposed principally by the Soviet Union. At that time the Soviet government was primarily interested in securing the approval of treaties with Romania, Hungary, and Bulgaria and was refusing also to agree to an Italian peace until these questions were settled. Although agreements were completed in February 1947, the Soviet government continued to delay the Austrian negotiations by supporting the extreme claims of the Yugoslav government, which asked for Carinthian territory, including Klagenfurt, embracing approximately 1,000 square miles and 190,000 people, and a reparation payment of $150 million.

Formal negotiations on the Austrian treaty commenced in January 1947 in London. Austrian representatives attended the meetings, but not as full members. In March and April 1947 the Austrian problems were discussed by the foreign ministers of the great powers in Moscow. This meeting ended without an agreement on the disposal of German property or the Yugoslav claims to border changes and reparations. The Western powers in these negotiations maintained a firm position against the Soviet and Yugoslav claims, since they did not wish to leave Austria open to full Soviet control.

Their concern became even stronger in 1948, when relations between the two power blocs worsened with the Berlin blockade and the Communist takeover of Czechoslovakia. The Western Allies did not want to leave Austria until the Marshall Plan had been given the opportunity to work and the economic and political situation was stable. Another meeting, held in London in February 1948, thus could make no progress. At this time the Soviet Union proposed as a solution to the German-assets problem that the Austrian government grant it rights in its oil production for fifty years, allow its participation in the Danube Shipping Company, and then pay $200 million for the remaining property in question.

The Austrian position was, however, considerably strengthened when a quarrel broke out between the Soviet and Yugoslav governments. After the war Josip Broz Tito had been able to establish a strong Communist government without Soviet assistance, but instead based on native support. In June 1948, rejecting Soviet attempts to control Yugoslav affairs, Tito embarked upon an independent course in foreign and domestic policy, which brought strong denunciations from the Soviet Union and the other Communist-bloc states. Subsequently, the Soviet government dropped its support of Yugoslav claims in Carinthia and accepted the Austrian borders of 1938. The Austrian government then entered into direct discussions with Belgrade on the question. Deprived of great-power support, Yugoslavia finally agreed to drop the territorial claims; in return the Austrian government guaranteed minority rights for the country's Croats and Slovenes and agreed that Austrian property in Yugoslavia should be confiscated for reparations. Although this major question was settled, the further intensification of the Cold War, with the establishment of the North Atlantic Treaty Organization (NATO) in April 1949, balanced by the

Soviet alliances with the East European countries, and the Korean conflict in 1950, postponed further the negotiation of an Austrian treaty.

Throughout this period the Austrian settlement remained closely tied to the evolution of events in Germany. In May 1949 the Federal Republic of Germany was established. The political organization of this state paralleled in many ways that of Austria. The two strongest parties were the Social Democrats and the Christian Democrats; the Communist vote ran around 6 percent. In October 1949, under Soviet sponsorship, the German lands under Russian occupation were organized as the German Democratic Republic. This pattern of partition was exactly what the Austrian government feared for its own state. Nevertheless, in the next years it continued to press strongly for a peace treaty, but still with little success. Both the Western states and the Soviet Union maintained their firm positions. The Soviet government linked the Austrian problem not only to Germany, but also, despite its hostility toward Tito, to a settlement of the fate of Trieste, a city disputed by Italy and Yugoslavia.

When Stalin died in March 1953, Soviet policy toward Austria, as toward other international problems, softened. In April of that year Figl was replaced at the head of the government by Raab; in November the Socialist leader, Bruno Kreisky, who favored a neutral policy, became state secretary for foreign affairs. The Soviet Union stopped billing Austria for occupation costs, a move that had been taken by the United States in 1947; the French and British followed this example in 1954. All of the occupying powers had by this time reduced their forces to a small number. In 1953 the last censorship regulations, imposed by the occupying states, were also canceled. The new Austrian leadership continued to press for treaty negotiations. At this time the possibility that Austria would assume a position of neutrality between the rival great-power blocs was introduced. In June Gruber, still in charge of foreign affairs, spoke with the Indian prime minister, Jawaharlal Nehru, in Switzerland in a conversation also attended by Krishna Menon, the Indian ambassador to Moscow. Menon subsequently informed the Russian government that Austria was willing to agree to permanent neutrality, which meant that it would neither make military pacts nor allow foreign military bases on its territory. The Russian foreign minister, V. M. Molotov, replied that this action was not sufficient.

Discussions continued through 1954, with the Russian position still closely linked to the German question. Molotov indicated that the Soviet Union did not intend to withdraw its troops from Austria until an agreement with Germany was signed. He also wished any treaty to include the declaration that Austria would not make alliances or allow military bases in the country, assurances that the Western powers opposed. After a year of negotiation, suddenly in February 1955 Molotov gave a speech in which he declared the Soviet desire not to delay the treaty further. The Russian government would no longer insist that its troops stay in Austria until the German treaty was made, but it demanded strong guarantees against a future Anschluss. In April, as a result of a Soviet invitation, a delegation including Raab, Figl, Kreisky, and Schärf flew to Moscow, where an agreement was reached on the final terms of the pact. The Austrian representatives gave assurances concerning the future neutrality of the state, and the Soviet Union agreed to withdraw its troops by December 31, 1955. The final Austrian State Treaty was signed in May 1955 in Vienna by the foreign ministers of the powers concerned – Molotov, John Foster Dulles, Harold Macmillan, Antoine Pinay, and Figl. The treaty, among other articles, repeated the declarations against an Anschluss, included safeguards for the Croatian and Slovenian minorities, and again forbade a Habsburg restoration. The last Allied forces left in October. Although this agreement was designated a "state" rather than a "peace" treaty, it was certainly the type of settlement usually imposed on a defeated enemy.

After the signing of the treaty the Austrian parliament proceeded in June to approve a constitutional amendment declaring that "Austria of her own free will declares herewith her permanent neutrality, which she is resolved to maintain and defend with all the means at her disposal . . . [and] will never in the future accede to any military alliances nor permit the establishment of military bases of foreign states on her territory."[25] Austrian neutrality was intended to be modeled on the Swiss example. However, in December 1955 Austria entered the United Nations, as Switzerland had not done. The neutrality declaration was not received enthusiastically by all sections of the West; Italy, a member of NATO, was now cut off from direct military communication with the other Allied forces in Germany. Many also feared that neutrality would open Austria to Soviet pressure in the future.

Although the final Soviet position marked a compromise of its previous views, that government had actually sacrificed little, if anything. Because the Warsaw Pact, concluded in May 1955 among the Socialist states, allowed the Soviet Union to maintain troops in Hungary and Romania, the Austrian base had lost its major value. In addition, by this year Austria had become an economic liability. With the development of the Soviet resources, Austrian oil was no longer necessary to the Soviet economy; the USIA industries generally were on the verge of collapse. In the final economic agreement the Austrian government agreed to deliver 1 million tons of oil yearly for ten years and to pay $2 million for

[25] Karl R. Stadler, *Austria* (New York: Praeger Publishers, 1971), p. 277.

the property of the Danube Steamship Company and $150 million for the return of the confiscated German assets.

Thus, ten years after the end of the Second World War, the Austrians became masters in their own house. They had, however, accomplished a great deal during the period of occupation. The process of recovery from the devastation of the war was well on its way; the government had been able to establish good relations with the victor powers; and the political framework of the 1920s had been restored. The question remained whether the state would use the bitter experiences of the past to build a functioning government and a prosperous economy. Much would depend on the attitude of the major parties and on their ability to end the destructive conflicts of the interwar era.

6

INDEPENDENT AUSTRIA: COALITION AND SINGLE-PARTY GOVERNMENTS, 1955–1970

THE two decades after 1955 were a great contrast to the preceding years. With the signing of the treaty and the adoption of a policy of neutrality Austria moved out of the center of European affairs. The dramatic events in international relations were henceforth to involve primarily the relationship between the two world powers, the United States and the Soviet Union, and, within the Soviet camp, the conflict between the small states and their giant protector. Austria's neutrality barred it from participation in the Cold War controversies. It should be noted that the neutral status had been adopted by the Austrian assembly in an independent decision; there were no outside guarantors. There were also few illusions, either in Austria or elsewhere, that in case of a major conflict the Austrian Army would be able to defend that neutrality against a great power.

Another major issue in past politics was settled, or at least put into abeyance for a long time to come: that of the German nature of the Austrian state. With the partition of prewar Germany, the question whether Austria was in 1955 a third German state, along with the Federal Republic and the Democratic Republic, or a nation in its own right was chiefly of academic interest. A reestablishment of the Greater Germany of the war years was not in the realm of the possible. Moreover, the close interlocking of the Austrian and West

German economies was to give a practical expression to common sympathies and interests and to show, in contrast to most nineteenth-century thought, that peoples with a common language and culture do not necessarily need a single political authority.

THE SECOND REPUBLIC: NEW INSTITUTIONS

In domestic politics the coalition government continued to guide Austrian affairs along a peaceful and productive path. The basic political structure of the 1920s was reintroduced; the constitution of 1920 with the changes of 1929 thus continues to form the basis of the government. To review its organization: at the head of state is the president, chosen by direct election every six years; his duties are largely representational. As before, the legislative branch of the government consists of two houses, the more important of which is the Nationalrat, whose members are elected directly every four years under the system of proportional representation. From 1959 to 1986 three parties held seats in the assembly; most laws were passed unanimously under the system to be described. Three presidents alternated in presiding over the sessions. The second house, the Bundesrat (Federal Assembly), is composed of representatives chosen indirectly by the legislatures of the nine provinces, with the chairmanship rotating among them.

Despite the similarity to the institutions of the First Republic, Austrian political life functioned in a quite different atmosphere after 1945. Of first importance was the change in the attitude and relationship of the major political parties. Instead of forming competing camps, they muted their ideological programs and adjusted their tactics to contribute to creating an era of cooperation and conciliation. As partners in a coalition government in a time of turmoil and distress, the

Socialists and the People's Party obviously could not continue their previous bitter controversies. The reorganized parties reflected the general recognition that modifications in their previous attitudes would have to be made. The Socialist Party of 1945, basically a revival of the prewar Social Democrats, was, as we have seen, at first headed by Karl Renner. An opponent of Bauer, who had died in 1938, Renner represented the right wing of his party. As the Cold War tensions heightened and as events in the neighboring Communist states increasingly alienated Austrian sympathies from Soviet-style systems, the party leadership became less tolerant of its own left wing and even stronger in its rejection of cooperation with the Communist Party. The former debate over the wisdom of supporting existing state institutions and joining in coalitions with middle-class parties was over. The Socialist Party was anxious to cooperate in rebuilding the country and, in particular, to encourage and assist in the development of a modern industrial economy. It also recognized the need to attract a wider group of voters and, where possible, to gain influence in rural districts. It could not, of course, move too far to the right and thus lose its basic constituency.

The People's Party, also founded in 1945, unlike the Socialists did not emphasize continuity with its prewar equivalent, the Christian Socials, even though many of its leaders had indeed been prominent in the activities of the old organization. Whereas the Socialist Party was the self-proclaimed representative of the working class, the People's Party was a combination of often competing interest groups, with voters coming from industry, business, agriculture, and the ranks of salaried employees. As in the interwar period, its chief strength lay not in Vienna, but in the provinces, where, however, some problems were to arise. As the economy shifted, with more people employed in industry and services, the number of those engaged in farming declined precipitously, so that an important base of party strength was eroded. A second stronghold of influence remained firm. Like the previous Christian Socials, the People's Party had a primary attraction for practicing Catholics, although the official connection with the church was ended. Representing its varied membership, the party program stressed traditional family values, property rights, and peasant interests, and it accepted a wide variety of social welfare legislation.

The weakest political coalition, the League of Independents, founded in 1949, did not participate in the government during the years of the grand coalition, but its importance for the possible founding of a small coalition was recognized by both the other parties. Organized by Herbert Kraus and Viktor Neimann, the League of Independents was composed of groups of a widely varying character. It represented not only the former German-national camp, but also Liberals, anticlerical conservatives, monarchists, and former Nazis, all voters who could not fit easily into the other parties. In 1956, after internal quarrels, the party was reorganized as the Freedom Party (Freiheitliche Partei Osterreichs, FPO). Its first leader was Anton Reinthaller, who had been a Nazi Party member and the minister of agriculture in the Seyss-Inquart cabinet after the Anschluss. After Reinthaller's death in 1958, Friedrich Peter, formerly an SS officer, headed the organization for the next twenty years. The party program declared that Austria was a German state and emphasized the positive side of the Austrian participation in the war. It also placed emphasis on family values, private property, and some aspects of the former Liberal program. Since an Anschluss was out of the question, the leadership called for a united Europe, which would join Austria and Germany within a larger framework.

The fate of the fourth party, the Communist, was determined by its close association with the Soviet Union. The influence of this small party, which obediently followed Moscow's directives, was effectively killed by the nature of the Soviet occupation and its intervention in the affairs of the other Communist states. Events in neighboring Czechoslovakia, Hungary, and Yugoslavia had a chilling effect on the Austrian electorate. The strongest showing occurred in the first postwar election, that of 1945, when the party won 5.42 percent of the vote; in 1949 this percentage declined to 5.08; in 1953 it was 5.28. In 1956 the figure dropped to 4.42; in 1959 to 3.27; and in 1962 to 3.04. In 1959 the party lost its representation in the parliament.

The successful conclusion of the peace treaty and the guidance of the country toward economic recovery were the work of the grand coalition. The two parties, under the pressure of extreme economic hardship and foreign occupation, were able to work out mechanisms for the smooth functioning of the government. Their cooperation was to continue for another eleven years, a period in which the country enjoyed an unprecedented period of economic prosperity and when no major domestic problems developed. Basic to this condition was the development of two institutions: first, the *Proporz* arrangements, that is, the proportional sharing of major government offices and positions open to state patronage; and second, after 1957, the establishment of the social partnership.

The Proporz system allowed the coalition to function with a minimum of friction. After each election a Coalition Committee, composed of delegations from the two parties, met to arrange a division of influence. The share of positions that each received was based on the results of the voting. The major offices were, of course, the ministries. In general, the People's Party received the Ministries of Education, Finance, Trade, Agriculture, and Defense, whereas the Socialists were given the Interior, Justice, Social Affairs, and Transport. Where a Socialist minister was appointed, he was seconded by a People's Party undersecretary, and vice versa. At first, the division of power was also reflected in the highest offices because the state president was a Socialist and the chancellor a conservative. Below these major appointments, proportional distribution was used to fill the many positions open to government patronage, such as those in the nationalized industries, the post office, the railroads, the banks, and the local and national administrations. The negotiations over the division of posts were always long and difficult. They concerned not only the appointments, but also the legislation to be introduced during the next years. The decisions in the Coalition Committee had to be unanimous.

This system, despite its obvious advantages, was strongly criticized because it did indeed limit the power of the legislature. Major decisions were made outside the normal parliamentary channels; the legislature usually accepted unanimously recommendations made by these outside committees. There was also no functioning political opposition; the Freedom Party represented only a small fraction of the total membership of the Nationalrat. With this close cooperation between the major parties the elections had as their primary result the readjustment of the index for the proportional distribution of offices.

Like the Proporz system, the new institutions of the social partnership were to prove extremely effective in securing domestic social peace. In March 1957, when the government was facing the problem of inflation, it established the Parity Commission for Prices and Wages. The intent was to avoid past disasters by bringing together representatives of the trade unions and the employers to make decisions in the common interest. The commission was composed of two representatives from each of the four great economic interest groups: the Chamber of Commerce, the Chambers of Agriculture, the Chamber of Labor, and the Austrian Trade Union Federation. They were joined by four government representatives: the chancellor and the ministers of interior, trade and industry, and social affairs, but after 1966 these members could not vote.

This commission, which became a second government for economic affairs, could function well because of the effectiveness of the associations that were already in existence. Of the four, the Chamber of Commerce was the eldest. Organized in 1848, it represented employers in industry, trade, and transport, including the nationalized sectors. The Chambers of Agriculture were established in the 1920s to support the interests of the small independent farmers. The Chamber of Labor, also dating from the 1920s, was divided into separate sections for industrial workers, salaried employees, and transport workers. These chambers were self-governing bodies with a compulsory membership for anyone connected with their activities; their dues were thus in effect taxes. More effective than private interest groups, they had legal powers over their members. The organizations were federally based, with separate chambers for each province.

The fourth partner, the Austrian Federation of Trade Unions, was the central office for fifteen unions, each organized on an industrial base. Although membership in a union was voluntary, about two-thirds of the Austrian work force was represented by the federation. As in the interwar years, organized workers, numbering 1.5 million, played a major political role in the state.

Although the basic task of the Parity Commission was to set wages and prices, it also established general economic policy. The commission's influence was to prove anything but revolutionary. In the next years it helped preserve a stable relationship between wages and profits, and it avoided any measures aiming at a redistribution of wealth. It was to the interest of all of the participants to increase production and to ensure the economic prosperity of the country so that there would be a greater share for all the social partners. The representatives also became adept at compromise, since here too agreement had to be unanimous.

The decisions reached by the commission were usually accepted with little opposition. They could also be enforced not only by government enactment, but also through the offices of the chambers and the OGB, whose representatives on the commission were usually the top officials of the associations. Since these members were chosen within their own organizations, they were in a different position from the representatives sent to the parliament, who had to give a full public accounting of their actions and who could be removed by the voters at the next election. The organizations also, as could be expected, had close ties with the major parties; the Chambers of Commerce and Agriculture were in touch with the People's Party, and the OGB with the Socialists. Although these relationships could all be criticized, the fact that the social partnership functioned well overrode other considerations.

Neither the coalition government nor the social partnership could have succeeded had not Austria enjoyed a period of economic prosperity. "The Austrian miracle," that is, the development of a modern industrial economy, arose out of postwar conditions that at first appeared bleak. In fact, the basis for a favorable development had already been laid in the years after the Anschluss when the Nazi leadership had at once acted to incorporate Austrian resources into its military economic program. The major achievement was the building up of heavy industry and the shifting of the industrial center westward. At this time a steel mill and other plants associated with the Hermann Göring Works were constructed at Linz, an aluminum plant was built at Ranshofen, and installations for hydroelectric power were placed in various regions. Austrian development was helped by its association with the German industrial economy, with its modern organization and techniques and its experienced personnel. Once the war commenced the government took control of mining, iron smelting, and steel and engineering works, all essential for military production. When Allied air attacks increased in frequency and severity after 1942, some German industries were moved to Austria. During this period there was also a shift toward a greater concentration of industry and an emphasis on the production of capital at the expense of consumer goods. All of these developments were to aid the postwar Austrian economy.

The division of Austria into zones after the war at first caused major economic difficulties. However, as we have seen, the Austrian economy benefited from the Cold War tensions and the determination of the Western powers to rebuild the European economy as a whole, including that of Austria and West Germany. Basic to the recovery was the Marshall Plan and the support given to the rebuilding and expanding of enterprises, many of which had been founded or reorganized during the Nazi period. The nationalization acts of 1946 and 1947 brought under state control property that was owned by German nationals or that had been expropriated by the German authorities, as well as those industries which had been founded in this period. Some difficulties were encountered because the nationalization was not systematic; property was often taken simply because it was defined as a German asset. An advantage to the state, however, was that the enterprises were acquired by what amounted to confiscation; only non-German owners were compensated. The Austrian state thus for a very small price came to control property whose value was estimated at over a billion dollars in 1960s currency. When Austria acquired the nationalized industries of the Soviet zone after 1955, it became the country with the highest degree of public ownership among the Western nations. From the prewar years, the state inherited control over public utilities, such as gas, water, electricity, and the railroads. After 1946 an enormous industrial empire came into its possession, including iron and steel works, petroleum refineries, and plants producing machinery, electrical equipment, and fertilizers. The government also had control over the banks, the major power resources, and the Danube Steamship Company.

Together with the previous acquisitions, the nationalization laws meant that by 1972, 20 percent of the gross national product came from enterprises in the public sector, which employed 29 percent of the labor force. About two-thirds of Austrian industry was controlled directly or indirectly by the state. These enterprises were organized in much the same manner as private institutions, with the exception that government officials rather than private owners or representatives of stockholders held the top managerial offices. These positions were at first assigned on the basis of Proporz, a system that often brought incompetent men into important positions. In its treatment of the nationalized property the coalition governments put the major emphasis not on making profits, but on maintaining full employment and on political and social harmony.

Although serious problems were to arise later, Austrian industry in the immediate postwar period benefited from the general European demand for its products, including machine tools, iron, steel, aluminum, nonferrous metals, and heavy machinery. The nationalized industries operated profitably, and the institution of the social partnership assured the cooperation of labor and management. Strikes were avoided and close control produced apparent social harmony.

It can thus be seen that in the postwar years Austria developed political, social, and economic institutions that were in many ways unique. The coalition government, the social partnership, and the large degree of public ownership created an interlocking system that brought material prosperity and a large degree of public satisfaction. The Austrian people, basically conservative, with a strong tradition of state regulation and reliance on public institutions for social services, supported the system, which was based on compromising radical stands and avoiding adventurous policies.

The primary role played by the parties and the large associations and the limitations that this condition placed on the parliamentary system need to be reemphasized. It is important to note that no law could even be introduced into the Nationalrat before it had been approved by the appropriate group: a chamber, the OGB, or a political or parliamentary committee. Moreover, in the assembly the representatives followed the directives of their party leaders. Thus important legislative decisions were in fact made before they were formally presented to parliament for public debate. This situation also explains why most measures were accepted unanimously.

In addition, there developed a substantial degree of overlapping among the members of the parties, the interest groups, and the bureaucracy. Officials in the chambers or the OGB were often the leaders of the political parties; many also became representatives in the assembly. In the same manner public employees could hold high positions in the parties and organizations and also enter parliament. There was in fact a tendency for civil servants as well as party and organization officials to run for office. It was estimated that 60 percent of the representatives in the Nationalrat had as their main occupation employment by the state, a party, or a special-interest association. A state employee who became a representative kept his salary. The management of the state-owned enterprises showed a similar pattern.

The intertwining of the political, social, and economic direction in the state and the presence of the same people in party, state, and organization offices caused, of course, many problems of policy and practice and left the door open for corruption. The system, nevertheless, worked during these years when Austria needed a period without controversy. It could only have been possible at a time when the political parties recognized the necessity of modifying their ideological programs and of placing major emphasis on cooperation and calm.

INTERNAL POLITICAL DEVELOPMENT, 1955–1966: THE GRAND COALITION

When considering Austrian politics in these years, the existence of the previously discussed institutions must be kept constantly in mind. To a large extent they account for the fact that only one controversy, that over the possible return of the Habsburg pretender, caused a major domestic uproar. Some incidents took place that made newspaper headlines, but they had no lasting effect on the functioning of state institutions. Up until this time the grand coalition had brought benefits to both the participating parties. Although at some time each had thought of forming a "small coalition" with the weak third party, neither had done so. Throughout this period the balance between the major parties remained very close. In the elections for the Nationalrat in 1956, 1959, 1962, and 1966 and for the presidency in 1957, 1963, and 1965, relatively small shifts in votes determined the outcome. As the years passed, however, there were increasing disagreements between the parties, and many began to criticize the coalition government and its restricting influence on parliamentary life.

The first election after the signing of the treaty took place in May 1956. The chief issue debated was the condition of the nationalized industries and their administration. The USIA concerns had now reverted to Austrian ownership, but after ten years of maladministration, they were in a poor condition and not competitive. The election resulted in a victory for the People's Party, which won an additional eight seats at the expense of the Freedom Party: the distribution of seats was eighty-two for the OVP, seventy-four for the Socialists, six for the Freedom Party, and three for the Communists. This success was regarded as a personal triumph for Chancellor Raab, who enjoyed the prestige of having negotiated the treaty. A coalition government was again formed, with a proportion of ten to eight. The question of the national industries was settled through a compromise solution by which these enterprises were placed under the jurisdiction of a special administration and a board on which both parties were represented. Three years later a further reorganization resulted in the placing of the industries under the direct authority of the chancellor.

Since the election cost the Socialists votes, they were forced to review their general position. Continuing their move toward the center, the party leaders recognized that they could not base their campaigns on appeals to the working class alone; they needed middle-class and Catholic votes to win a majority in the future. In May 1958 a new party program with this aim was accepted; it was the work of a committee under the chairmanship of Bruno Kreisky. Meanwhile, in January 1957 Körner died; in the succeeding election for the presidency the Socialist candidate Schärf won, but by only 100,000 votes.

Bruno Pitterman replaced Schärf as head of the party and vice-chancellor in the coalition government.

The elections of May 1959 marked definite gains for the Socialists. As in 1953 they won more votes than their opponents, but because of the electoral system, they again gained a minority of the seats. The division was seventy-nine for the People's Party, seventy-eight for the Socialists, and eight for the Freedom Party. The Communists were left without a single place. Their decline was a direct result of the Soviet suppression of the Hungarian revolution. Thereafter, this party was to play an insignificant role in Austrian politics. With this close balance between the SPO and the OVP parties the cabinet remained much as before, except that Kreisky was appointed foreign minister. His leadership in negotiating the South Tirol controversy and in meeting the difficult problem of joining the European economic associations will be discussed later. He also in June 1960 succeeded in reaching an accord with the Vatican. After Raab resigned, he was replaced in May 1961 by Alphons Gorbach, who added two younger men from the People's Party to his government, Josef Klaus for finance and Karl Schleinzer for defense.

In the election of November 1962 the People's Party regained some of its losses, but it still did not command an absolute majority. The distribution was eighty-one seats for the People's Party, seventy-six for the Socialists, and eight for the Freedom Party. In March 1963 Gorbach, now quarreling with those in his party who wanted reforms, reorganized his government without Klaus, but including the controversial Socialist politician Franz Olah as minister of interior. New presidential elections in April 1963 resulted in the reelection of Schärf, with 55 percent of the vote, and the defeat of Raab, who had run with the strong backing of Gorbach.

This setback was reflected in the People's Party meeting in Klagenfurt in September 1963. Already, after the losses in

1959, there had been criticism of the party leadership. At this time the reformers, led by Klaus and Hermann Withalm, triumphed. Klaus was elected as party chairman although he did not have a government position. This younger group was to prove less willing to compromise with the Socialists. One of the strengths underlying the grand coalition had been the fact that the leaders of both parties were united by their war experiences; many in fact had been in prison together. This generation, whether belonging to the left or the right, was determined to assure that the events of 1934 would never again occur. The men who were coming to power did not share this feeling to so great an extent. They saw the negative aspects of coalition rule, and they came to prefer a one-party government. Moreover, the postwar leaders were leaving: Raab died in 1964; Schärf and Figl in 1965. In April 1964 this change of leadership was shown in a reorganization of the government; Gorbach was replaced by Klaus, with Bruno Pitterman as vice-chancellor.

The Socialists were also having internal quarrels, the most important of which involved the activities of Franz Olah, who was the president of the OGB from 1959 until he resigned to become minister of interior in 1963. An ambitious and powerful figure, he came into conflict with the majority of his party and was expelled. In September 1965 he then formed the Demokratisch-Fortschrittliche Partei (Democratic Progressive Party), which was to campaign in the elections of 1966 and 1970. At this time the Socialists, despite these problems, were able to keep control of the presidency. After the death of Schärf, the office was contested by Gorbach and Franz Jonas, the mayor of Vienna, who won by less than sixty-four thousand votes.

By the elections of 1966 many in both parties were becoming increasingly critical of the coalition. Moreover, the association had broken down already on the very controversial issue of the return of the Habsburg heir to Austria, a question that dominated politics in the early 1960s. Although members of the Habsburg family had been expelled by a law of 1919, they could return if they gave a declaration of loyalty to the republic, an action that many had taken. This measure was repealed during the Schuschnigg regime, but Otto had made no attempt to take advantage of the favorable situation, because he was aware of the adamant position of the Little Entente and Nazi Germany toward a possible Habsburg restoration. After the Second World War, the Habsburg exclusion again became law, and it was included in the State Treaty. The Habsburg question also involved a possible return of some of the confiscated property. Otto was perfectly aware that he could not ever become emperor or regain lost Habsburg possessions, but he did want to return to Austria. He was willing to make a declaration of loyalty, but he would not promise to desist from political activities.

The entire question had major political repercussions, and it aroused strong emotions in particular among the older generation of politicians with roots in the prewar period. The Socialist position was clear: the party opposed returning property or allowing Otto to enter the country. The question was more difficult for the People's Party, since it had a monarchist right wing. In July 1961 Otto's lawyers presented his declaration renouncing his rights to the throne. The government split; after an evenly divided vote in the Ministerial Council of seventy-nine to seventy-eight, it was decided that a simple lack of agreement would be registered. Otto then turned to the courts, and in May 1963 the Administrative Court of Justice found that his declaration was in order. Nevertheless, in June the Socialist Party and the Freedom Party joined to express their disapproval of Otto's return. The coalition thus broke on the question. In order to make the situation easier for the People's Party, Otto agreed not to press the issue until new elections were held. He finally made a visit in 1967, when a purely People's Party government was in control.

The elections of March 1966 were to have a special significance, since they marked the end of the coalition that had run Austrian affairs since 1945. In this election the Socialists started with some handicaps. Olah, as we have seen, had formed a separate party, which was to take away almost 150,000 votes, a significant number when the closeness of Austrian elections is considered. Moreover, after its failures in previous elections, the Communist Party decided to contest only one seat and advised its adherents to vote for the Socialists. When this support was not firmly rejected by the Socialists' leaders, the People's Party found that it could exploit the electorate's anti-Communist sentiments. The Socialists also lost votes in connection with an incident known as the Fussach affair, which involved the minister for communications and electricity, the Socialist Otto Probst. In his position he had control of the shipping on Lake Constance. When a new ship was built for this service, his ministry named it *Karl Renner* after a man who was, after all, not only a Socialist, but also a great Austrian statesman. Nevertheless, enormous protests came from Vorarlberg, a traditionally conservative region, which reached their height in a demonstration against Probst when he visited Fussach in November 1964. The name of the ship was subsequently changed to *Vorarlberg*.

In the campaign Klaus called for an end to the coalition; the Socialists supported its continuation since they had less hope of gaining a majority. In the elections the People's Party won an absolute majority of eighty-five seats, whereas the Socialists received seventy-four and the Freedom Party six. Negotiations were then carried on for the possible maintenance of the coalition. As the clear victor, the People's Party naturally wished a larger measure of control in the government. Although both Pitterman and Kreisky supported the continuation of the association, the majority of the Socialist Party rejected the conditions presented. As a result, Josef Klaus organized the first one-party government since the war and brought the great coalition to an end.

FOREIGN POLICY

During the period of the great coalition the Austrian government was able to conduct what was in general a successful foreign policy, within the limitations imposed by its neutral status. The division of Europe into two armed camps had particularly dangerous implications for Austria, given its geographic position. There were few illusions about what another war would mean in an age of nuclear weapons even for nations not involved in actual combat. As far as specific problems were concerned, the great coalition had to deal with three major ones: the South Tirol question, the possibility of association in the European Economic Community, and the adjustment of relations with the Communist eastern neighbors.

South Tirol   After 1955 the fate of South Tirol was the problem that aroused the most feeling among the Austrian public. It dominated the first four years of the 1960s and was one of the chief controversies with which Raab had to deal during his period in office. The issue involved chiefly the status of the Italian province of Bozen (Bolzano), which under Habsburg rule had formed the southern half of the province of Tirol. In 1961 the region had a population of 232,717 Germans, 128,271 Italians, and 12,594 Ladins, who speak a Latin-based language. All but 7,000 of the Italians had arrived after 1910. The strong provincial self-consciousness of the German population was concentrated chiefly in the Catholic peasantry.

After the First World War, as we have seen, Italy was given South Tirol in a gross violation of the principle of self-determination so that Italy would have a strong strategic frontier. During the Nazi period Hitler had abandoned claims to the area in order to maintain his friendship with Mussolini. During the war the population had developed some quite unrealistic expectations. Since Italy was just as much a defeated enemy power as Germany, the Tiroleans thought that the victorious Allies might either award their land to Austria or give it wide rights of autonomy. Soon after the end of the war the Austrian government tried to obtain one of these alternatives. Karl Gruber, who was in charge of foreign policy then, was himself a Tirolean. Austrian hopes were again disappointed because of the obvious requirements of power politics. For both East and West, Italy, with its population of 45.6 million, was a nation far more important to placate in the sharp differences of the time than Austria. The Soviet Union did not wish to alienate Italy's strong Communist Party; the United States did not want to offend either the anti-Communist Italians or the Italian-American voter at home. Faced with this difficult situation, Gruber met with the Italian foreign minister, Alcide de Gasperi, and negotiated in September 1946 an agreement that left the area under Italian control, but granted Bozen province wide autonomous rights. The agreement was annexed to the Italian peace treaty in 1947. The intent of the pact was, however, negated by Italian actions. The Italian constitution of 1948 included the entire area under discussion in a region called Trentino-Alto Adige. The enlargement of the administrative divisions placed the Tiroleans under a jurisdiction in which there were twice as many Italians as Germans. As the industrialization of the area increased, it could be expected that more Italians would arrive.

Dissatisfied with their conditions, the Tiroleans turned to Vienna for support. Very little could be done for them until after 1955, when Austria again became an independent state. From that time on the status of South Tirol became not only an international, but also a domestic issue. Austrian public opinion compelled the government to back Tirolean claims vigorously. In October 1956 it sent a memorandum to Rome suggesting that a committee be set up to investigate the situation. The Italian government replied that this matter concerned only its own internal affairs and that the Gruber–de Gasperi agreement had been fulfilled. This exchange marked the beginning of a long period of controversy. Unable to make any progress on a bilateral basis, the Austrian government took the matter to the General Assembly of the United Nations in October 1960; this body adopted a resolution directing the two sides to negotiate. Beyond the fact that the Austrian right to intervene was thus recognized, this action did little to aid the Austrian position. Meanwhile, within the area the ardent national groups started a campaign of terror bombings. Since these measures had worked elsewhere, notably in Cyprus, the activists hoped to attract world attention to their problems. Many of these groups gained supplies from and used as a sanctuary both Austrian and German territory.

In September 1961 the Italian government took a step toward solving the problem. A committee of nineteen moderates, including seven recognized South Tirolean leaders, was set up to try to reach a settlement. Although its final report of April 1964 became the basis of the agreement attained five years later, some questions still had to be met, including the right of Austria to continue to intervene and

support Tirolean grievances. When another period of stalemate followed, the terror tactics were again renewed. The
Italian government was extremely dissatisfied with what it
regarded as the intentionally lax Austrian border control. In
June 1967 Italy vetoed Austria's association with the Common Market as a reprisal.

A settlement was not reached until the end of 1969, when
all sides involved agreed to a 137-point program that gave
wider autonomous rights to Bozen, including the use of German as an official language. The agreement was to be worked
out step by step on the basis of a timetable. When each stage
had been completed, Austria and Italy were to acknowledge
formally its fulfillment; at the end Austria was to make a
final declaration. The Austrian government agreed that the
International Court at The Hague would judge disputes and
that it would not intervene during this period. This settlement was accepted by a South Tirolean assembly in November 1969 by a vote of 52.9 percent in favor, 44.5 percent
against, and 2.6 percent abstaining. The agreements were
then approved by the Italian and Austrian parliaments in
December. Many Austrians were not enthusiastic about the
pact because of the limitation of the Austrian right to intervene. Since both the Socialists and the Freedom Party took
this attitude, the treaty was accepted by the narrow margin
of eighty-three to seventy-nine.

The European Economic Associations   Although the Austrian
declaration of neutrality had enabled the government to obtain Soviet consent to a peace treaty, this condition brought
up certain problems. It was obvious that the state could not
associate itself in military organizations such as NATO, but
in the 1950s the West European states formed economic as
well as political associations, which it was to Austria's advantage to join. In April 1948 the nations participating in

the Marshall Plan formed a permanent group, the Organization for European Economic Cooperation (OEEC), with its headquarters in Paris. Austria had representatives on the council of the organization. This Western action was countered by the formation of the Council for Mutual Economic Assistance (COMECON) among the Socialist-bloc nations in 1949. After the end of the Marshall Plan in 1952 the OEEC continued its functions and became the center of a move to integrate the West European economies. On this basis six nations – France, West Germany, Italy, Belgium, the Netherlands, and Luxemburg – went a step further. In 1951 they had already formed the European Coal and Steel Community, which had been successful; in May 1957 the same six nations established the European Economic Community (EEC), also called the Common Market. The original idea of the association was that the nations over a period of years would work to eliminate all the barriers between them and to amalgamate their economic systems. Each member surrendered a degree of its sovereignty in certain areas. The Common Market thus had a political as well as an economic significance.

The close relationship of these states and the relative success of the endeavor were harmful to the nonmember states. Britain, with its involvement with its own Commonwealth nations, was in a particularly difficult situation. In January 1960 seven European states – Britain, Denmark, Norway, Sweden, Switzerland, Portugal, and Austria – set up the European Free Trade Association, or EFTA, a combination without the political implications of the Common Market. The problem for Austria was that its main partners in trade were Italy and Germany, and the EEC was the stronger association. Austrian neutrality, however, made the question of participation doubtful; Article 224 of the Rome agreement establishing the Common Market provided that the obligations would apply also in time of war. Already the Austrian government had decided that it could not join the Coal and Steel Community for similar reasons.

The position of the EFTA members became more difficult when in 1961 Britain decided that it would have to apply for association with the EEC, but with special stipulations. In October 1961 the three neutrals, Switzerland, Sweden, and Austria, decided to seek associate membership with limited obligations. The Soviet government immediately protested the Austrian action as a violation of neutrality and of treaty provisions forbidding political and economic associations with Germany. The Austrian government replied that since the neutral status was a matter of Austrian law alone, it would be the sole judge of the definition of the terms, a position that was henceforth maintained in answer to repeated Soviet objections. The French veto of the British application in 1963 did not prevent the continuation of the Austrian negotiations. As we have seen, Italy vetoed Austria's entrance and maintained this position until 1969, although its intransigence was not the sole hindrance to Austrian adherence.

The question of Austrian membership in the EEC became a matter of party conflict. At first the chief proponent was the People's Party. Over half of the Austrian trade was with the members of the "inner six"; most of the agricultural exports went to these countries. Moreover, at first, with Konrad Adenauer and Charles de Gaulle in charge, the chief EEC countries had comparatively conservative governments. For this reason the Socialists were at first suspicious of what seemed an organization with a definite political orientation. However, when the British Labour Party and the German Social Democrats, under the leadership of Willy Brandt, supported the association, the Austrian Socialists also changed. The Freedom Party, which was against the neutrality statute anyway, was highly favorable to the EEC, which would bring Austria closer to West Germany. Most Austrians of all parties were convinced that if the EEC continued the process of economic integration, EFTA could not survive the competition.

In 1971 Britain finally entered the Common Market. In July 1972 agreements were signed by the EEC with Austria and other members of EFTA, which gave those states certain tariff privileges. The Socialist position at this time was that Austria could not be a full member of the Common Market, unless a general European community were established, without violating the neutrality stipulations. Such a condition could not occur without an agreement between the Eastern and Western blocs, a remote possibility at this time.

Relations with the Socialist Bloc   Although the Austrian constitution called for political neutrality, this stipulation was always modified by the recognition that the term could not mean moral neutrality. The sympathies of all political parties, except, of course, the Communist, were with the Western nations. Two events on Austria's borders were bound to influence Austrian public opinion decisively – the Soviet interventions in Hungary in 1956 and in Czechoslovakia in 1968. The first event, coming so soon after the signing of the State Treaty, showed the difficulties of neutrality. The Austrian government officials, the press, and the three major parties all denounced the action. The KPO was severely damaged by the intervention and lost a third of its members. The chief practical problem for the government was the control of the borders, since the Hungarians fought the Soviet Army. Streams of refugees crossed the frontiers; Austria received about 170,000 for at least a short stay.

The problem was not so difficult in 1968 because the Czechs did not fight. Nevertheless, Austria gave temporary asylum to over 90,000 people. This second intervention by the Soviet Army did even greater damage to the Austrian Communist Party. The Central Committee at first condemned the action and thus split the group. Later, after the victory of the pro-Soviet faction, Ernst Fischer, the leading theoretician, was expelled from the party for his continued criticism of Soviet actions.

Despite the ideological differences the Austrian government did have considerable connections with both the Soviet Union and the East Bloc countries. Moreover, in 1962, for example, 14.8 percent of the Austrian exports went to Eastern Europe. In 1964 the share of Austrian trade with COMECON states was 17.5 percent. This outlet was particularly important for the disposal of the products of the former USIA industries, which were not competitive with those of the West and were dependent on the Eastern trade. Despite the repeated Soviet warnings about Austrian cooperation with the Common Market, relations with the Soviet Union were not unfavorable. In July 1958 Raab went to Moscow, where he was granted a 50 percent reduction in the oil deliveries owed to the Soviet Union under the treaty.

Moreover, the Austrian government did take certain actions that were either favorable to the Soviet position or at least in line with the upholding of its neutrality against Western pressure. In 1948 an international conference of both Eastern and Western representatives was held in Belgrade to formulate new regulations to control the Danube River. Austria was allowed only to send an observer. The Western Allies wanted to restore the Danube's previous status as an international waterway under the authority of a commission that had British, French, and Italian representatives, as well as those of the riparian governments. At the meeting the Soviet Union used the principle of majority rule to gain the settlement it wished. The river was to be regulated by a commission of riparian states to the exclusion of outside powers. Although most of the Western states refused to sign the final agreement, Austria in 1960 joined the Soviet-dominated Danube Commission, which included Czechoslovakian, Hungarian, Yugoslav, Romanian, Bulgarian, and Soviet members, with West Germany admitted only as an observer with no voting rights.

Only one flagrant violation of Austrian neutrality occurred. In July 1958 U.S. Air Force planes flew over the country without permission in an action connected with the Lebanon crisis of that year. The Austrian government protested and an official U.S. apology was delivered. Permission for return flights was requested and granted. Austria's determination to maintain its neutral status against both the Western and the Communist camps was thus demonstrated.

THE PEOPLE'S PARTY GOVERNMENT, 1966–1970

The OVP administration that came to power in 1966, under the leadership of Josef Klaus, had the bad luck to be in office during a period of relative economic decline. The long period of Austrian prosperity, which had commenced in 1953, at this time showed signs of weakening, with the low point reached in 1967. Old fears of unemployment were reawakened. To meet this situation the government raised some taxes, reduced services, and accepted a larger budget deficit. It should be noted that although the Socialists were now a genuine opposition party, a new experience for post-1945 Austria, both parties were careful not to disturb the political climate.

The OVP government also had to accept the responsibility for the implementation of a reorganization of the state industries; these measures had been agreed to by the Socialists under the coalition government, but they were not put into effect until December 1966. The number of enterprises was reduced to twenty-four, but this sector of the economy still employed over a hundred thousand people, that is, more than a fifth of those in industry. The state enterprises at this time accounted for over a fourth of Austrian production.

In this period the People's Party was also faced with other political difficulties. The labor unions were at the height of their strength, with the OGB representing about 1.5 million workers. In the second half of 1968 they began to press for the introduction of the forty-hour week. Supported by the SPO, the unions backed an initiative petition that gained nine hundred thousand signatures. December 1969 saw the passage of the first acts that were to lead to the introduction of the forty-hour week by January 1975.

While facing an increasingly strong labor opposition, the People's Party government saw its farm constituency steadily declining. Whereas about 23.7 percent of the population was engaged in farming in 1959, that number was to sink to 9.9 percent by 1977. Despite the obvious need to attract a larger segment of the population, in particular salaried employees, the party kept its traditional program, with the emphasis on Christian and family values and property rights. The next election, held in 1970, was a defeat for the party and demonstrated the need for a wider program and a more aggressive policy.

The first fifteen years of Austrian affairs after the regaining of independence in 1955 should perhaps be compared with the similar period after 1918 in order to appreciate the considerable achievements of the second era. Although the Second Republic adopted the political institutions of its predecessor, the spirit in which they were administered was quite different. In the first years after World War II both parties were led by men who had lived through the turbulent interwar and wartime period; the conviction of "never again" dominated their thinking. The coalition certainly did not function without friction, but the conflicts were not great enough to prevent constructive cooperation. The proportional division of offices and the social partnership, by providing a framework within which economic and social problems could be worked out, also contributed to the tranquility of the country.

The contrast in economic development to the post–World War I period was also impressive. Without the burden of major reparation payments and with Marshall Plan assistance, the industrial base of the country was expanded. Labor problems were largely avoided by the cooperation of the parties and the offices of the social partnership. Although agriculture was declining, adequate food supplies were available. In foreign policy, despite the limitations imposed by neutrality, Austria became an associate member of the EEC, and a settlement was reached over South Tirol. After independence, as we have seen, the country was governed by the great coalition, followed by four years of People's Party rule. A Socialist government was now to come to power to hold office for an even longer time.

7

THE SOCIALIST
GOVERNMENTS:
THE KREISKY ERA

THE Socialist defeat in 1966 had demonstrated the divisions within the party and the declining appeal of its program to the electorate. It had not been able to win supporters among the farmers or, even more important, among the middle class whose votes would be essential for victory in the future. Socialist and Marxist slogans of the past would obviously not attract this group, which was also increasingly influenced by its aversion to events in the neighboring Communist-dominated countries. The Socialist program of 1958 made some moves toward meeting this problem when it declared itself for all the working people, including the self-employed, agricultural workers, and those in the professions. The program also emphasized democratic values, renounced dictatorship, and stood for a mixed economy. However, it still continued the Socialist support of ending class differences and redistributing wealth; the statement of policy concluded: "The party fights for a new classless society and thus for a new Socialist humanism."[26]

The major problem faced by both the SPO and the OVP was that the social basis of their constituencies was changing. As in all modern industrial societies the population in

[26] Melanie A. Sully, *Political Parties and Elections in Austria* (London: C. Hurst and Co., 1981), p. 61.

Austria was shifting in a direction that made the interwar programs of the great parties to some extent obsolete. By 1977, 49.3 percent of the working population was employed in the service sector of the economy. Although another 40.8 percent was employed in manufacturing and mining and a relatively small 9.9 percent in agriculture and forestry, it was obvious, given the close balance between the parties, that elections would be determined by the votes of salaried workers, government employees, those who ran small businesses, and others in the service sector.

The need for a new political orientation that would hold the middle ground and attract the swing vote was recognized by the Socialist Party and discussed at the party congress held in January 1967. The aim was to win this central group of voters, which was composed to a great extent of salaried employees aged between twenty and thirty-five who were not ideologically oriented, but who were chiefly concerned with those matters which affected them personally, such as full employment, economic growth, and ever-higher living standards. To gain their support the party obviously had to change its image as an aggressive working-class party devoted to the struggle with the bourgeoisie; certainly Marxist slogans about the "class struggle" and religion as "an opium for the people" had to be abandoned. The party needed to make it possible for the middle class, including the Catholics, to vote Socialist.

The shift in emphasis, in fact, the abandonment of most of the previous ideological base of the party, was accompanied by a change in leadership. Pitterman had been too doctrinaire and had supported programs that had failed. The new course was to be represented by Bruno Kreisky, who had a pragmatic approach and stood for an open party. At this conference he was elected to head the party by a strong majority; Pitterman thereafter directed the activities in the

Nationalrat. Kreisky was supported by the unions and the provincial organizations; after his selection a reorganization gave more power to the local leaderships as against Vienna, which had previously dominated party affairs.

KREISKY BECOMES CHANCELLOR

Bruno Kreisky was to become not only the leading Austrian political figure of the next years, but also a major influence in international affairs. Born in Vienna in 1911, he came from a wealthy middle-class family of Moravian origin. Although of a Jewish background, he declared himself an agnostic. As a member of a Socialist youth group, he had become acquainted with the poverty and misery connected with the massive unemployment of the interwar years. Because of his association with the illegal Socialist Party, he spent time in prison during the period of authoritarian rule in the 1930s and after the Anschluss. He was, however, allowed to emigrate to Sweden, where he worked as a journalist and was active in Socialist circles. In exile he became acquainted with and was particularly attracted to Swedish Socialist policy. In 1940 he met the German Social Democratic leader, Willy Brandt, with whom he was to continue to have a close association in the future. After the war he returned to Austria and entered state service. He was actively engaged in the major diplomatic negotiations of the time, including those in regard to the State Treaty, South Tirol, and the European economic associations. In 1953 he became state secretary for foreign affairs; in 1959 he was made foreign minister in the government of Julius Raab.

At the same time he rose rapidly through the party ranks. In 1956 he entered parliament as a deputy for St. Pölten in Lower Austria. His successes in foreign policy gave him prestige, but also the reputation of being primarily a diplomat.

Bruno Kreisky

After his assumption of party leadership in 1967, he made a great effort to travel through the country to establish personal links with the Socialist voters and the party officials. Within a year he was able not only to secure his personal authority, but also to bring a divided party together and give it a new appearance.

In many ways Kreisky was an ideal political leader for the time. With the growing importance of television in campaigning, he was able to project an attractive and popular image; he gave the impression of having both tolerance and humor. He was also able and willing to carry on the type of campaign familiar in the United States. He traveled around the country and talked directly to the electorate. He was to become the most popular Austrian political figure of the postwar era.

The Kreisky leadership was backed by a modified party program. Although the previous stand was not entirely rejected, a new direction was taken with the aim of winning the middle, but at the same time not losing the left to the Communist Party or causing a party split. With the realization that the majority of votes were not cast by industrial workers, an emphasis was placed on ideas that would attract everyone, such as the importance of the individual in the Austrian concept of social democracy and the superiority of democratic government over Communist dictatorship. Attempts were also made to attract voters on the right and to appeal to those who, while not approving of all aspects of the program, would nevertheless vote for Socialist candidates. Once again the SPO was declared the party of all the working people, white collar, blue collar, and self-employed alike.

In the electoral campaign in 1970 the Socialist Party thus adopted a vague and noncontroversial "center" program designed to win as many voters as possible. Kreisky campaigned "for a modern Austria," promising reform but no revolutionary changes. Speaking at a time when the Soviet invasion of Czechoslovakia was still in the public mind, he strongly denounced Communism. In a speech given in Eisenstadt, close to the Hungarian border, in October 1969, he spoke against dictatorships whether they were Fascist or Communist. His party also firmly rejected Communist support.

In the elections of March 1970 the Socialists won a plurality of 81 seats as against 79 for the OVP, with 5 for the FPO. Since the Freedom Party leader, Peter, had during the campaign rejected the idea of a coalition with the Socialists, they carried on negotiations to revive the great coalition. With the failure to achieve agreement, Kreisky chose a minority government. In this administration Rudolf Kirchschläger, a practicing Catholic affiliated with no party, became foreign minister. In October 1971, in a second election under a new electoral law, the Socialists gained the majority, with 50.04 percent of the votes. In an assembly of 183 seats the Socialists held 93, the OVP 80, and the FPO 10. After providing the nonvoting speaker, the SPO was left with a majority of 2. The Communist Party still did not have a seat, although its share of the vote had risen from 0.98 percent to 1.35 percent. After this victory Kreisky did not consider the formation of a coalition. Kirchschläger continued as foreign minister; Fred Sinowatz entered the government as minister for education.

The SPO not only controlled the parliament, but continued to elect the presidents. In April 1971 Franz Jonas defeated Kurt Waldheim, who then was chosen the general secretary of the United Nations. After Jonas died in April 1974, he was replaced by another Socialist-supported candidate, Kirchschläger, who, it will be remembered, was nonparty. In the election held in June 1974 he received 51.7 percent of the votes; in May 1980 his reelection was unopposed.

In control of the government, the Socialists introduced a program of social reform whose main provisions called only for moderate changes that were generally approved of by the electorate at large. The party rhetoric, vague and noncontroversial, emphasized that the goal was "a modern, just, and humane society." Many of the measures represented

302

merely the extension of existing programs or had already been accepted by the OVP and the social partners through the existing system. Since no proposals were introduced that would upset any large group, most of the changes passed unanimously in the Nationalrat. Thus benefits to workers and employees were extended; the term for military service was reduced from nine to six months; the age of majority was cut from twenty-one to nineteen years; legislation on the equality of men and women was passed; the administration of the state-owned radio and television was reformed. In education free textbooks and travel were provided for students, and changes were introduced in the organization and governance of institutions of higher education. In 1975 the forty-hour week, previously passed, came into effect.

At this time also a new criminal code was adopted, some sections of which caused a strong reaction. The major protests were over the measures concerning abortion, which provoked a storm of controversy that continued unabated over the years. Before the reform, laws dating from the previous century designated abortion as a crime carrying a prison sentence of one to five years. The question was under discussion during the interwar years, but no changes were made. In the 1970s the Socialist Party supported legislation approving abortions on the mother's request through the third month of pregnancy (the so-called *Fristenlösung*). In November 1973 the measure passed, but over the combined opposition of the OVP and FPO. The vehemently critical stand of the Catholic church and other groups led to the organization of the movement called Action Life and the circulation of a petition that obtained almost nine hundred thousand signatures. In March and April 1976 the Nationalrat again discussed the issue, but did not change the decision.

At this time the Socialist government benefited from the generally good economic conditions. The budgets showed the largest deficits yet, but the general public was satisfied with the situation. At the time of the 1975 elections unemployment was down and the inflation rate of 9 percent was perceived as low in comparison to that in other countries. The agreements with the EEC, signed in 1972, brought benefits that were felt at this time. The reorganization of the state industries was also under way.

In the electoral campaign the SPO presented its previous program and also made full use of the personal popularity of Kreisky. Directing its appeals to the center, the party placed emphasis on its achievements and campaigned on issues such as the improvement of working conditions, the safeguarding of individual rights, the protection of the environment, and similar broad themes. Since it stood for the same things, the People's Party had difficulty conducting its campaign. In addition, shortly before the elections the fifty-one-year-old Karl Schleinzer, the party leader since 1971 and the OVP candidate for chancellor, was killed in a car accident. His successor, forty-two-year-old Josef Taus, was not well known, and in contrast to his opponent, he proved a colorless leader. With these handicaps the OVP could not hope to capture the votes it needed. Although it was recognized that the former emphasis on Christian values and the family had lost some of their appeal, a new program was difficult to formulate. The two parties were very close to each other; both talked about social justice, democracy, and a neutral foreign policy. The OVP certainly could not use red-scare tactics against Kreisky; he in fact was making great efforts to attract Catholic voters.

Under these circumstances it was not surprising that in the elections of October 1975 the SPO kept its ninety-three seats, with eighty for the OVP and ten for the FPO. After his victory Kreisky repeated his assurances that no radical changes would be made. The Socialist Party still recognized the importance of the floating voter, estimated at 6 percent of the electorate, and it continued to hope to win Catholics and farmers. Some moderate reforms were passed in 1976 and 1977, for instance, the establishment for four-week vacations, rising to five, as standard, but most of these measures were passed unanimously since they had the approval of the social partners. In 1978 even further changes were made in the Socialist Party program; emphasis was placed not only on social justice, but also on "Christian values." In a supporting speech, Kreisky in May 1978 stated that Marx had made contributions to socialist thought, but that some of his teachings were out of date, a statement that could not have been made by an SPO leader previously and certainly could not be made at the time in the neighboring Communist states.

When the next electoral period came in May 1979, the SPO had little to fear. Because their candidate was so popular, the party ran on the slogan "Austria needs Kreisky" and on its record of job security. Economic conditions continued to be excellent, although budget deficits were allowed to rise in the effort to hold down unemployment. The social partnership was working well; there were few strikes. The labor unions under the leadership of Anton Benya cooperated with the government and with management; they accepted the principle of the linking of wage increases with the rise in labor productivity. Some criticism did indeed come from the left wing of the party from those who pointed out that basic socialist ideals were being compromised; for instance, the distribution of income was becoming more and not less unequal. However, the majority of the electorate was clearly more interested in securing continuing prosperity that would give each individual a comfortable and happy personal life than in seeing the revival of the former ideological and class conflicts. The Socialist victory in 1979 was impressive: the SPO increased its representation to ninety-five, with seventy-seven seats for the OVP and eleven for the FPO. The Austrian public obviously liked Kreisky and his policies.

Although there were no major destructive controversies, certain issues did disturb the domestic scene in the 1970s. The disagreement over the abortion laws has been described. Two other important questions arose: the first involved the protection of the environment and the use of nuclear energy; the second concerned the position of the Austrian Slovenes and their minority rights.

As in other industrial nations the 1970s saw grave concern in Austria about energy resources. The sharp rise in petroleum prices, together with the cutoff of supplies from Iran, brought into question the future of a country that needed to import two-thirds of its requirements, including all its oil from the Middle East, most of its gas from the Soviet Union, and 90 percent of its coal from the East Bloc. The economic development of the country and the maintenance of full employment were tied to the assurance of adequate supplies. These imports were also a heavy charge on the Austrian balance of payments. The fear of possible shortages, cutoffs, or another sharp increase in prices united the trade unions and the manufacturers in an effort to find alternative sources of energy. The obvious choice was the development of nuclear or hydroelectric plants.

The question was, at first, not a party matter. The decision to build a nuclear plant was made by the Klaus government in the late sixties with Socialist support; once in office Kreisky made plans to build three more by 1990. The first plant was constructed at Zwentendorf, approximately forty miles from Vienna, at a cost of about $650 million (9 billion schillings). It was intended to provide up to 12 percent of Austrian needs and to save $77 million in foreign exchange. Both the SPO and the trade unions gave strong support to the project. The question did not become a national issue until 1977 and 1978, when the construction was almost complete.

By 1978 the Europe-wide environmental movement had focused attention on the safety of nuclear power. Already the problem of disposing of wastes had come up in Austria; no province would accept them. Additional fears were generated by the fact that the plant was situated near a fault line; the possible effects of an earthquake thus also had to be considered. The intense public opposition that arose crossed party lines, but it affected the SPO in particular. The environmental movement was especially appealing to segments of the population, such as the youth, whose allegiance the Socialists wished to hold. They were also concerned about the possible development of an Alternative-Green Party, such as existed in West Germany, that might endanger their majority, which could be affected by a relatively small swing in voting patterns.

Nevertheless, despite the political dangers Kreisky met the question directly. Both parties agreed that a referendum, the first in the republic, should be held. Taking a strong affirmative position, Kreisky turned the issue into a vote of confidence for himself, suggesting that he might resign should the measure be defeated. In the referendum of November 1978 the parties took different stands. The Socialists expected to win, but they could not control some of their provincial voters, particularly in Vorarlberg, where environmental concerns were strong. The People's Party leaders instructed their supporters to follow their own inclinations, but they appeared to be unfavorable. The Freedom Party joined the opposition. The final vote was close: 64 percent of the electorate voted, with 50.47 against the opening of the plant and 49.53 for it. Despite this defeat, Kreisky did not resign. In December the Nationalrat passed a bill closing the entire operation; it would take a two-thirds majority to override this decision.

A similar controversy arose when the government made plans to build a hydroelectric power plant at Hainburg, thirty miles east of Vienna. Once again a coalition of government officials, unions, and industry joined against the environmentalists, who had the support of the largest Austrian newspaper, *Kronen Zeitung*. The opposition argued that the plant would destroy Europe's last remaining natural marshland. When, in the late fall of 1984, the government decided to go ahead with its plans, demonstrations and protests forced a reconsideration of the question. In January 1985 construction was halted so that the issue could be discussed further.

The public reaction, which, of course, did nothing to meet the vital question of energy resources, can be better understood when it is remembered that Austria as a tourist country needs to protect its landscape. By the 1980s problems of industrial pollution had become serious. Any observer could see that pine and fir trees throughout the Alpine regions were dying. The presence of industries in mountain areas where harmful chemical emissions could not disperse was clearly having a bad effect on the countryside. The automobile too was a major culprit, but catalytic converters and lead-free gasoline were not made requirements until 1986. These problems by the middle 1980s were recognized as international in scope, since pollutants observed no national boundaries.

Another question that aroused public interest and even passion concerned the minority rights of the Slovenes in Carinthia and the Croats in Burgenland. It was estimated that there were approximately twenty-five thousand Croats and twenty to fifty thousand Slovenes, forming together less than 1 percent of the Austrian population of 7.5 million. In the State Treaty the Austrian government had accepted specific obligations in regard to the minorities, including their right to organize, to have their own press, and to use their languages in elementary and secondary schools. In Carinthia, Burgenland, and Styria, where Slovenes and Croats lived, their languages as well as German were to be official, and where there was a concentration of population "topographical terminology and inscriptions shall be in the Slovene or Croat language as well as in German."

The major controversy over these stipulations arose in July 1972 when the Nationalrat passed a law providing that dual-language signs were to be placed wherever there was a minority of at least 20 percent. As a result, signs in Slovene as well as German were put in 205 of the 2,900 villages and towns in Carinthia. The German-speaking population, remembering the Yugoslav claims to the province after both wars, reacted with violence and tore the signs down. These actions had the support of local German organizations and of the police, army, and local officials. These events were naturally observed in neighboring Slovenia and embittered Austria's relations with Yugoslavia, which delivered a note of protest in November.

In July 1976 the government again tried to deal with the problem. The major difficulty was that no one really knew how many Slovene-speakers lived in Carinthia. In order to determine the numbers, it was decided that a census would be taken, a move that was strongly opposed by Slovene representatives. It was obvious that the Slovene-speaking population had dropped dramatically from 1914, when one in four inhabitants was a Slovene. Although this figure had clearly changed radically, a decision about dual-language signs or about the use of the Slovene language in the schools could not be made without a count. Despite continued Slovene objections and the call for a boycott, the census was held in November. In Carinthia 86.4 percent of those eligible voted;

98.6 percent declared themselves Germans, and 0.9 percent, Slovenes. Because of the circumstances surrounding the vote, in particular the strong protests of the Yugoslav government and Slovene groups, who argued that the results did not reflect the true conditions, no useful results were obtained.

Nevertheless, in July 1977, in an attempt to solve the problem, the government put into effect the Ethnic Groups Act of 1976, which applied to both Slovenes and Croats. It was decided that dual-language signs should be set up where more than a quarter of the population was not German-speaking. At this time in Carinthia eighty-five elementary and twenty-four secondary schools had Slovene as a language of instruction; the state also subsidized two Slovene newspapers, and broadcasts in Slovene were transmitted from Klagenfurt.

ECONOMIC POLICY

Although economic questions have been covered in the previous pages, some special aspects of Austrian development should be emphasized. The years after 1955, as we have seen, produced no economic crises of the type that caused so much distress before 1938. Indeed, throughout this period Austria remained a prosperous small industrial country enjoying steady economic growth. From 1950 to 1960 the gross national product increased an average of 6 percent annually; from 1960 to 1970 it rose by 4.7 percent annually, and from 1970 to 1979 by 4.3 percent. The great concern of the Austrian public was always unemployment; the memory of the interwar years lingered. In the 1960s this figure was held below 3 percent, and in the 1970s it stayed below 2 percent. Austria had full employment in 1960–1961. Thereafter, foreign "guest workers" were brought in to fill, in general, menial jobs, such as those in the tourist industry and domestic service, and as unskilled factory workers. The number reached a height of 227,000 in 1973; most of these immigrants were Turks or Yugoslavs. The inflation rate was also kept down, at least in comparison with other countries: in 1974 it was 9.5 percent, but it was reduced to 3.6 percent in 1978. Austria too was affected by the general recession in 1974–1975 caused by the worldwide oil crisis. In 1975 Austrian economic conditions worsened, but the government and the institutions of the social partnership were able to handle the accompanying problems; some foreign workers were sent home.

During the Kreisky period the changes in the social structure that have been noted previously were accelerated. The number of industrial workers grew slightly, but the farm population, which had amounted to 23.7 percent in 1959, fell, as we have seen, to 9.9 percent in 1977. Despite this decline agricultural methods were so efficient that the country not only could feed itself, but produced surpluses of milk and wheat. Austrian agriculture was heavily subsidized both for political and for economic reasons. The government also saw the necessity of supporting the rural population, particularly in the Alpine regions, in order to maintain the countryside in the interests of tourism. The greatest shift was among those in the service sector of the economy, with an increase from 35.1 percent of the population in 1959 to 49.3 percent in 1977.

In any discussion of the Austrian economy a special place must be given to tourism, which, of course, accounted for part of the rise in the number of those engaged in service occupations. Endowed with gorgeous Alpine scenery, Austria experienced a period of rapid growth in tourism in the 1950s and 1960s. Although there was a slowdown after 1972, a height was reached in the late 1970s. In 1980 foreign visitors accounted for 84,825,000 overnight stays, with Vienna and the three provinces of Tirol, Salzburg, and Carinthia the most popular centers. Tourism not only became a major employer of labor and a source of profit, but also helped balance the trade deficit, caused by the necessity of importing energy resources as well as by the Austrian taste for foreign luxury items, such as automobiles.

As before, Austrian trade ties were primarily with the West European states. A member of the Organization for Economic Cooperation and Development (OECD), which replaced OEEC in 1961, the state was part of an association that included among its members the United States and Canada. About 70 percent of Austrian trade was with these states, and around 12 percent with COMECON. Among the European powers particular attention should be given to the unique and predominating role that West Germany played in the Austrian economy. Some figures for selected years clearly demonstrate the close relationship. In 1972 German investment in Austria totaled 1.22 billion marks, but it was partially balanced by some Austrian investment in Germany. In 1984 105,000 Austrian workers were employed in German-owned industries, a number that compares with those working for state enterprises. In 1976, 23.4 percent of Austrian exports went to West Germany, while 41.1 percent of the imports came from there. The tourist industry, as in the prewar years, was strongly dependent on Germans, who constituted about three-quarters of the foreign visitors in the 1970s. With the border between the countries open, there were few hindrances to close economic cooperation.

Although the Austrian economy was thus stable, and a good life was provided for the average citizen, certain problems existed. Austria was (as it has remained) a welfare state; along with the standard package of social benefits the government offered many extras, such as payments on marriage and the birth of each child, whose cost was high. Moreover, the same principle of social welfare was applied to the state industries. Particular difficulties were met in the management and operation of the iron and steel industry, which in the 1980s was not producing competitive products. After the government took over the industries and some banks in 1946, they were organized as joint stock companies with the state in the position of a stockholder. In 1970 a holding company, the Austrian Corporation for Industrial Administration (Osterreichische Industrieverwaltung, OIAG), was formed. In addition to the companies included in this organization, the nationalized banks also controlled certain industries. The state was thus by far the largest employer, with approximately 110,000 workers in the OIAG firms and an additional 60,000 in industries run by the banks. In an attempt to meet growing problems of organization and management in the iron and steel industries, in the 1970s some companies were merged to form the United Austrian Iron and Steel Works (Vereinigte Osterreichische Eisen- und Stahlwerke, VOEST-Alpine) and the United Specialty Steel Works (Vereinigte Edelstahlwerke, VEW). However, the state enterprises, open to political influences, continued to have problems difficult to solve: they could not easily fire redundant labor, close uneconomical plants, or quickly adjust to new conditions. By the middle of the 1980s VOEST-Alpine, the largest Austrian employer, with 70,000 workers, continued to suffer financial losses. Throughout this period the shortage of energy resources also affected the economic situation, but, as we have seen, environmentalist opposition prevented the building of even hydroelectric plants.

FOREIGN RELATIONS

The main lines of Austrian international relations had been determined before Kreisky became chancellor. As we have seen, the major questions of the previous era, the association

with the EEC and the problem of South Tirol, while continuing to cause some controversies, had been dealt with by the
agreements previously concluded. As before, international
affairs were largely determined by the continuing division of
the world into camps and the conflict between the United
States and the Soviet Union. However, during most of the
1970s some signs of an amelioration of international tensions were apparent. After the withdrawal of the United States
from Vietnam, the U.S. and Soviet governments entered into
negotiations on some outstanding problems. Most important were the inauguration of negotiations concerning the
control and limitation of arms, leading to the conclusion of
the SALT I (Strategic Arms Limitation Talks) agreement in
1972 and SALT II in 1979, which was, however, never rati-
fied. One of the major events of this period of détente was
the holding of the Helsinki Conference on security and cooperation in Europe, in which Austria participated along with
thirty-four other states, including Canada and the United
States. The Final Act, signed on August 1, 1975, obligated
the participants to accept the map of Europe established at
the end of the war: "The participating States regard as in-
violable all one another's frontiers as well as the frontiers of
all States in Europe, and therefore they will refrain now and
in the future from assaulting these frontiers."[27]

This period also brought about new developments in the
German question. In 1969 Kreisky's friend and associate, Willy
Brandt, became the German chancellor. Abandoning the
previous West German attitude, Brandt accepted the division of Germany into two states and inaugurated a program
of *Ostpolitik* (Eastern Policy), which led to a series of agreements with the Soviet Union, Poland, and the German Dem-

---

[27] Text of the Final Act in James Mayall and Cornelia Navari, *The End of
the Post-War Era: Documents on Great-Power Relations, 1968–1975* (Cambridge: Cambridge University Press, 1980), p. 296.

ocratic Republic. Kreisky approved of this approach, since he saw no practical alternative.

The period of détente came to an end in 1979 with the Soviet invasion of Afghanistan and the subsequent pressure on Poland. As a neutral nation, Austria was not involved in the controversy that arose over the stationing of additional U.S. missiles in Europe. Kreisky, who never concealed his anti-Communist opinions, was in favor of a strong U.S. military presence in Europe, but he was very critical of many U.S. actions, such as the attitude taken toward Socialist movements in Central America.

In other European affairs, the Austrian position was similar to that of its fellow neutrals, Switzerland and Sweden. The closest ties remained with the Western economic partners; relations with the Communist world varied. After the wounds caused by the suppression of the Hungarian revolt of 1956 were healed, Vienna and Budapest reestablished good relations. In contrast, a similar friendship was not possible with Prague. In February 1976 Kreisky became the first Austrian chancellor in the postwar years to make an official visit to Czechoslovakia, but many issues remained unsettled between them. Except for the controversy over Slovene minority rights, neutral Austria and nonaligned Yugoslavia had many similar views in foreign policy; both sought to stay outside the spheres of influence of the two great armed camps.

Although Austria's weakness and neutrality limited its possibilities, Kreisky, like previous Austrian leaders, wanted his country to take an active part in world affairs. As a former foreign minister, he took a particular interest in international relations, and he favored close participation in the work of the United Nations. Here Austria could cooperate with other small states and with the new nations that had emerged after the disintegration of the great Western colonial empires. To this end the government invested a large amount in constructing the Vienna International Center, called UN City, which was designed to house UN agencies and to make Vienna the third official city after New York and Geneva. Already some agencies, such as the International Atomic Energy Organization in 1957 and the Industrial Development Organization in 1967, had made Vienna their headquarters. Austria in 1970 became one of the nonpermanent members of the UN Security Council; Kurt Waldheim was twice elected secretary general, in 1971 and in 1976. Austrian troops formed part of UN contingents in Cyprus and on the Golan Heights. In addition to the UN agencies, Vienna was also the headquarters for other international organizations, such as the Organization of Petroleum Exporting Countries (OPEC), and the International Institute for Applied Systems Analysis was established at Laxenberg in 1973. Austria's neutral status also made Vienna an excellent site for negotiations between the Soviet Union and the United States. John F. Kennedy and Nikita Khrushchev met there in 1961; the negotiations for SALT I and SALT II were held in the Hofburg.

Kreisky personally attracted international attention in particular when he became involved in the Arab and Israeli controversies, which he did both in his position as Austrian chancellor and as an active participant in the activities of the Socialist International. Although he supported the maintenance of the security of Israel, he was sharply critical of its policies toward the Palestinians, and he opposed the annexation of territories occupied after the 1967 war. Since he did not believe that time was on the Israeli side, he believed its government should make concessions to achieve a settlement with its Arab neighbors. His outspoken attitude drew sharp criticisms not only from his Socialist colleague Golda Meir, but even more from Menachem Begin and the members of the Likud government in office after June 1977.

Vienna also became a center of terrorist activity. The first major incident occurred in September 1973, when Arab activists seized three Jewish emigrants from the Soviet Union and an Austrian customs official. Vienna had by this time become the transit point for thousands of Jews coming from the Soviet Union, most of whom were on the way to Israel. After Kreisky agreed to the terrorists' demands and promised to close the transit camp that the Jewish Agency was running at Schönau Castle, the hostages were freed and the terrorists were flown to Tripoli. Kreisky's actions in this crisis drew criticism in particular from the United States and Israel. Jewish emigration, however, was not affected, because another camp, under Austrian Red Cross jurisdiction, was subsequently opened at Wöllersdorf.

After the October 1973 Egyptian–Israeli war, the Socialist International set up a Fact-Finding Mission to the Middle East, with Kreisky as chairman. At this time he, as well as other European Socialist leaders, favored the recognition of the Palestine Liberation Organization (PLO) as the official representative of the Palestinians. In July 1979 he and Willy Brandt received the PLO leader, Yassir Arafat, in Vienna; in February 1980 Kreisky and Arafat met again. In March the PLO received de facto Austrian recognition, when an accredited agent was accepted in Vienna. In the next years the Austrian government continued its support of the PLO as the legitimate representative of the Palestinian people and of Arafat as its leader.

The relationship of Kreisky with Arab leaders drew a strong Israeli reaction; the Austrian chancellor had no hesitation about replying in strong terms or about attacking the activities of Jewish agencies in Austria. In October 1975, at the time of the election, Simon Wiesenthal, representing Jewish groups, accused FPÖ leader Peter of having served with an SS unit that was responsible for widespread atrocities. Peter had never denied membership in the SS, but he emphasized that he had not participated in such activities. Kreisky strongly resented the Wiesenthal accusations, which he took as a personal attack. In reply, he brought into question Wiesenthal's war record, even implying that he had been a German agent.

In December 1975 Vienna suffered its worst terrorist attack. This time the target was the Vienna headquarters of OPEC, where Arab leaders were meeting; three men were killed, many were wounded, and thirty-three hostages were taken. Again the Austrian government conceded to the demands; the terrorists were allowed to fly to Algiers, where the hostages were released. Another incident occurred in December 1985, when three men, belonging to a radical group that had broken from the PLO, attempted to take hostages from among the passengers at the Vienna airport awaiting an El Al Israeli Airlines flight. Three people, including one of the terrorists, were killed and dozens wounded. A similar attack was made at the Rome airport.

THE END OF THE KREISKY ERA

These years of Socialist government were, as can be seen, a period of domestic prosperity and moderate reform. Although no major controversies troubled the political scene, it was also obvious that the Socialist Party and its leadership had changed. No longer the militant organization of the prewar years, its leaders, enjoying the good life, had become separated from the working-class constituency they claimed to represent. The scandals that usually are attached to any government long in power also appeared here. This situation was well represented by what one journal had called

"Austria's longest-running political comedy thriller,"[28] the public controversy over the income and life-style of Hannes Androsch, the vice-chancellor and minister of finance and Kreisky's heir-apparent. Androsch, the man heading the office responsible for tax collecting, was shown to have, together with his wife, a 75 percent share in a tax-consulting office, whose main task, of course, was to advise clients how to avoid paying taxes. He and his friends were also accused of involvement in other questionable activities. In defending himself, Androsch declared that his father-in-law was actually running the business, although his wife did work there. Although in December 1978 the SPO issued a statement that he had done nothing illegal, Androsch transferred a 51 percent interest in his company to three trustees. Popular with his associates, Androsch was difficult to remove from his powerful positions. Finally, in January 1981, he resigned his government offices, but he was put at the head of the Creditanstalt, Austria's largest nationalized bank. Fred Sinowatz then replaced him as second to Kreisky.

The greatest scandal of the Second Republic, however, broke out in 1980 and was connected with the construction of a general hospital of over two thousand beds, which had commenced in 1960. From its inception there were attacks on the design, the organization, and the facilities to be provided. The question of corruption was even more important; it was soon shown that officials had accepted bribes from companies that wanted construction contracts. A Nationalrat committee undertook an investigation that led to a trial at which the defendants received jail sentences.

The hospital and Androsch scandals were exploited to the full by the popular press. The Socialist regime was often made

---

[28] *Economist,* January 24, 1981, p. 47.

to appear as if it were staffed by officials whose primary concern was to advance their own interests and who were involved in underhanded deals. Nevertheless, despite these vulnerable points, the Socialists had reason to face the elections of April 1983 with optimism. The state was in a prosperous and stable condition, with a low, 5.4 percent, inflation and a 3.7 percent unemployment rate. The SPO expected a challenge from the new Green Party, but not from the others. The election results were thus a surprise to many. The SPO, receiving only 90 seats out of the total of 183, lost its absolute majority; the People's Party increased its representation by 4 to 81; the Freedom Party gained 1 for a total of 12. The Greens, with only 3 percent of the vote, did not win a place.

Before the election Kreisky had announced that he would not join a coalition. Thus, after thirteen years at the head of the government, he resigned. In May a small coalition was formed with Fred Sinowatz as chancellor and Norbert Steger of the FPO as vice-chancellor. The People's Party, now under the leadership of Alois Mock, remained in opposition. In October an SPO party congress elected Sinowatz also as party chairman. Although the Kreisky era was over, the former chancellor remained active in Austrian and international affairs. Moreover, his successors made no immediate changes in the policies or personnel of his period in office.

In comparison with the relatively placid preceding period, 1986 was a tumultuous year in Austrian politics. The continuing decline in SPO popularity was shown again in the presidential elections of June 1986. For the first time in the Second Republic an OVP candidate, Kurt Waldheim, winning by a comfortable majority of 53.8 percent of the votes, defeated his Socialist opponent, Kurt Steyrer. The campaign was clouded by charges, particularly from the World Jewish Congress, concerning Waldheim's wartime activities in the

Balkans, where he had served in the German Army. Although the question received wide publicity, particularly in the U.S. press, and the final vote was probably affected to some extent by an Austrian aversion to outside pressure, the results reflected more directly a move to the right in domestic politics that was soon to be apparent also in subsequent events.

After this electoral defeat the Socialist leadership recognized that a major reorganization was necessary to prepare the party to face the parliamentary elections, which were scheduled at first for April 1987. Fred Sinowatz, although remaining head of the party, was replaced as chancellor by the former minister of finance, Franz Vranitzky. With a background in banking and representing the center of the party, Vranitzky, it was hoped, could attract the middle-of-the-road voter, who now appeared to be more conservatively inclined. Moreover, should a further shift in electoral patterns force the Socialists to attempt to re-form a coalition with the OVP, the new leadership was better suited to participate in such negotiations.

Such an event occurred sooner than expected. In September 1986 Jörg Haider, the head of the FPO in Carinthia, replaced Steger as party leader. After this choice of a right-wing nationalist, Vranitzky ended the coalition partnership and announced that new elections would be held in November. During the subsequent campaign the major issues were economic, including the necessity of cutting the budget deficit, tax reform, and the reorganization of the nationalized industries, particularly those requiring large subsidies. Since these measures would involve reducing the high welfare costs and holding the line on wages, the SPO faced the danger of losing workers' votes. The OVP opposition continued to be led by Mock, who was closely associated with Waldheim both before and after his controversial election. Already during the campaign there was much discussion of reviving the grand coalition of 1945–1966; both of the major parties muted their campaign rhetoric so that an accommodation would be possible should neither receive a clear victory.

The elections, held on November 23, brought losses for both major parties. The SPO won 43.1 percent of the votes, with eighty seats, and the OVP took 41.3 percent and seventy-seven seats, a difference of only three places. Other parties increased their percentages. The FPO, with 9.7 percent, had eighteen representatives instead of the previous twelve. The environmentalist Greens, under the leadership of Freda Meissner-Blau, with 4.8 percent and eight seats, entered parliament as a fourth party, the first since the Communist Party lost its representation in 1959.

Immediately after the results were clear, Waldheim asked Vranitzky to form a government. Although it was expected that the grand coalition would be revived, the negotiations extended over almost two months. A program for the future as well as a division of offices had to be decided upon. Finally, on January 16, 1987, an agreement was announced which, in essence, marked a division of power in the new government. In a cabinet of seventeen members, the partners each received eight positions; of the important posts the SPO obtained the Ministries of Finance, Interior, Social Affairs, and Transport and State Industries; the OVP held Defense, Agriculture, Science, Trade, and, most important, Foreign Affairs. Vranitzky became chancellor, with Mock as vice-chancellor and foreign minister. After much debate it was decided that a nonparty jurist should be appointed minister of justice, since this office would be involved in the investigation of the scandals connected with the previous SPO regime.

The program endorsed by both parties was designed to last for the four-year parliamentary period. Recognizing the seriousness of the domestic problems, the partners agreed upon measures to bring the state finances in order and to reduce the budget deficit. Although the coalition had the advantage that the government could take unpopular but necessary measures with both parties in theory sharing public displeasure, it will be noted that the SPO held the ministries that would be most affected by the reforms. Despite the speculation at the time whether the partners would be able to take the necessary strong steps, or if indeed the coalition would last, this combination was the only possible alternative given the results of the election. Under the circumstances a small coalition between the OVP and the FPO or between the SPO and the Greens was not practical.

These decisions, as could be expected, were not greeted favorably by all. Bruno Kreisky, for instance, resigned his honorary presidency of the SPO in protest against the assignment of Foreign Affairs to the OVP. He evidently feared that his acomplishments during his period in office, including the assurance of an active and positive Austrian role in world affairs and strict neutrality, were in jeopardy. Vranitzky had already demonstrated that his major interest was directed toward domestic policy; Mock was known to favor closer relations with the EEC.

Even with this fairly even sharing of power within the coalition, the SPO remained the strongest single party. Despite the fears of many conservatives in previous years, the period of Socialist leadership had certainly not brought about revolutionary changes. There was, in fact, little to differentiate this period from the earlier years of the first grand coalition or the single-party rule of the OVP. The Socialist Party had not attempted to widen the sphere of public ownership in economic life or to equalize incomes. Its officials worked with the trade unions and with the institutions of the social partnership, where the other party was well represented.

Moreover, few fundamental disagreements existed between the two major parties. On the broad scale their programs were often difficult to tell apart, a situation that, of course, provided a favorable environment for future cooperation within the grand coalition.

Conclusion

AUSTRIA IN THE 1980S

THE preceding pages have charted the changes in the lives of the German-speaking people who inhabit the territory of present-day Austria. We have seen how Austrian Germans moved from being citizens of a multinational empire, one of Europe's great powers, to being residents of a small neutral state. We have also observed how this change led to the establishment of a prosperous and stable society, whose condition compares favorably with that of other West European nations and most emphatically with that of other successor states of the Habsburg Empire.

Certainly, for the Austrian Germans the breakup of the Habsburg Empire had come as an unexpected shock. Holding the strongest historic position among the nationalities, the Germans had not felt it necessary to organize militant societies to achieve definite goals. Their position had been essentially defensive; they sought primarily to keep the privileges they enjoyed. In 1918 they received what few wanted. Although the First Republic inherited many beneficial attributes from the monarchy — including its legal system, its constitutional political principles, and its trained bureaucracy — it did not gain a spirit of "Austrianism" as such. Individuals usually felt a close connection with their home provinces and a patriotic loyalty to the monarchy; they also considered themselves to be part of a larger German cultural

325

nation. In addition to this lack of basic support, the terrible conditions after the war gave rise to a conviction that Austria as an independent state was simply not economically viable. With the alternatives of the re-creation of the Habsburg Empire or its replacement by a Danubian federation excluded by the international conditions of the time, most Austrians came to support union with Germany as the answer to their national aspirations and to the harsh economic realities of the time. Overwhelming popular support for an Anschluss was only partially dampened by the coming to power of the National Socialist regime in Berlin in 1933.

The independent state was also placed in a humiliating position after the first war. Burdened with the responsibility for the conflict and forced to beg for loans to survive, the Austrian leaders coulld not conduct an independent foreign policy. Austria was at first subject to French and British pressure; in the 1930s Fascist Italy exerted an often determining influence on both internal and external affairs, a condition that lasted until Mussolini in 1938 assented to the Anschluss. This condition of dependency and weakness was not easy to accept for a people with an imperial and glorious past. As Seipel wrote in 1928: "To cultivate our own little garden and to show it to foreigners in order to make money out of it are no proper tasks for the inhabitants of the Carolingian Ostmark and the heirs of the conquerors of the Turks."[29] The union with Germany, which joined Austria with the strongest Continental military power, in a sense reversed this situation, but it also drew the country into a devastating war that resulted in a crushing defeat.

The conditions under which the Second Republic was established, including economic ruin and burned-out cities, in

---

[29] Seipel to Dr. W. Bauer, private letter, Hütteldorf, July 30, 1928, in Paul Sweet, "Seipel's Views on the *Anschluss:* An Unpublished Exchange of Letters," *Journal of Modern History* 19 (1947):323.

fact provided a basis for what was to be a relatively fast and stable recovery. The ill-fated association with Nazi Germany effectively crushed any possibility for a continuation of union with that country. Moreover, faced with a possible punitive settlement and another giant reparations bill, the Austrian leaders quite practically wished to present themselves as victims of Nazi conquest rather than as defeated enemies. Immediately after the war they also made a determined effort to emphasize that there was indeed an Austrian nation apart from the larger German concept. After 1945 there was, of course, no single "German fatherland." The close cultural, economic, and political ties that developed between Austria and the Federal Republic of Germany and their common membership in general European associations, such as the OECD, give both states the advantages of union without any accompanying difficulties.

Despite its officially neutral status Austria is in fact an integral part of Western Europe, sharing its common political, economic, and cultural principles. The idea of a participation in a Danubian Federation, popular between the wars, is no longer a practical alternative. The Communist-run governments of the other successor states, with their depressed economies and their repressive political and cultural policies, offer no attraction to Austrians, who enjoy both a representative government and a comfortable life. In foreign policy only one issue, that of South Tirol, has caused strong reverberations among the public. It is interesting to note that although the rights of the Tirolean Germans under Italian rule are defended, the government has made little attempt to concern itself with the fate of other Germans, such as those in Transylvania or Czechoslovakia, who similarly inhabit former Habsburg lands. Situated in a strategic position between the two great-power blocs, Austria is, of course, limited in its freedom of action in foreign policy; it cannot pursue grand designs or large goals. The status of neutrality, however, frees its government from involving itself too deeply in the great controversies dividing the Soviet Union and the United States. Its leaders, as we have seen, nevertheless have not hesitated in making decisions unpopular with one or another of the giant adversaries. For instance, they denounced the Soviet intervention in Hungary and Czechoslovakia, and they have recognized the PLO despite U.S. disapproval.

Although no longer closely associated with other former Habsburg lands, Austria almost alone among the successor states has remained proud of its Habsburg traditions, which it celebrates in frequent museum exhibitions and public festivals. The desire to continue to play the role of a major power in world affairs is shown in the welcome that has been extended to international organizations and to gatherings of world leaders. Great efforts have also been made to preserve the great cultural heritage of the imperial past and to continue it into the present. The state generously supports art, music, education, literature, and the theater. The contributions of Habsburg history are thus incorporated into the concept of the specifically Austrian character.

Although preserving an almost nostalgic attitude toward the past, the Second Republic has been able to accomplish what the First could not: successful adjustment to the life of a small state. In 1918 independent Austria had certain distinct advantages: its citizens were joined together by their common language, Catholic religion, history, and culture. In the First Republic these cohesive elements were not exploited. Instead of cooperating to meet the challenges of the time, the two major political parties, the Social Democrats and the Christian Socials, formed opposing camps, each with its own armed auxiliaries, and they fought for control of the state. In the post–1945 period not only were the lessons of the past taken to heart, but the parties themselves were deeply affected by the changing social composition of their constituencies, determined by the new economic conditions.

The great accomplishment of the Second Republic is undoubtedly its establishment of a prosperous modern economic system, despite the limited resources of the country. As one authority has written: "In terms of the performance of the Austrian economy in the 1970s and the rapidity with which its industry has changed since 1960, Austria surpasses all countries except Japan."[30] Austria thus shares in the general prosperity enjoyed by the West European states. Not only has its industrial base been built up, but despite the decrease in numbers of those engaged in agriculture, the country is self-sufficient in food.

Industrialization, the decline of agriculture, and the growth of service enterprises have, as we have seen, changed the social composition of the electorate and deeply influenced party programs. With the relative decrease in the percentage of the population in industry, the Socialists could no longer emphasize a "class struggle," but had to adopt policies that would attract the support of middle-class salaried employees. The People's Party was affected by the reduction of the farm population. The move of both parties to the center has produced a political scene quite different from that of the interwar years.

Most important in promoting social harmony and political tranquility has been the development of the institutions of the social partnership, which have allowed the economy to progress without frequent strikes or labor discord. Given a voice in major decisions, the unions have adopted a realistic attitude toward wage increases and have understood the ba-

---

[30] Peter J. Katzenstein, "Commentary," in Sven W. Arndt, ed., *The Political Economy of Austria* (Washington, D.C.: American Enterprise Institute, 1982), p. 151.

sic economic problems of the country. Workers have shared with the rest of the population a general desire, based on the remembrance of the horrors of unemployment in the interwar years, for full employment and social welfare measures; that is, they prefer security to a freely competitive system. The population in general is thus willing to limit demands in the interest of the general economy, and the majority prefer a cradle of social benefits to large wage increases. The social partnership also reflects what has been an Austrian preference for corporate institutions, that is, for representation through economic interest groups as well as through political associations.

The Austrian condition, of course, provides basic problems. As a small state in a strategic location, it is open to outside military interference. Its economy, dependent on imported energy resources and the tourist trade, can be severely damaged by world events. Nevertheless, in the mid-1980s Austria was a fine example of a successful adaptation by a state to modern realities after 1945. With a prosperous economy, a stable political life, and an electorate divided by no great issues, it was indeed "a small house in order."[31] Whether this favorable situation can be maintained in the future depends, of course, on the avoidance of major political or economic crises, the continuation of the basic public agreement on domestic goals, and a tranquil world order.

[31] "A Small House in Order," *Economist,* March 15, 1980, country survey on Austria.

BIBLIOGRAPHY

This bibliography consists of a listing of books in English; it is selective and obviously does not cover all of the publications available on Habsburg and Austrian history. Although it has not been possible to include German-language materials, the following books not only cover the subjects under consideration, but also have excellent bibliographies. Erich Zöllner, *Geschichte Osterreichs* (Vienna: Verlag für Geschichte und Politik, 1970), and the four volumes of Hellmut Andics's *Osterreich, 1804–1875* (Augsburg: Wilhelm Goldmann Verlag, 1980) deal with the entire period. Hugo Hantsch, *Die Geschichte Osterreichs* (Graz: Verlag Styria, 1962), in two volumes, surveys Habsburg history to 1918; Hanns Leo Mikoletzky, *Osterreich im 20. Jahrhundert* (Vienna: Austria-Edition, 1962), is concerned primarily with the First Republic. Heinrich Benedikt, ed., *Geschichte der Republik Osterreich* (Vienna: Verlag für Geschichte und Politik, 1954), and Walter Goldinger, *Geschichte der Republik Osterreich* (Vienna: Verlag für Geschichte und Politik, 1962), similarly emphasize events before 1945. Two large collections of special studies deserve particular attention, both edited in two volumes by Erika Weinzierl and Kurt Skalnik: *Osterreich, 1918–1938* (Graz: Verlag Styria, 1983) and *Osterreich: Die Zweite Republik* (Graz: Verlag Styria, 1972). In addition, for important articles, reviews, and information on Austrian history, the reader should consult the successive volumes of *Austrian History Yearbook*, published by the Center for Austrian Studies, University of Minnesota.

THE HABSBURG EMPIRE

General Histories

Crankshaw, Edward. *The Fall of the House of Habsburg.* New York: Popular Library, 1963.

Jászi, Oscar. *The Dissolution of the Habsburg Monarchy.* Chicago: University of Chicago Press, 1929.

Bibliography

Kann, Robert A. *The Habsburg Empire: A Study in Integration and Disintegration.* New York: Praeger Publishers, 1957.

A History of the Habsburg Empire, 1526–1918. Berkeley: University of California Press, 1974.

The Multinational Empire: Nationalism and National Reform in the Habsburg Monarchy, 1848–1918. 2 vols. New York: Columbia University Press, 1950.

Kann, Robert A., and Zdeněk V. David. *The Peoples of the Eastern Habsburg Lands, 1526–1918.* Seattle: University of Washington Press, 1984.

Macartney, C. A. *The Habsburg Empire, 1790–1918.* London: Weidenfeld and Nicolson, 1968.

The House of Austria. Edinburgh: Edinburgh University Press, 1978.

May, Arthur J. *The Hapsburg Monarchy, 1867–1914.* Cambridge, Mass.: Harvard University Press, 1951.

Tapié, Victor L. *The Rise and Fall of the Habsburg Monarchy.* Translated by Stephen Hardman. New York: Praeger Publishers, 1971.

Taylor, A. J. P. *The Habsburg Monarchy, 1809–1918.* London: Hamish Hamilton, 1948.

Wandruszka, Adam. *The House of Habsburg.* Garden City, N.Y.: Doubleday and Co., Anchor Books, 1965.

Internal Affairs

Bernard, Paul P. *Jesuits and Jacobins: Enlightenment and Enlightened Despotism in Austria.* New York: Oxford University Press, 1985.

Blum, Mark E. *The Austro-Marxists, 1890–1918: A Psychobiographical Study.* Lexington: University Press of Kentucky, 1985.

Bottomore, Tom B., and Patrick Goode. *Austro-Marxism.* Oxford: Oxford University Press, Clarendon Press, 1978.

Boyer, John W. *Political Radicalism in Late Imperial Vienna: Origins of the Christian Social Movement, 1848–1897.* Chicago: University of Chicago Press, 1981.

Carsten, Francis L. *Fascist Movements in Austria: From Schönerer to Hitler.* Beverly Hills: Sage Publications, 1977.

Evans, R. J. W. *The Making of the Habsburg Monarchy, 1550–1700.* Oxford: Oxford University Press, Clarendon Press, 1979.

Gerschenkron, Alexander. *An Economic Spurt That Failed.* Princeton, N.J.: Princeton University Press, 1977.

Good, David F. *The Economic Rise of the Habsburg Empire, 1750–1914.* Berkeley: University of California Press, 1984.

Haas, Arthur G. *Metternich: Reorganization and Nationality, 1813–1818.* Wiesbaden: Franz Steiner Verlag, 1963.

Ingrao, Charles W. *In Quest and Crisis: Emperor Joseph I and the Habsburg Monarchy.* West Lafayette, Ind.: Purdue University Press, 1979.

Bibliography

Jenks, William A. *Austria under the Iron Ring, 1879–1893*. Charlottesville: University Press of Virginia, 1965.

Vienna and the Young Hitler. New York: Columbia University Press, 1960.

Knapp, Vincent J. *Austrian Social Democracy, 1889–1914*. Washington, D.C.: University Press of America, 1980.

Koenigsberger, H. G. *The Habsburgs and Europe, 1516–1660*. Ithaca, N.Y.: Cornell University Press, 1971.

Komlos, John. *The Habsburg Monarchy as a Customs Union: Economic Development in Austria-Hungary in the Nineteenth Century*. Princeton, N.J.: Princeton University Press, 1983.

May, Arthur J. *The Passing of the Hapsburg Monarchy, 1914–1918*. 2 vols. Philadelphia: University of Pennsylvania Press, 1966.

Murad, Anatol. *Franz Joseph I of Austria and His Empire*. New York: Twayne Publishers, 1968.

Orton, Lawrence D. *The Prague Slav Congress of 1848*. Boulder, Colo.: East European Monographs, 1978.

Palmer, Alan. *Metternich*. New York: Harper and Row, 1972.

Rath, R. John. *The Viennese Revolution of 1848*. Austin: University of Texas Press, 1957.

Redlich, Joseph. *Emperor Francis Joseph of Austria*. New York: Macmillan Publishing Co., 1929.

Rothenberg, Gunther E. *The Army of Francis Joseph*. West Lafayette, Ind.: Purdue University Press, 1976.

Rozenblit, Marsha L. *The Jews of Vienna, 1867–1914: Assimilation and Identity*. Albany: State University of New York Press, 1983.

Rudolph, Richard L. *Banking and Industrialization in Austria-Hungary: The Role of Banks in the Industrialization of the Czech Crownlands, 1873–1914*. Cambridge: Cambridge University Press, 1976.

Sked, Alan. *The Survival of the Habsburg Empire: Radetzky, the Imperial Army, and the Class War, 1848*. London: Longman, 1979.

Spielman, John. *Leopold I of Austria*. London: Thames and Hudson, 1977.

Valiani, Leo. *The End of Austria–Hungary*. New York: Alfred A. Knopf, 1973.

Wangermann, Ernst. *The Austrian Achievement, 1700–1800*. New York: Harcourt Brace Jovanovich, 1973.

Whiteside, Andrew Gladding. *Austrian National Socialism before 1918*. The Hague: Martinus Nijhoff Publishers, 1962.

Foreign Policy

Bridge, F. R. *From Sadowa to Sarajevo: The Foreign Policy of Austria-Hungary, 1866–1914*. London: Routledge and Kegan Paul, 1972.

Great Britain and Austria-Hungary, 1906–1914. London: Weidenfeld and Nicolson, 1972.

Bibliography

Hanak, Harry. *Great Britain and Austria-Hungary during the First World War.* London: Oxford University Press, 1962.

Jelavich, Barbara. *The Habsburg Empire in European Affairs, 1814–1918* Chicago: Rand McNally and Co., 1969.

Jenks, William A. *Francis Joseph and the Italians, 1849–1859.* Charlottesville: University Press of Virginia, 1978.

Katzenstein, Peter J. *Disjointed Partners: Austria and Germany since 1815.* Berkeley: University of California Press, 1976.

Kraehe, Enno E. *Metternich's German Policy.* Vol. I: *The Contest with Napoleon, 1799–1814.* Princeton, N.J.: Princeton University Press, 1963. Vol. II: *The Congress of Vienna, 1814–1815.* Princeton, N.J.: Princeton University Press, 1983.

Roider, Karl A., Jr. *Austria's Eastern Question, 1700–1790.* Princeton, N.J.: Princeton University Press, 1982.

Schroeder, Paul W. *Austria, Great Britain and the Crimean War.* Ithaca, N.Y.: Cornell University Press, 1972.

Metternich's Diplomacy at Its Zenith, 1820–1823. Austin: University of Texas Press, 1962.

Silberstein, Gerard E. *The Troubled Alliance: German-Austrian Relations, 1914–1917.* Lexington: University Press of Kentucky, 1970.

Treadway, John D. *The Falcon and the Eagle: Montenegro and Austria-Hungary, 1908–1914.* West Lafayette, Ind.: Purdue University Press, 1983.

Zeman, Z. A. B. *The Break-Up of the Habsburg Empire, 1914–1918.* London: Oxford University Press, 1961.

Cultural History

Field, Frank. *The Last Days of Mankind: Karl Kraus and His Vienna.* London: Macmillan Press, 1967.

Gartenberg, Egon. *Vienna: Its Musical Heritage.* University Park, Pa.: Pennsylvania State University Press, 1968.

Gay, Peter. *Freud for Historians.* New York: Oxford University Press, 1985. *Freud, Jews, and Other Germans: Masters and Victims in Modernist Culture.* New York: Oxford University Press, 1978.

Hanson, Alice M. *Musical Life in Biedermeier Vienna.* Cambridge: Cambridge University Press, 1985.

Hofmann, Werner. *Gustav Klimt.* Translated by Inge Goodwin. Greenwich, Conn.: New York Graphic Society, 1971.

Janik, Allan, and Stephen Toulmin. *Wittgenstein's Vienna.* New York: Simon and Schuster, 1973.

Johnston, William M. *The Austrian Mind: An Intellectual and Social History, 1848–1938.* Berkeley: University of California Press, 1972.

Vienna, Vienna: The Golden Age, 1815–1914. New York: Crown Publishers, 1981.

Bibliography

Kann, Robert A. *A Study in Austrian Intellectual History: From Late Baroque to Romanticism.* New York: Praeger Publishers, 1960.

Luft, David S. *Robert Musil and the Crisis of European Culture, 1880–1942.* Berkeley: University of California Press, 1980.

McGrath, William J. *Dionysian Art and Politics in Austria.* New Haven, Conn.: Yale University Press, 1974.

Morton, Frederic. *A Nervous Splendor: Vienna 1888/1889.* Boston: Little, Brown and Co., 1979.

Powell, Nicolas. *The Sacred Spring: The Arts in Vienna, 1898–1918.* Greenwich, Conn.: New York Graphic Society, 1974.

Rosen, Charles. *The Classical Style: Haydn, Mozart, Beethoven.* New York: Viking Press, 1971.

Schorske, Carl E. *Fin-de-siècle Vienna: Politics and Culture.* New York: Alfred A. Knopf, 1980.

Schweiger, Werner J. *Wiener Werkstätte: Design in Vienna, 1903–1932.* Translated by Alexander Lieven. New York: Abbeville Press, 1984.

Shedel, James. *Art and Society: The New Art Movement in Vienna, 1897–1914.* Palo Alto, Calif.: Sposs, 1981.

Ungar, Frederick, ed. *Handbook of Austrian Literature.* New York: Frederick Ungar Publishing Co., [1973].

Vergo, Peter. *Art in Vienna, 1898–1918: Klimt, Kokoschka, Schiele and Their Contemporaries.* London: Phaidon Press, 1975.

Waissenberger, Robert, ed. *Vienna, 1890–1920.* New York: Rizzoli, 1984.

Vienna Secession. New York: Rizzoli, 1977.

THE REPUBLIC OF AUSTRIA

General Histories

Barker, Elizabeth. *Austria, 1918–1972.* Coral Gables: University of Miami Press, 1973.

Stadler, Karl R. *Austria.* New York: Praeger Publishers, 1971.

The First Republic and the Anschluss to 1945

Bauer, Otto. *The Austrian Revolution.* London: Leonard Parsons, 1925.

Brook-Shepherd, Gordon. *Dollfuss.* London: Macmillan Press, 1961.

Bullock, Malcolm. *Austria, 1918–1938: A Study in Failure.* London: Macmillan Press, 1939.

Diamant, Alfred. *Austrian Catholics and the First Republic, 1918–1934.* Princeton, N.J.: Princeton University Press, 1960.

Edmondson, C. Earl. *The Heimwehr and Austrian Politics, 1918–1936.* Athens: University of Georgia Press, 1978.

Gehl, Jürgen. *Austria, Germany and the Anschluss, 1931–1938.* London: Oxford University Press, 1963.

335

Bibliography

Gulick, Charles A. *Austria: From Habsburg to Hitler.* 2 vols. Berkeley: University of California Press, 1948.

Kitchen, Martin. *The Coming of Austrian Fascism.* Toronto: McGill–Queen's University Press, 1980.

Klemperer, Klemens von. *Ignaz Seipel: Christian Statesman in a Time of Crisis.* Princeton, N.J.: Princeton University Press, 1972.

Low, Alfred D. *The Anschluss Movement, 1918–1919, and the Paris Peace Conference.* Philadelphia: American Philosophical Society, 1974.

The Anschluss Movement, 1931–1938, and the Great Powers. Boulder, Colo.: East European Monographs, 1985.

Luža, Radomir. *Austro-German Relations in the Anschluss Era.* Princeton, N.J.: Princeton University Press, 1975.

The Resistance in Austria, 1938–1945. Minneapolis: University of Minnesota Press, 1984.

Maass, Walter B. *Assassination in Vienna.* New York: Charles Scribner's Sons, 1972.

Country without a Name: Austria under Nazi Rule, 1938–1945. New York: Frederick Ungar Publishing Co., 1979.

Pauley, Bruce F. *Hitler and the Forgotten Nazis.* Chapel Hill: University of North Carolina Press, 1981.

Rabinbach, Anson, ed. *The Austrian Socialist Experiment: Social Democracy and Austromarxism, 1918–1934.* Boulder, Colo.: Westview Press, 1985.

The Crisis of Austrian Socialism: From Red Vienna to Civil War, 1927–1934. Chicago: Chicago University Press, 1983.

Rusinow, Dennison I. *Italy's Austrian Heritage, 1919–1946.* Oxford: Oxford University Press, Clarendon Press, 1969.

Schuschnigg, Kurt von. *Austrian Requiem.* New York: G. P. Putnam's Sons, 1946.

The Brutal Takeover. London: Weidenfeld and Nicolson, 1971.

My Austria. New York: Alfred A. Knopf, 1938.

Stadler, K. R. *The Birth of the Austrian Republic, 1918–1921.* Leyden: A. W. Sijthoff, 1966.

Starhemberg, Ernst Rüdiger von. *Between Hitler and Mussolini.* New York: Harper and Bros., 1942.

Suval, Stanley. *The Anschluss Question in the Weimar Era.* Baltimore: Johns Hopkins University Press, 1974.

The Second Republic

Alcock, Antony E. *The History of the South Tyrol Question.* Geneva: Michael Joseph, 1970.

Allard, Sven. *Russia and the Austrian State Treaty.* University Park, Pa.: Pennsylvania State University Press, 1970.

Bibliography

Arndt, Sven W., ed. *The Political Economy of Austria.* Washington, D.C.: American Enterprise Institute for Public Policy Research, 1982.

Bader, William B. *Austria between East and West, 1945–1955.* Stanford, Calif.: Stanford University Press, 1966.

Bauer, Robert A., ed., *The Austrian Solution.* Charlottesville: University Press of Virginia, 1982.

Bluhm, William T. *Building an Austrian Nation: The Political Integration of a Western State.* New Haven, Conn.: Yale University Press, 1973.

Cronon, Audrey Kurth. *Great Power Politics and the Struggle over Austria, 1945–1955.* Ithaca, N.Y.: Cornell University Press, 1986.

Katzenstein, Peter J. *Corporatism and Change: Austria, Switzerland, and the Politics of Industry.* Ithaca, N.Y.: Cornell University Press, 1984.

Schlesinger, Thomas O. *Austrian Neutrality in Postwar Europe.* Vienna: Braumüller, 1972.

Shell, Kurt L. *The Transformation of Austrian Socialism.* New York: State University of New York Publishers, 1962.

Steiner, Kurt, ed. *Modern Austria.* Palo Alto, Calif.: Sposs, 1981.

Sully, Melanie A. *Political Parties and Elections in Austria.* London: C. Hurst and Co., 1981.

Waldheim, Kurt. *The Austrian Example.* London: Weidenfeld and Nicolson, 1973.

Whitnah, Donald R., and Edgar L. Erickson. *The American Occupation of Austria: Planning and Early Years.* Westport, Conn.: Greenwood Press, 1985.

Wright, William E., ed. *Austria since 1945.* Minneapolis: Center for Austrian Studies, University of Minnesota, 1982.

INDEX

Index

Index

Index